Additional Praise for

MY OWN WORDS

"At the heart of *My Own Words* is an abiding commitment to civility, to institutional norms, to the infinite possibilities of dialogue and cooperation, and to the now-dubious notion that protecting outsiders and others is a core American value. . . . Above all, always in her own methodical way, what shines through these essays is Ruth Bader Ginsburg, feminist, who truly could not conceive of a world without meaningful gender parity in the 1970s. . . . As a collection of thoughtful writing about perseverance and community and the law, it is a tonic to the current national discourse."

—*The Washington Post*

"Ginsburg has used her words to promote equality and stem discrimination as well as to express gratitude and to celebrate others who did so before and with her. . . . Exceedingly readable, thanks to Ginsburg's characteristically precise and unembellished prose."

—*Newsweek*

"The Notorious RBG makes it even harder to ponder her eventual absence with a look at gender inequality, the Supreme Court's inner workings, and the too-little-remarked-upon intersections of law and opera."

—*New York Magazine*

"The selection showcases her astonishing intellectual range, from law and lawyers in opera, to tributes to Louis Brandeis, William Rehnquist, and Gloria Steinem, to the significance and form of dissenting opinions. The book also includes a number of revealing speeches Ginsburg has given about her historical heroines."

—*The New Republic*

"A collection of her writings that will offer even more. . . . Justice Ginsburg's impact not only on the legal profession but also on young women contemplating such a career path is undeniable."

—*Library Journal*

"Much recommended as a Christmas gift for smart, ambitious nieces. And nephews, too."

—*The Guardian*

"[*My Own Words*] reveals a more personal side of the unlikely icon who has inspired operas, tattoos, T-shirts and millions of young women who never knew that the law was once reserved for male lawyers."

—CNN.COM

"No sitting Supreme Court justice has the adoring fan base Ruth Bader Ginsburg has. . . . the amicus briefs, and, later, bench announcements included here are recognizably impressive, even to civilians, in their lucidity, calm persuasiveness, and avoidance of jargon on one side and distracting captiousness on the other. The more informal writings in *My Own Words* share those qualities while adding charm."

—*Bookforum*

MY OWN WORDS

Justice Ginsburg speaks at the Conference of Court Public Information Officers in the West Conference Room at the Supreme Court on August 8, 2011.

MY OWN WORDS

Ruth Bader Ginsburg

With Mary Hartnett and Wendy W. Williams

SIMON & SCHUSTER PAPERBACKS

New York London Toronto Sydney New Delhi

Simon & Schuster Paperbacks
An Imprint of Simon & Schuster, Inc.
1230 Avenue of the Americas
New York, NY 10020

First Simon & Schuster trade paperback edition August 2018

SIMON & SCHUSTER PAPERBACKS and colophon are registered trademarks of Simon & Schuster, Inc.

Frontis photo: Steve Petteway, Collection of the Supreme Court of the United States.

Book design by Ellen R. Sasahara

Manufactured in the United States of America

9 10 8

The Library of Congress has cataloged the hardcover edition as follows:

Names: Ginsburg, Ruth Bader, author. | Hartnett, Mary Eileen, 1959– author. |Williams, Wendy W. (Writer on law) author.
Title: My own words / Ruth Bader Ginsburg with Mary Hartnett and Wendy W. Williams.

Description: New York : Simon & Schuster, 2016. | Includes bibliographical references and index.
Identifiers: LCCN 2016031635| ISBN 9781501145247 (hardback) | ISBN 9781501145254 (trade paperback)
Subjects: LCSH: Ginsburg, Ruth Bader. | Women judges—United States—Biography. | Women lawyers—United States—Biography. | United States. Supreme Court.—Biography. | BISAC: BIOGRAPHY & AUTOBIOGRAPHY / Lawyers & Judges. | BIOGRAPHY & AUTOBIOGRAPHY / Women. | POLITICAL SCIENCE / Government / Judicial Branch.
Classification: LCC KF373.G565 G56 2016 | DDC 347.73/2634—dc23
LC record available at https://lccn.loc.gov/2016031635

ISBN 978-1-5011-4524-7
ISBN 978-1-5011-4525-4 (pbk)
ISBN 978-1-5011-4526-1 (ebook)

To Marty, dear partner in life and constant uplifter

Contents

Part Two ✦ Tributes to Waypavers and Pathmarkers

Part Three ✦ On Gender Equality: Women and the Law

Part Four ✦ A Judge Becomes a Justice

Part Five ✦ The Justice on Judging and Justice

A Note on Sources

My Own Words includes a variety of materials, including speeches that have no citations, and legal briefs and law review articles that are rife with citations. Our publisher recommended that instead of including the full citations in the print edition of the book, it would benefit the environment and most of our readers to instead house the majority of the legal citations from briefs and articles on the book's website MyOwnWordsBook.com. We have retained notes from the introductory text and the *Scalia/Ginsburg* opera excerpt in the print edition.

Preface

MAY I TELL YOU, good readers, how this book came to be. In the summer of 2003, Wendy Williams and Mary Hartnett visited me in chambers. They had a proposal: "People will write about you, like it or not. We suggest that you name as your official biographers authors you trust. The two of us volunteer for that assignment." Wendy and I were in the same line of business in the 1970s. We were engaged in moving the law in the direction of recognizing women's equal-citizenship stature. Wendy was a founder of the San Francisco–based Equal Rights Advocates. I was on the opposite coast as cofounder of the American Civil Liberties Union's Women's Rights Project. We understood and aided each other's public education, legislative, and litigation efforts. Wendy and I remained in close touch when she joined the faculty of Georgetown University Law Center. Mary was an adjunct professor at the Law Center, and director of the center's Women's Law and Public Policy Fellowship Program. Well traveled, wise, and what the French call *sympathique*, Mary seemed to me a fit partner for Wendy in the biographical venture. Without hesitation, I said yes to their proposal.

My Own Words would follow after publication of the biography, we anticipated. But as my years on the Court mounted, Wendy and Mary thought it best to defer final composition of the biography until my Court years neared completion. So we flipped the projected publication order, releasing first the collection now in your hands.

"Did you always want to be a judge" or, more exorbitantly, "a Supreme Court Justice?" Schoolchildren visiting me at the Court, as they do at least weekly, ask that question more than any other. It is a sign of huge progress made. To today's youth, judgeship as an aspiration for a girl is not at all outlandish. Contrast the ancient days (the fall of 1956) when I entered law school. Women were less than 3 percent of the legal profession in the United States, and only one woman had ever served on a federal appellate court.* Today about half the nation's law students and more than one-third of our federal judges are women, including three of the nine Justices seated on the U.S. Supreme Court bench. Women hold more than 30 percent of U.S. law school deanships and serve as general counsel to 24 percent of Fortune 500 companies. In my long life, I have seen great changes!†

How fortunate I was to be alive and a lawyer when, for the first time in U.S. history, it became possible to urge, successfully, before legislatures and courts, the equal-citizenship stature of women and men as a fundamental constitutional principle. Feminists, caring men among them, had urged just that for generations. Until the late 1960s, however, society was not prepared to heed their plea.‡

What enabled me to take part in the effort to free our daughters and sons to achieve whatever their talents equipped them to accomplish, with no artificial barriers blocking their way? First, a mother who, by her example, made reading a delight and counseled me constantly to "be independent," able to fend for myself, whatever fortune might have in store for me. Second, teachers who influenced or encouraged me in my growing-up years. At Cornell University, professor of European literature Vladimir Nabokov changed the way I read and the

---

* Florence Allen, appointed by President Franklin D. Roosevelt to the U.S. Court of Appeals for the Sixth Circuit in 1934.

† See "Women's Progress at the Bar and on the Bench," p. 69.

‡ See "Advocating the Elimination of Gender-Based Discrimination: The 1970s New Look at the Equality Principle," p. 154.

way I write. Words could paint pictures, I learned from him. Choosing the right word, and the right word order, he illustrated, could make an enormous difference in conveying an image or an idea. From constitutional law professor Robert E. Cushman and American Ideals professor Milton Konvitz I learned of our nation's enduring values, how our Congress was straying from them in the Red Scare years of the 1950s, and how lawyers could remind lawmakers that our Constitution shields the right to think, speak, and write without fear of reprisal from governmental authorities.*

At Harvard Law School, Professor Benjamin Kaplan was my first and favorite teacher. He used the Socratic method in his civil procedure class always to stimulate, never to wound. Kaplan was the model I tried to follow in my own law teaching years, 1963–80. At Columbia Law School, professor of constitutional law and federal courts Gerald Gunther was determined to place me in a federal court clerkship, despite what was then viewed as a grave impediment: on graduation, I was the mother of a four-year-old child. After heroic efforts, Gunther succeeded in that mission. In later years, litigating cases in or headed to the Supreme Court, I turned to Gunther for aid in dealing with sticky issues, both substantive and procedural. He never failed to help me find the right path.

Another often-asked question when I speak in public: "Do you have some good advice you might share with us?" Yes, I do. It comes from my savvy mother-in-law, advice she gave me on my wedding day. "In every good marriage," she counseled, "it helps sometimes to be a little deaf." I have followed that advice assiduously, and not only at home through fifty-six years of a marital partnership nonpareil. I have employed it as well in every workplace, including the Supreme Court of the United States. When a thoughtless or unkind word is spoken, best tune out. Reacting in anger or annoyance will not advance one's ability to persuade.

---

* See "Wiretapping: Cure Worse than Disease?," p. 20.

Advice from my father-in-law has also served me well. He gave it during my gap years, 1954–56, when husband Marty was fulfilling his obligation to the Army as an artillery officer at Fort Sill, Oklahoma. By the end of 1954, my pregnancy was confirmed. We looked forward to becoming three in July 1955, but I worried about starting law school the next year with an infant to care for. Father's advice: "Ruth, if you don't want to start law school, you have a good reason to resist the undertaking. No one will think the less of you if you make that choice. But if you really want to study law, you will stop worrying and find a way to manage child and school." And so Marty and I did, by engaging a nanny on school days from 8:00 a.m. until 4:00 p.m. Many times after, when the road was rocky, I thought back to Father's wisdom, spent no time fretting, and found a way to do what I thought important to get done.

Work-life balance was a term not yet coined in the years my children were young; it is aptly descriptive of the time distribution I experienced. My success in law school, I have no doubt, was due in large measure to baby Jane. I attended classes and studied diligently until four in the afternoon; the next hours were Jane's time, spent at the park, playing silly games or singing funny songs, reading picture books and A. A. Milne poems, and bathing and feeding her. After Jane's bedtime, I returned to the law books with renewed will. Each part of my life provided respite from the other and gave me a sense of proportion that classmates trained only on law studies lacked.

I have had more than a little bit of luck in life, but nothing equals in magnitude my marriage to Martin D. Ginsburg. I do not have words adequate to describe my supersmart, exuberant, ever-loving spouse. He speaks for himself in two selections chosen for this book.* Read them and you will see what a special fellow he was. Early on in our marriage, it became clear to him that cooking was not my strong

---

* See "Marty Ginsburg's Favorite Subject," p. 25; "How the Tenth Circuit Court of Appeals Got My Wife Her Good Job," p. 126.

suit. To the everlasting appreciation of our food-loving children (we became four in 1965, when son James was born), Marty made the kitchen his domain and became Chef Supreme in our home, on loan to friends, even at the Court.*

Marty coached me through the birth of our son, he was the first reader and critic of articles, speeches, and briefs I drafted, and he was at my side constantly, in and out of the hospital, during two long bouts with cancer. And I betray no secret in reporting that, without him, I would not have gained a seat on the U.S. Supreme Court. Then–Associate White House Counsel Ron Klain said of my 1993 nomination: "I would say definitely and for the record, though Ruth Bader Ginsburg should have been picked for the Supreme Court anyway, she would not have been picked for the Supreme Court if her husband had not done everything he did to make it happen."† That "everything" included gaining the unqualified support of my home state senator Daniel Patrick Moynihan and enlisting the aid of many members of the legal academy and practicing bar familiar with work I had done.‡

I have several times said that the office I hold, now for more than twenty-three years, is the best and most consuming job a lawyer anywhere could have.§ The Court's main trust is to repair fractures in federal law, to step in when other courts have disagreed on what the relevant federal law requires. Because the Court grants review dominantly when other jurists have divided on the meaning of a statutory or constitutional prescription, the questions we take up are rarely easy;

---

* As a memorial to Marty, the spouses of my colleagues, under the superintendence of Martha-Ann Alito, compiled and published, the year after his death, a collection of his recipes titled *Chef Supreme* (Washington, DC: Supreme Court Historical Society, 2011).

† Interview by Mary Hartnett with Ron Klain (Nov. 30, 2007) (on file with authors).

‡ For Marty's own account, see "Some Reflections on Imperfection," 39 *Arizona State Law Journal* 949 (2007).

§ See "Workways of the Supreme Court," p. 201.

they seldom have indubitably right answers. Yet by reasoning together at our conferences and, with more depth and precision, through circulation of, and responses to, draft opinions, we ultimately agree far more often than we divide sharply. Last Term (2015–16), for example, we were unanimous, at least on the bottom-line judgment, in 25 of the 67 cases decided after full briefing and argument. In contrast, we divided 5–3 or 4–3 (Justice Scalia's death reduced the number of Justices to eight) only eight times.*

When a Justice is of the firm view that the majority got it wrong, she is free to say so in dissent. I take advantage of that prerogative, when I think it important, as do my colleagues.† Despite our strong disagreements on cardinal issues—think, for example, of controls on political campaign spending, affirmative action, access to abortion—we genuinely respect each other, even enjoy each other's company. Collegiality is key to the success of our mission. We could not do the job the Constitution assigns to us if we didn't—to use one of Justice Scalia's favorite expressions—"get over it!" All of us revere the Constitution and the Court. We aim to ensure that when we leave the Court, the third branch of government will be in as good shape as it was when we joined it.

Earlier, I spoke of great changes I have seen in women's occupations. Yet one must acknowledge the still bleak part of the picture. Most people in poverty in the United States and the world over are women and children, women's earnings here and abroad trail the earnings of men with comparable education and experience, our workplaces do not adequately accommodate the demands of childbearing and childrearing, and we have yet to devise effective ways to ward off sexual harassment at work and domestic violence in our homes. I am optimistic, however, that movement toward enlistment of the talent of all who compose "We, the People," will continue.

---

* See "Highlights of the U.S. Supreme Court's 2015–16 Term," p. 317.

† See "Remarks on the Role of Dissenting Opinions," p. 278.

As expressed by my brave colleague, the first woman on the Supreme Court of the United States, Justice Sandra Day O'Connor:

> For both men and women the first step in getting power is to become visible to others, and then to put on an impressive show. . . . As women achieve power, the barriers will fall. As society sees what women can do, as women see what women can do, there will be more women out there doing things, and we'll all be better off for it.*

I heartily concur in that expectation.

Ruth Bader Ginsburg
July 2016

---

* See "Sandra Day O'Connor," p. 89.

Timeline

1933
March 15: Joan Ruth Bader born in Brooklyn, New York.

1934
June 6: Older sister Marilyn Bader dies of meningitis at the age of six.

1938
Enters kindergarten at Public School 238 in Brooklyn. Because several students in her class are named Joan, starts going by "Ruth" in school and is nicknamed "Kiki" at home.

1946
Graduates from PS 238 and enters James Madison High School in Brooklyn. Mother Celia is diagnosed with cancer.

1950
Sun., June 25: Mother dies of cancer.
Tues., June 27: High school graduation (does not attend due to mother's death).

1950–54
Attends Cornell University.
Fall of 1950: Meets Martin D. ("Marty") Ginsburg on a blind date.
June 14, 1954: Graduates from Cornell.
June 23, 1954: Marries Marty in his parents' Long Island home.

1954–56
Lives in Fort Sill, Oklahoma, where Marty fulfills Army service as artillery school instructor. Works in several clerical positions including at Lawton, Oklahoma, Social Security office.
July 21, 1955: Daughter, Jane, is born.

1956–58
Attends Harvard Law School (1 of 9 women in class of approximately 500).

1958–59

Attends Columbia Law School (1 of 12 women).
May 1959: Graduates from Columbia Law School (tied for first in class).

1959–61

Judicial clerk to Judge Edmund Palmieri, U.S. District Court for the Southern District of New York.

1961–63

Research associate and then associate director of Columbia Law School Project on International Procedure. Divides time between New York and Sweden.

1963–72

Professor at Rutgers School of Law, State University of New Jersey.
Sept. 8, 1965: Son, James, is born.
June 20, 1968: Father, Nathan, dies.
1971: Coauthors first Supreme Court brief in *Reed v. Reed*.

1972–80

Professor at Columbia University School of Law. Director of and counsel to ACLU Women's Rights Project.
Jan. 17, 1973: First Supreme Court oral argument (*Frontiero v. Richardson*).

1980–93

Judge, U.S. Court of Appeals for the D.C. Circuit (appointed by President Jimmy Carter).

1993 forward

Associate Justice, U.S. Supreme Court (appointed by President Bill Clinton).

2010

June 27: Beloved husband and "life partner" Marty Ginsburg dies of cancer.

Part One

Early Years and Lighter Side

Introduction

Ruth Bader Ginsburg *began writing at an early age, with the first piece in this collection being published in her school newspaper when she was barely thirteen years old. Her childhood experiences helped shape the writer, person, and judge she went on to become.*

Born on March 15, 1933, Joan Ruth Bader was the second daughter of Celia and Nathan Bader. Older sister Marilyn called her active baby sister "Kiki," because she was "a kicky baby," and the nickname stuck. Justice Ginsburg, however, has no memories of the sister who nicknamed her. Marilyn died of meningitis at the age of six, just fourteen months after Kiki's birth.

Kiki Bader grew up in a working-class neighborhood among Irish, Italian, and Jewish neighbors, where quiet tree-lined residential streets with brick and stucco row houses bumped up against busy thoroughfares like Coney Island Avenue and Kings Highway with their grocers, dry cleaners, and car repair shops. Her parents rented the first floor of a small gray stucco row house; their landlady lived on the second floor. During the winter, coal was delivered and shoveled into the furnace to keep the small home warm, but there was no air-conditioning to temper the hot Brooklyn summers. Her mother washed the family's clothes by hand and hung them out to dry on a clothesline that went out her bedroom window. They had a refrigerator with coils on top, and a Victrola in the living room, where Kiki and her cousin Richard later learned to dance to records they bought at a tiny store in the Times Square subway stop.[1]

Kiki Bader attended her neighborhood's public schools, starting with Brooklyn Public Elementary School No. 238, a square brick building just over a block from her home. Because there were several other Joans in her kindergarten class, her mother suggested to the teacher that confusion could be avoided by calling Kiki by her middle name, Ruth. From that time forward, she was Kiki to family and friends, and Ruth for more official purposes. Ruth and her cousin Richard, who lived just up the street, would usually walk to school together. After school each day, as she grew older, she and Richard could often be found with their friends in the neighborhood riding bikes, roller-skating, jumping rope, or playing stoopball. Ruth's neighbor and best friend, who like her sister was named Marilyn, was Italian Catholic. Ruth loved to play jacks on her front steps with Marilyn, and to be invited over to Marilyn's house for dinners of spaghetti and meatballs.

Ruth Bader was, throughout her education, an enthusiastic and outstanding student. She loved learning to read, but learning to write was traumatic: left-handed Ruth was reduced to tears when her teacher tried to "convert" her into a right-hander. The result was a D in penmanship. Ruth vowed then that she would never write another word with her right hand, and she never did. She never got another D, either.

Like most children, Ruth enjoyed gym class and recess, and skinned her knees in the schoolyard skipping rope and playing dodgeball. She went on school field trips to local museums and attended Friday assemblies where the girls and boys wore red, white, and blue: white shirts and red ties for everyone, blue skirts for the girls, and blue pants for the boys.[2] *While Ruth enjoyed her English, history, and social studies classes, she was not, she confesses, especially fond of math. Nor was home economics, where girls learned cooking and sewing in preparation for their future as housewives and homemakers, her cup of tea: "I remember envying the boys long before I even knew the word* feminism, *because I liked shop better than cooking or sewing. . . . The boys used to make things out of wood, and I thought that was fun, to use the saw, and I didn't think it was fun to sew, and my cooking never came out the way it was supposed to." The sewing assignment for the eighth-grade girls was to make their own graduation dresses. Ruth ruefully recalls her creation: "Mine was a mess."*[3] *Ruth's mother saved the day, having the dress "fixed" by a local dressmaker before graduation.*

Friday afternoons found Ruth at her local library, which was housed above a Chinese restaurant and a beauty parlor. While her mother had her hair done downstairs, Ruth would savor her time in the library, the delicious smell of spices wafting up from the restaurant while she read Greek myths and books such as The Secret Garden and Louisa May Alcott's Little Women. (Of all the March sisters, Ruth loved the lively independent intellectual Jo the best.) Ruth was also a fan of the Nancy Drew detective books. Unlike scary films, which gave her nightmares, she was not frightened by the mystery stories. She loved Nancy Drew because "Nancy was a girl who did things. She was adventuresome, daring, and her boyfriend was a much more passive type than she was."[4] For similar reasons, Amelia Earhart, the first woman to fly solo across the Atlantic, also captured her imagination. Earhart had taken her historic flight the year before Ruth was born and went missing over the Pacific five years later; Ruth was drawn to Amelia's courage and sense of adventure.[5]

Ruth was not only an avid reader, she also created stories of her own—her younger cousins remember her as a gifted and dramatic storyteller.[6] She was also fond of poetry, both reading and memorizing it. A few of her childhood favorites were Emma Lazarus' famous words inscribed at the foot of the Statue of Liberty ("Give me your tired, your poor, / Your huddled masses yearning to breathe free"); Shakespeare's Henry V Epilogue ("Small time, but, in that small, most greatly lived / This star of England"); and the A. A. Milne poem "Disobedience" ("James James Morrison Morrison"). She loved Robert Louis Stevenson's poetry collection, A Child's Garden of Verses, and was particularly fond of "the Jabberwocky" by Lewis Carroll ("Twas brillig, and the slithy toves").[7]

Ruth very much admired her mother, who encouraged Ruth to be independent and self-sufficient. Ruth believes that this was at least in part because her mother, wishing she'd had the chance to further her own education and career, and somewhat resentful of the fact that the scarce family resources had been allocated entirely to her brother's education, wanted to ensure that her gifted daughter would have no such regrets. "My mother was very strong about my doing well in school and living up to my potential. Two things were important to her and she repeated them endlessly. One was to 'be a lady,' and that meant conduct yourself civilly, don't let emotions like anger or envy get in your way. And the other was to be independent, which was an unusual message for mothers of that time to be giving their daughters."[8]

The year Ruth was born, Adolf Hitler became chancellor of Germany and gave orders for the first concentration camp in Dachau. As Ruth grew *from childhood to adolescence in the shadow of World War II, her protective parents tried to shield her from photographs of death camps and emaciated survivors. "Nobody wanted to believe what was really happening. People thought that Hitler hated Jews and had these repressive laws, but . . ."*[9] *And, although most of Ruth's childhood memories of her multiethnic Brooklyn neighborhood were positive, she became increasingly aware of anti-Semitism close to home. Two elderly women living on her block housed foster boys and told them that it would bring bad luck if they brought a Jew into the house, especially at lunchtime.*[10] *Other children on the street repeated the myth that matzo was made from the blood of Christian boys, and taunted Ruth and her Jewish friends, calling them "kikes."*[11] *On one drive in the Pennsylvania countryside, Ruth and her family passed an inn with a sign on the lawn: "No Dogs or Jews Allowed."*[12]

Eight-year-old Ruth was with her parents on a Sunday drive to Queens on December 7, 1941, sitting in the backseat and listening to the car radio, when the regularly scheduled broadcast was interrupted and a stunned Ruth heard the radio announcer report that the Japanese had just attacked Pearl Harbor.[13] *The next day, Americans across the country turned on their radios to hear President Franklin Roosevelt confirm what they feared but still hoped was not true: America was at war. As was the case for most Americans, Ruth's world changed immediately and dramatically the moment the United States entered the war. Her cousin Seymour ("Si"), a happy-go-lucky eighteen-year-old college student at the time of Pearl Harbor, was inducted into the Army the following May. Si ended up serving in Europe and in the Pacific, and Ruth worried about him and sent him letters using Victory mail, also known as "V-mail." Ruth would scrawl as much news from home as she could fit onto the small prescribed letter form, and then fold it, address it, and place it in the mail. It was then microfilmed and sent overseas, where it would be reproduced and censored, before finally being delivered to Si.*

Shrieking sirens for air raid drills routinely interrupted Ruth's activities at home and school. At home after dark, Ruth would run to turn off the lights, and at school the young pupils were herded together into the assembly room. Ruth's Brooklyn neighborhood had an air raid warden, and sections of particular streets were arranged into smaller zones, each with its own captain.[14]

Ruth's family was allotted ration coupons for gasoline, so they took fewer and more carefully planned weekend excursions outside of Brooklyn. Ruth and her classmates helped to plant and tend a "victory garden" of carrots, radishes, and other vegetables at their elementary school, and they would knit squares each morning during homeroom period to be made into afghan blankets for the troops.[15] *One day each week was "stamp day," when Ruth and her classmates could bring in their allowance money to buy twenty-five-cent stamps to paste into a savings bond book with proceeds used to support the war effort.*[16] *Ruth and her classmates also helped fulfill their patriotic duty by chewing lots of gum, and then peeling off the silver gum wrappers and wadding hundreds of them into tinfoil balls for contribution to the "Aluminum for Defense" drives. Ruth loved the posters of Rosie the Riveter, portraying a strong and able woman supporting the war effort with her factory work.*[17]

On the afternoon of April 12, 1945, Franklin Roosevelt, who had been president for twelve-year-old Ruth's entire young life, died suddenly in Warm Springs, Georgia, of a cerebral hemorrhage, and Harry Truman became president. Two and a half weeks later, on April 30, Adolf Hitler committed suicide in his bunker, shooting himself in the right temple as Allied forces closed in. Berlin fell on May 2, and less than one week later, on May 8, 1945, Ruth watched as New Yorkers danced in the streets to celebrate V-E (Victory in Europe) Day.[18]

Ruth remembered V-J (Victory over Japan) Day later that summer much differently, since it came just after the United States dropped atomic bombs on Hiroshima and Nagasaki:

> *Well, it was stunning, something we had no idea was in the making and then it was in the paper . . . tremendous clouds . . . the horror that we had killed so many people and people were burned and scarred for life. . . . There was that pall over V-J day. Even though it was the end to it, everybody realized the instrument of destruction that had been launched and, I suppose, feared for the future with such a weapon like that. So I remember V-E day as being total jubilation but V-J day affected very much by the bomb.*[19]

1

Editorial for the School Newspaper

Highway Herald, June 1946

ELEANOR ROOSEVELT *had been the first lady throughout most of Ruth Bader's childhood. Ruth's mother, who deeply admired the first lady, often read Mrs. Roosevelt's "My Day" newspaper columns aloud to Ruth. Eight months after President Roosevelt's death, Eleanor Roosevelt was appointed by President Truman as a U.S. delegate to the newly established United Nations General Assembly. The UN Charter, in its preamble, declared as one of its aims "to regain faith in fundamental human rights, in the dignity and worth of the human person, in the equal rights of men and women and of nations large and small." Eleanor Roosevelt, pursuant to that goal, became in April 1946 the first chairperson of the newly created U.N. Commission on Human Rights. In the wake of World War II, Ruth and her mother followed closely as Eleanor Roosevelt led the efforts that would result, in 1948, in the adoption of the Universal Declaration of Human Rights, a document Roosevelt celebrated as "the international Magna Carta for all mankind."*

Two months after Eleanor Roosevelt was chosen to head the UN Commission on Human Rights, Ruth Bader, by then a thirteen-year-old eighth grader and editor of her school newspaper, the Highway Herald, *wrote a column of her own. Her column, the first piece in this collection, was a sign of things to come. While other students wrote about the circus, school plays, and the glee club, Ruth discussed the Ten Commandments, Magna Carta, Bill of Rights, Declaration of Independence, and United Nations Charter.*

Highway Herald, June 1946
Published by Pupils of Elementary Public School 238, Brooklyn, New York
Editorial by Ruth Bader, Grade 8B1

Since the beginning of time, the world has known four great documents, great because of all the benefits to humanity which came about as a result of their fine ideals and principles.

The first was the Ten Commandments, which was given to Moses while he was leading the Israelites through the wilderness to the land of Canaan. Today people of almost every religion respect and accept them as a code of ethics and a standard of behavior.

Up until the thirteenth century, conditions under the kings of Europe were unbearable for the commoners. Taxation was high, living conditions poor and justice unknown. It was then, in 1215 AD, that the barons and peers of England met and drew up a charter called the Magna Carta. After forcing King John to sign it, the document was declared the governing law of the land. This gave the English peasants the first rights ever granted to them.

When William of Orange, a Dutchman, was offered the English throne, his chief ambition was to use the military powers of Britain to aid his beloved Holland in its war with Spain. In accepting this offer, he had to grant certain concessions to the English people. So, in 1689, he signed the Bill of Rights. This limited the King's powers and gave much of the government control to parliament, another important stride in the history of the world.

The Declaration of Independence of our own U.S. may well be considered one of the most important steps in the shaping of the world. It marked the birth of a new nation, a nation that has so grown in strength as to take its place at the top of the list of the world's great powers.

And now we have a fifth great document, the Charter of the United Nations. Its purpose and principles are to maintain international peace and security, to practice tolerance, and to suppress any acts of aggression or other breaches of peace.

It is vital that peace be assured, for now we have a weapon that can destroy the world. We children of public school age can do much to aid in the promotion of peace. We must try to train ourselves and those about us to live together with one another as good neighbors for this idea is embodied in the great new Charter of the United Nations. It is the only way to secure the world against future wars and maintain an everlasting peace.

Highway Herald

June 1946

Published by pupils of P. S. 238, Brooklyn.

Page 3

PROSPECTIVE GRADUATES

Boys

Aliciakos, William
Anzini, Bert J.
Assael, Bernard S.
Bavaro, Dominic
Berger, Jack
Berko, Jerome
Bernstein, Barry A
Biblowitz, Robert
Bloukos, Nicholas
Boosin, Walter G.
Brand, Jack
Brownstein, Irving
Campbell, Thomas
Carmody, Michael
Connors, William
Cordova, Simon
Denmark, Burton
Di Orio, Jerome N.
Drucker, Howard
Dundish, Harold
Ferraro, Anthony J.
Fischer, Eugene
Frey, Ira
Fromm, Harold
Gates, Norman
Glener, Howard H.
Grassi, Mario
Goldberg, Robert
Harmetz, Ronald
Hornreich, Norman
Jonas, George
Kaplan, Eugene
Kessler, Robert
Klein, Jerome
Kluger, Jacob
Koppel, William
Laing, Charles
Lein, Marvin
List, Irwin
Lobel, Roger
Luca, Ralph
Mc Carthy, Donald R.
Milstein, Stanley
Oran, Frederick
Pearlman, Jacob
Plafker, Herbert L.
Rabia, Michael
Randazzo, Anthony
Rankus, Philip
Richmond, Sheldon
Rizzuto, Joseph
Roth, Harvy
Salzman Richard S.
Shafer, Donald
Schiraldi, Pasquale
Schleier, Herbert L.
Schnopper, Herbert
Schumsky, Stanley
Seiff, Gerald
Singer, Edwin
Slatkin, Gerald
Smirk, Richard
Sofferman, Stanley
Stamberg, Stanley
Svasek, Arthur
Unger, Stanley M.
Waltzer, Bruce C.
Weinberger, Lawrence
Weiss, Robert
Yankowitz, David
Zimmerman, Stuart

Girls

Accardy, Roberta
Agresta, Anna P.
Aguila, Diana
Babkes, Irene
Bader, Ruth
Berg, Stella
Birnbaum, Gloria
Birnbaum, Jacqueline
Birnberg, Gloria
Braunhut, Arlene S.
Braverman, Dolores B.
Cutler, Susan
De Lutio, Marilyn
Denker, Constance
Denmark, Marylin
Emanuele, Frances A.
Epstein, Florence R.
Fayer, Jane
Finkelstein, Adele
Firestone, Roma
Fischetti, Florence
Foreman, Myrna
Franklin, Jeanne
Fried, Phyllis
Friedlander, Jean
Gappell, Millicent
Garvis, Evelyn
Gilberto, Rosaline F.
Godfrey, Sybil
Goldman, Carole
Goodman, Carol
Gorden, Harryette
Greenberg, Janet
Grosky, Sally
Hudyma, Mary Ann
Hyman, Arlene
Kantrawitz, Rhoda
Koff, Judith
Kosta, Marcia
Kotkin, Marilyn
Kwies, Joan
Landrum, Lillian
Leviant, Beverley
Lipkin, Sylvia J.
Maese, Rita
Marrone, Marie M.
Mausner, Claire S.
Mayo, Sydelle
Medici, Dolores
Moskowitz, Sandra
Pascucci, Rita D.
Reagusa, Sophie
Reisman, Florence
Rice, Shirley P.
Rubin, Myrna A.
Samet, Sandra
Schuchman, Elaine
Schwartz, Judith
Schwartz, Ruth
Scotto, Michela
Shanneck, Anne
Sherlip, Frances
Shimsky, Ruth R.
Smith Barbara
Tauro, Maria
Teitlebaum, Judith
Timin, Helen
Weintraub, Gloria
Weisinger, Marilyn
Wellins, Arlene
Zehall, Dorothy
Zeichner, Leona

2

Highway Herald

ARTHUR BOWIE
Assistant Superintendent

W. CAMPBELL, Faculty Advisor

OUR STAFF

Our Staff

Editor- Ruth Bader 8B1
Assistant Editor- Richard Salzman 8B1
Secretary- Barbara Smith 8B3
Art Editor- Norma Dienst 8A1
Humor Editor- Shelmay Getz 8A3
Sports Editor- Donald Saltzman 8A1
Girls Sports Editor- Phyllis Morse 8A4
Chief Assembler- Marilyn DeLutio 8B1
Club Editor- Bernice Galitzer 8A1
Dramatic Editor- Rita Klein 7A4

Typists:
Shelmay Getz 8A3
Barbara Smith 8B3
Richard Salzman 8B1

Reporters:
Harold Fromm 8B4
Marilyn Kotkin 8B4
Roma Firestone 8B4
Lorraine Weisen 8A3
Marvin Simms 8A4
Evelyn Jourdan 7B1
Thalia Schnipper 7B1
Linda Singer 7B4
Joel Shapiro 7B3
Karen Gold 7B3
Noami Heimer 7B3
Iris Kowatt 7B4
Lorraine Tabak 7B4
Rona Kessner 7A1
Harris Rosenberg 7A1
Martin Wallace 7A3
Ronald Schapiro 7A3
Stanley Goodman 7A3
Rita Klein 7A4
Esther Zuckor 7A4
Elaine Shanus 7A4

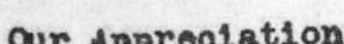

Our Appreciation

The Newspaper Club of June 1946, wishes to thank Shelmay Getz of 8A3 for all she has given us by typing the stories and articles.

Dear Boys and Girls of P.S. 238:-

Let us all join in congratulating and extending our best wishes to the boys and girls of our June, 1946, graduating class. We shall miss them but we feel confident they are going to do well in the high schools of their choice and will reflect honor on P. S. 238.

The sudden passing of our beloved principal, Mr. Hunt, brought grief to every boy and girl and to every teacher in P. S. 238. He was an inspiration to all. His kindly sense of humor and his insistance on fair play endeared him to everyone. Let us try to display in our lives those fine traits of high honor, justice, tolerance, conscientious hard work, and the kindly, helpful spirit which Mr. Hunt so well exemplified.

Some classes wanted to do somethi special in Mr. Hunt's memory. Knowing h he loved boys and girls, they sent contributions to the Junior Red Cross a Boys' Town so that they would be doing something for other boys and girls. Thi was a beautiful way of expressing their regard for Mr. Hunt.

Vacation time is here again,-- a time for rest, relaxation and fun. Even though you won't be in school, here are few things I should like you to remembe

1- Be alert. Practice your safety lessons. There will be many more cars o the streets. Be very careful.

2- Remember the starving millions in other parts of the world. Do not was food of any kind.

3- You live in a beautiful sectio of our great city. Keep it clean, order and neat. Cooperate with the Department of Sanitation in every way you can.

4- The Post Office Department has tremendous job and does it very well. Help them by seeing that you always use the zone number on every letter you ser

May each one enjoy a happy summer and return to P. S. 238 in the fall, ha py, rested and ready for work.

Sincerely,
Emily L. Reed

EDITORIAL

Since the beginning of time, the world has known four great documents, great because of all the benefits to humanity which came about as a result of their fine ideals and principles.

The first was The Ten Commandments, which was given to Moses while he was leading the Israelites through the wilderness to the land of Canaan. Today people of almost every religion respect and accept them as a code of ethics and a standard of behavior.

Up until the thirteenth century, conditions under the kings of Europe were unbearable for the commoners. Taxation was high, living conditions poor and justice unknown. It was then, in 1215 A.D., that the barons and peers of England met and drew up a charter called The Magna Carta. After forcing King John to sign it, the document was declared the governing law of the land. This gave the English peasants the first rights ever granted to them.

When William of Orange, a Dutchman, was offered the English throne, his chief ambition was to use the military powers of Britain to aid his beloved Holland in its war with Spain. In accept-ing this offer, he had to grant certain concessions to the English people. So, in 1689, he signed The Bill of Rights. This limited the King's powers and gave much of the government control to parlia-ment, another important stride in the history of the world.

The declaration of Independence of of our own U.S. may well be considered one of the most important steps in the shaping of the world. It marked the birth of a new nation, a nation that has so grown in strength as to take its place at the top of the list of the worlds great powers.

And now we have a fifth great document , The Charter of United Nations Its purpose and principles are to maintain international peace and security, to practice tolerance and to suppress any acts of aggresion or other breaches of peace.

It is vital that peace be assured, for now we have a weapon that can destroy the world. We children of public school age can do much to aid in the promotion of peace. We must try to train ourselves and those about us to live together with one another as good neighbors for this idea is embodied in the great new Charter of the United Nations. It is the only way to secure the world against future wars and maintain an everlasting peace.

by Ruth Bader 8B1

Page 3

I Am An American Day

I am ever so proud to be, a citizen of
country so great,
Of a country that is destined for so
wonderful a fate.
I am ever so proud to be able to say,
This on "I Am An American Day."

A country so large and so grand,
One up to which all people stand.
A country so fine and so very pure,
America offers a chance for rich and
poor.

Giving opportunities for citizens
naturalized and true,
The country so prosperous and grew,
I am an American, I can say on "I Am An
American Day."

by Audrey Rothbart 8A[illegible]

Treasure of the Heavens

The sun's a golden halo,
The star's a diamond chain,
The moon's a silver locket,
With links from drops of rain.
A satin sky of lightest blue, with
plumes of fleecy white,
A deeper velvet blue,
Comes out in darkest night.
Thus, you see the heavens,
Carved by God's fine tools,
Sewn with tiny stitches,
Priceless, by God's rare jewels.

by Naomi Heimer 7B3

For a United Brotherhood

Now the war is over and the thunder of guns is silent. We should try to keep these guns silent forever by cooperating with our friends and neighbors. We should try to prove to the world that friendship is the key to our policy; and that stirring up hatred between religions is wrong. Inter group hatred slowed up teamwork and democratic spirit in many parts of the world.

It is just as hard to keep peace as it is to fight wars, and the way we can keep peace is by not fighting amongst ourselves. There are still people like Hitler that try to keep people of different religions from being friendly with each other. If everyone is friendly with one another this could all come to an end. Let us all unite in an American Brotherhood.

by Jack Belove 6-1-2

2

One People

Editorial, *East Midwood Bulletin* (June 21, 1946)

ALTHOUGH RUTH'S *immediate family was not devoutly religious, Jewish traditions were very much a part of her childhood. Her mother, Celia, lit candles every Friday night, and at Hanukkah all the grandchildren gathered to receive one silver dollar each as Hanukkah "gelt" (money) from their grandfather. Ruth and her parents regularly joined the annual gathering of aunts and uncles and cousins for the Seders held by her paternal grandparents on the first and second nights of Passover.*[1] *Her fondest memories were those Seders when she got to ask the traditional Seder questions, beginning with "Why is this night different from all other nights?"*

"That," Ruth later remarked, "was always the best part of the Seder for me, that the youngest child, which I was for a time, got to ask the questions and then the whole rest of the evening was providing answers."[2] *(This may have been the first sign of Ruth's future role as one of the most active and precise questioners on the United States Supreme Court bench.)*

From childhood onward, Ruth especially valued the reverence for justice and learning that was part of her Jewish heritage. She enjoyed studying Hebrew and the history of the Jews, and was especially moved by the life of Deborah, the general, judge, and prophet, as recounted in Judges 4–5 and in the Song of Deborah:

Awake, awake, Deborah;
Awake, awake, strike up the song!
Up, Barak, and take your captives,
O son of Abinoam![3]

But from a young age, Ruth also resented what she saw as sometimes rigid adherence to seemingly hypocritical rules and the inferior role assigned to women. Her mother, Celia, told her stories about Celia's Orthodox father, including a childhood memory of what started out as a happy Saturday afternoon. Celia watched her brother ride his shiny new bicycle, which he had bought with hard-earned dollars and dimes, but the happy afternoon dissolved into an anger- and tear-filled evening when their father destroyed the bicycle with an ax as punishment for bike riding on the Sabbath.[4] *And Ruth could not understand, in those days when only Jewish boys were ushered into adulthood with a religious celebration when they turned thirteen, why her cousin Richard got to have a bar mitzvah, "but there was no comparable ceremony for me."*[5]

Ruth attended various synagogues during her childhood (first a Reform temple and then an Orthodox synagogue where the women were relegated to the balcony) before finding the best fit at a Conservative temple, the East Midwood Jewish Center. There she spent Sunday mornings learning about Jewish history, holidays, and ceremonies, gained a beginner's acquaintance with the Hebrew language, and at age thirteen was confirmed (a ceremony introduced in part to entice girls to continue their religious studies since only boys could be bar mitzvahed). Ruth and her classmates talked about the creation of a Jewish state, and placed coins in their Tzedeka boxes to pay for planting trees in Israel. Ruth also authored two pieces in the East Midwood Bulletin*'s 1946 religious school graduation issue. One was a biographical tribute to Rabbi Stephen S. Wise on the occasion of his seventy-second birthday, which included thirteen-year-old Ruth's praise of Rabbi Wise's work for women's suffrage: "He was champion of every righteous cause. Jew and Gentile alike came to hear him. He was a valiant fighter for woman suffrage and among the first American Zionists."*[6] *The other piece, the lead article in that issue of the* Bulletin, *follows.*

Bulletin of the East Midwood Jewish Center
1625 Ocean Avenue, Brooklyn, N.Y.
Vol. XIII, June 21, 1946—Sivan 22, 5706, No. 42

ONE PEOPLE

The war has left a bloody trail and many deep wounds not too easily healed. Many people have been left with scars that take a long time to pass away. We must never forget the horrors which our brethren were subjected to in Bergen-Belsen and other Nazi concentration camps. Then, too, we must try hard to understand that for righteous people hate and prejudice are neither good occupations nor fit companions. Rabbi Alfred Bettleheim once said: "Prejudice saves us a painful trouble, the trouble of thinking." In our beloved land families were not scattered, communities not erased nor our nation destroyed by the ravages of the World War.

Yet, dare we be at ease? We are part of a world whose unity has been almost completely shattered. No one can feel free from danger and destruction until the many torn threads of civilization are bound together again. We cannot feel safer until every nation, regardless of weapons or power, will meet together in good faith, the people worthy of mutual association.

There can be a happy world and there will be once again, when men create a strong bond towards one another, a bond unbreakable by a studied prejudice or a passing circumstance. Then and only then shall we have a world built on the foundation of the Fatherhood of God and whose structure is the Brotherhood of Man.

RUTH BADER
Grade VIII

THE BULLETIN
of the
East Midwood Jewish Center

Telephone NAvarre 8-3800
1625 Ocean Avenue

Published weekly from the beginning of Temple activities in the fall to the end of Temple activities in the spring.
Subscription Price—$1.00 per Annum
Entered as second-class matter April 18, 1933 at the Post Office at Brooklyn, 30 N.Y. under the Act of March 3rd, 1879.

DR. HARRY HALPERN .... *Rabbi*
HARRY L. ABRAMS .... *President*

Editors
Seymour B. Liebman. *Chairman*
Dr. Harry Halpern Henry R. Goldberg
J. B. Rosenfeld Milton B. Perlman

Robert Gabbe .... *Exec. V. P.*

Vol. XIII June 21, 1946 No. 42

GRADUATION ISSUE

Editorial Staff

Ruth Bader Norman Potash
Fred Goldin Anita Ryder
Rboert Handros Henry Tulgan

ONE PEOPLE

The war has left a bloody trail and many deep wounds not too easily healed. Many people have been left with scars that take a long time to pass away. We must never forget the horrors which our brethren were subjected to in Bergen-Belsen and other Nazi concentration camps. Then, too, we must try hard to understand that for righteous people hate and prejudice are neither good occupations nor fit companions. Rabbi Alfred Bettleheim once said: "Prejudice saves us a painful trouble, the trouble of thinking." In our beloved land families were not scattered, communities not erased nor our nation destroyed by the ravages of the World War.

Yet, dare we be at ease? We are part of a world whose unity has been almost completely shattered. No one can feel free from danger and destruction until the many torn threads of civilization are bound together again. We cannot feel safer until every nation, regardless of weapons or power, will meet together in good faith, the people worthy of mutual association.

There can be a happy world and there will be once again, when men create a strong bond towards one another, a bond unbreakable by a studied prejudice or a passing circumstance. Then and only then shall we have a world built on the foundation of the Fatherhood of God and whose structure is the Brotherhood of Man.

RUTH BADER
Grade VIII

THE MESSIANIC IDEAL

It is fascinating that the religious (and perhaps the national) development of Judaism has been a series of humanizations. It started with the humanization of God, by removing the apathy and transcendentalism that had been associated with Him and making Him loving and eventually able to be loved — not feared. And then followed a humanization of the interpretation of Him and His ways, and so on.

Each of these attainments opened up a new era of thought, hope and consolation. And the latest of this series of humanizations is that of the Messiah. In the modern conception of the Messiah is contained the key to the sustenance and flourishing of Judaism today.

The idea of the Messiah started in the Middle Ages when the afflictions of the Jews made them turn their hopes to the ascent of a mighty leader who would save them from their misery. While it is easy to understand the conception of such a character, it is just as easy to understand why the Jews have never and will never accept a single man as a Messiah.

(Continued on Page 10)

Thirteen-year-old Ruth Bader at her confirmation at the East Midwood Jewish Center in June 1946. Ruth is immediately to the left of Rabbi Harry Halpern, center, and Ruth's childhood friend and college roommate Joan Bruder [Danoff] is immediately to his right.

June 1946, when the above piece was published, was a joyous time for Ruth's parents. The long war years were finally over, Ruth had just been confirmed by Rabbi Harry Halpern—the same rabbi who had married her parents nearly twenty years earlier—and on June 24 they watched with pride as Ruth and her classmates marched into the auditorium for their eighth-grade graduation. The school orchestra played Sir Edward Elgar's "Land of Hope and Glory." Ruth, first in her class of 144 students, gave the valedictory speech.

The family's happiness was short-lived. Just as Ruth entered adolescence and started high school, her mother was diagnosed with cervical cancer. Celia had her first operation when Ruth was thirteen, and Ruth's high school years were punctuated by her mother's hospital stays and haunted by her pain. In the 1940s there was no such thing as chemotherapy, and by the time the doctors diagnosed the cancer, it had already spread. At that time such a diagnosis was almost always a death sentence, and many family members would not even say the word cancer, *referring to it only as "C."*[7]

Instead of letting her mother's illness interfere with her studies, Ruth immersed herself in academics and extracurricular activities, relying on a routine of hard work, discipline, and little sleep to "carry her along," a pattern she would repeat during times of adversity throughout her life. In addition to being an honor roll student and earning top grades, Ruth was active in student government and was a cello-playing member of the high school orchestra. She also belonged to the "Go-Getters" booster club, whose members sold tickets to school sporting events and in return were awarded coveted shiny black jackets with gold letters. She was also a "twirler," performing with her baton at football games and even twirling her way through a Manhattan parade.

Her serious study habits and academic achievements notwithstanding, Ruth's classmates did not think of her as a "nerd" or "bookworm." One classmate recalled that Ruth was "beautiful, outgoing, and friendly—not buddy-buddy with the world but she was very popular."[8] *According to another classmate, "She had this very quiet warmth, and a kind of magnetism."*[9]

As Ruth neared the end of her senior year, her mother's health took a sharp turn for the worse. In a futile attempt to prolong Celia's life, the doctors gave her an aggressive round of radiation treatment, which did nothing to relieve her pain but instead made her violently ill and increased her suffering. The week before Celia died she learned that Ruth, slated to graduate the following Tuesday, June 27, near the top of her class, had been chosen as one of a select few to be on a "Roundtable Forum of Honor" that would present commencement remarks at graduation. Neither Ruth nor Celia would be able to attend. Celia Bader died at home that Sunday, June 25, 1950, at the age of forty-eight. She was buried Monday afternoon next to her firstborn daughter, Marilyn. Ruth missed Tuesday's high school graduation ceremony to stay home with her grieving father.

3

Wiretapping: Cure Worse than Disease?

Letter to the Editor, *Cornell Daily Sun* (Nov. 30, 1953)

In the fall *of 1950, a few months after her mother's death, Ruth and her father packed her possessions into his aging Chevrolet and headed upstate to Cornell University, where Ruth had been awarded a full scholarship. Ruth's college years at Cornell as a government major would prove key to her intellectual and personal development. The two teachers who influenced her most were very different people: Vladimir Nabokov, a novelist and professor of European literature, and Robert E. Cushman, a political scientist and constitutional scholar.*

According to Ruth, Nabokov changed the way she read and wrote: "He used words to paint pictures. Even today, when I read, I notice with pleasure when an author has chosen a particular word, a particular place, for the picture it will convey to the reader." Ruth remembers Nabokov as a great showman and a spellbinding teacher, and recounted how his wife, Véra, would sit in the back of the third-floor lecture hall with its tall wooden doors and shake her head when he said something particularly outrageous. Ruth, whose judicial and scholarly writing is distinctively concise and well crafted, credits Nabokov: "I try to give people the picture in not too many words, and I strive to find the right words."[1]

But it was the eminent constitutional scholar and writer on civil liberties, Robert Cushman, who first encouraged Ruth to go to law school. He may also have sowed in her the first seeds of the legal activism that characterized her work on behalf of gender equality under law in the 1970s. Professor Cushman supervised her independent studies project and then hired her as his research assistant. The early 1950s were the heyday of the Cold War and Senator Joseph McCarthy's destructive campaign against those he labeled "card-carrying communists." Before encountering Professor Cushman, Ruth confessed, "I didn't want to think about these things; I really just wanted to get good grades and become successful—but he was both a teacher and a consciousness raiser."[2] *Cushman, who assigned her to research McCarthy's assault on civil liberties, "wanted me to understand two things," Ruth recalls. "One is that we were betraying our most fundamental values, and, two, that legal skills could help make things better, could help to challenge what was going on."*[3]

Ruth understood. In November of her senior year, she made her first foray into the realm of published legal argument, penning a letter to the editor of the Cornell Daily Sun *on the admissibility of wiretapping evidence in espionage cases. Her piece was a response to a letter to the editor by two Cornell law students, expressing their support for Attorney General Herbert Brownell's proposal, inspired by what Brownell said were recent "disclosures of successful communist espionage penetration in our government," that Congress enact a law allowing federal prosecutors to introduce wiretap evidence when trying espionage cases. The law students cited a 1928 Supreme Court case,* Olmstead v. United States, *holding that wiretapping of private telephone calls by federal agents without a search warrant is not a search and seizure in violation of the Fourth Amendment. The law students argued that wiretapping in such situations was not only constitutional but in the interests of national security: "Today . . . we find ourselves facing a rising 'crime' wave. No person, whether he be an adherent of McCarthyism or not, should righteously attempt to protect people who can be proved guilty of crimes by preventing the use of damning evidence."*

While lawyer, judge, and Justice Ruth Bader Ginsburg would go on to craft hundreds of legal arguments and opinions, certain hallmarks of her legal writing and thought—her care in choosing words, her wariness of politically motivated prosecution, her concern that shortcuts in the name of efficiency often reduce effectiveness in the long run, and her unswerving commitment to individual rights and the presumption of innocence—shone through even in that first letter to her college newspaper. And, in classic Ruth Ginsburg fashion, the letter displayed none of the shrillness, bombast, or ideological fer-

vor that can sometimes characterize the writings of college students and even some judges. This was not by accident. "I hope you noticed," Justice Ginsburg remarked, when asked about her letter to the editor some five decades later, "how moderate I was!"[4]

Cornell Daily Sun
Monday, November 30, 1953
Letter to the Editor
Wiretapping: Cure Worse than Disease?

To the Editor:

Perhaps, as was argued by two law students in Tuesday's issue, the Supreme Court wanted the regulation of wiretapping to be left to Congress, and therefore, upheld the constitutionality of wiretapping in the *Olmstead* case. However, few would agree that what is deemed constitutional is necessarily worthy or wise.

Of course, society is interested in apprehending criminals, but the protection of the innocent has always been basic to our concept of justice. Both these ends must be weighed and balanced as to their relative merits before any conclusion can be reached about Mr. Brownell's proposal to admit evidence obtained by wiretapping in federal criminal trials.

What did the law students mean by telling us that we are faced with a rising "crime" wave? Were they speaking about an increase in the activities of gangsters and racketeers, or the growing number of cases in which individuals are being prosecuted for political crimes against the state? Particularly in the case of political crimes, the value of making it easier to apply the criminal sanction, when the conduct in question often involves slight danger and little conscious wrongdoing, should be seriously reflected.

In the first place, what is the purpose of the criminal sanction? Is it just to put a man behind bars, or is it to attach the moral condemnation of the community to certain forms of behavior? Unless moral judgment is involved, the cost of enforcing the criminal code might well be employed in other areas.

Today, restraints have been imposed in areas where individual free choice was formerly permitted. To a large extent, restrictions have been necessary for the good of society. However, the criminal sanction is still the most extreme measure that is available to the government, and it should not be lightly employed if other satisfactory alternatives can be substituted. We may regard something as an emergency measure today, but we should remember that the criminal law not only reflects the moral outlook of the community, but may very well alter or create moral attitudes. When attempts to prevent certain forms of behavior may place individual rights and liberties in peril, the criminal sanction should be saved as a last resort.

Wiretapping may save the government investigators a good deal of time and effort by making it unnecessary to seek other sources of proof. A thorough investigation of cases may seem like a burdensome task, especially when the shortcut of wiretapping can achieve more immediate results. As an officer in India once said, "It is far pleasanter to sit comfortably in the shade rubbing red pepper into a poor devil's eyes than to go out in the sun hunting the evidence."

But, even if the situation today demands increased vigilance on the part of the government, restraints on individual rights in the field of individual privacy, morality, and conscience can be a cure worse than the disease. We may be anxious to reduce crime, but we should remember that in our system of justice, the presumption of innocence is prime, and the law cannot apply one rule to Joe who is a good man, and another to John, who is a hardened criminal.

The general good Mr. Brownell's proposal is expected to accomplish seems to me to be outweighed by the general harm it may well do.

RUTH BADER '54

PAGE FOUR — CORNELL DAILY SUN — MONDAY, NOVEMBER 30, 1953

The Georgia Press . . .

Freedom Is for Sissies

'Way down south in Georgia everyone licks hambones, eats candied yams, cracks pecan nuts and remains complacently happy throughout his terrestial stay. Every once in a long while, though, somebody pipes up against the long-hallowed institutions that provide for the complacent happiness. And when there is such an occurrence, brother there's fireworks.

Handful Of Squirts

Such was the reason for the ranting editorial remarks of a mature newspaper publisher and former speaker of the state legislature of Georgia recently. His target was two editors of the University of Georgia weekly student newspaper who had dared to take a "liberal" view of questions concerning racial segregation in public schools. Of course, said Mr. Roy C. Harris, weekly newspaper publisher, member of the Board of Regents and one of the state's foremost political powers, anybody expressing these views are nothing but "a little handful of sissy, misguided squirts."

And furthermore:

"Every time I see one of these little sissy boys hanging around some college, the more I think every one of them ought to be made to play football.

". . . the time has come to clean out all of these institutions of all communist influences and the crazy idea of mixing and mingling of the races which was sponsored in this country by the Communist Party."

Mr. Harris went on to say: "The state of Georgia pays a big price to educate its college students. If the state is willing to spend this money, it has the right to control what is taught and what is done at the University."

Prior to Mr. Harris's published remarks, he told the student paper editors that one-third of their $15,000 would be cut if there were any more editorials attacking segregation. The next day the students published a story telling how Mr. Harris had threatened to "put us out of business."

This, Mr. Harris denied. "I didn't threaten them," he said. "I just told them what was going to happen."

Students Apologize

Following this exchange, the student editors met with University officials, the result being a written letter of apology by the students who expressed concern over the fact that they had created "an embarrassing situation for the university or for the Board of Regents . . ."

The students signed the letter to show their interest in the university's "growth and development." The result of the affair has been an attempt to set up a system of student-faculty approval for controversial editorials that will "allow for some measure of student expression."

This whole incident is just so remote from the Cornell way of life that it appears almost laughable. But it isn't so very funny when one considers that the individual's and the newspaper's right to free expression were squelched within the bounds of this nation.

Easily Forgotten

Mr. Harris and his kind are deeply embued in tradition. As educated persons, they've been exposed to documents upon which a rich tradition has been built in this country. What do they think of when they refer to "the crazy idea of the mixing and mingling of races?" How can they so easily forget that this nation was founded on the premise that "all men are created equal?" And how can they use freedom of the press, guaranteed to them by another great tradition, to quelch another person's use of that same freedom?

Of course this can all be brushed off very easily with something to the effect that "well that's the way things are in the South but the situation is improving every day."

This isn't the case, however. Only last week, the press's right to free expression and discretion was subverted by one Joseph McCarthy, senator from Wisconsin, who, subtlely using the threat of an investigation, forced the nation's radio and television operators to accord him free time to refute political utterances against him. He was granted free time, $300,000 worth in fact, which he used only incidentally to refute the charges but more specifically to hurl new vitriolic brickbats at indiscriminate targets.

It is too coincidental that George D. Stoddard, former president of the University of Illinois, recently noted "a discernible shift toward bigotry" in the United States today. He went on to warn of "the paranoid state of mind that once perpetrated the Inquisition, the Salem witch-hunt, the Ku Klux Klan."

Mr. Harris, Senator McCarthy, et al—take note of tradition not numbered in your catalog as outlined by Dr. Stoddard:

"Freedom is indivisable, to invade it at one place is to degrade it everywhere."

Good Morning, Kiddies

Albert's Pride and Abner's Fall

Albert was just coming to the realization that he was on the receiving end of a beanbag and not a football as we left the swamp critters. All ready to join in the fun, however, his high hopes were dashed as he was told that he would have to wear a middie blouse and bloomers.

"Big time bean bag requires correct attire!" exhorted his buxom coach, with the additional hint that Albert could "turn in his sneakers" if he persisted in his refusal to don the traditional bean bag togs.

"Doggone, coach, I'll be the laughing stock of the Rose Bowl," Albert insists, overlooking the fact that Michigan State has already accepted.

The faithful dog, already attired in the proper regalia, responds, realistically, "We'll more likely go into the Orange Bowl . . . on account it's closer."

"Finally Albert succumbs: "Well, okay, middie blouse but no bloomers."

The next day, apparently due to Albert's modesty and consequent reluctance to change his clothes in front of the readers, we find him in both blouse and bloomers, warming up his best bean-bag arm.

"By jing, I don't see how the country is sudden gone bean bag crazy," says Albert, apparently still not wholly convinced that the bloomers are worth it all.

The repartees are quick and effective: "They sniggered when ma invented mah jong," says the loyal Beauregard, while the winged coach points out that "When L'il Abner Doubleday sat down to play baseball everybody laughed."

But artist Kelly has not forgotten that the bean-baggers are still students, or rather professors, in Owl's newly founded university.

"Phoo," the dejected founder mutters, his hands dejectedly held behind his bowed back. "The harebrains of this swamp is unculturable . . . We got no students in our college . . . just perfessors an' all of them playing games. If somebody was to give the school a million dollars they'd go an' build a stadium."

"Why not a liberry? We already is loaded with comic books . . ." Owl questions the bat triplets. Again the repartees are quick and effective: "A stadium will hold 60,000 screaming cash customers, but who ever saw 60,000 souls throwing down hard money to stampede into a liberry?"

For the details of the construction of the new bean bag stadium (a prediction based on the not too reasonable assumption that Kelly evolves his strip in a straight line) turn to page 6.

PHOO! THE HAREBRAINS OF THIS SWAMP IS UNCULTURABLE... WE GOT NO STUDENTS IN OUR COLLEGE...JES' PERFESSORS AN' ALL OF THEM IS PLAYIN' GAMES!
HOWDY, OWL.
I GOT SIX JACKS I WIN.
HOW COME? I GOT SEVEN.
11-28

Abner failed his son. In four words can be summed up the failure of Al Capp's leading man to live up to his duties and responsibilities as a father. We knew the marriage was a mistake.

Nightmare Alice's conjuring up an imaginary beast lead Abner to grab his assailant, thereby making it not a little easier for her to grab him.

"Nightmare Alice played a trick on me only a fathead would of fell fo'," moans the dejected father to Daisie Mae as he is led across the finish line. "An' you fell fo' it?' she asks. "Natcherly," Abner sobs in reply, his patriarchal dignity seemingly shattered.

Marryin' Sam again enters the scene, asks for his $2.00 in advance (justifying the unusually high price with the prediction that "when they grow up an' finds what ah done to 'em they takes pot-shots at me!"), and the wedding continues—on page 6.

Letters to the Editor

Wiretapping: Cure Worse Than Disease?

To the Editor:

Perhaps, as was argued by two law students in Tuesday's issue, the Supreme Court wanted the regulation of wire tapping to be left to Congress, and therefore, upheld the constitutionality of wire tapping in the Olmstead case. However, few would agree that what is deemed constitutional is necessarily worthy or wise.

Of course, society is interested in apprehending criminals, but the protection of the innocent has always been basic to our concept of justice. Both these ends must be weighed and balanced as to their relative merits before any conclusion can be reached about Mr. Brownell's proposal to admit evidence obtained by wire tapping in federal criminal trials.

What did the law students mean by telling us that we are faced with a rising "crime" wave? Were they speaking about an increase in the activities of gangsters and racketeers, or the growing number of cases in which individuals are being prosecuted for political crimes against the state? Particularly in the case of political crimes, the value of making it easier to apply the criminal sanction, when the conduct in question often involves slight danger and little conscious wrongdoing, should be seriously reflected.

In the first place, what is the purpose of the criminal sanction? Is it just to put a man behind bars, or is it to attach the moral condemnation of the community to certain forms of behavior? Unless moral judgment is involved, the cost of enforcing the criminal code might well be employed in other areas.

Today, restraints have been imposed in areas where individual free choice was formerly permitted. To a large extent, restrictions have been necessary for the good of society. However, the criminal sanction is still the most extreme measure that is available to the government, and it should not be lightly employed if other satisfactory alternatives can be substituted. We may regard something as an emergency measure today, but we should remember that the criminal law not only reflects the moral outlook of the community, but may very well alter or create moral attitudes. When attempts to prevent certain forms of behavior may place individual rights and liberties in peril, the criminal sanction should be saved as a last resort.

Wire tapping may save the government investigators a good deal of time and effort by making it unnecessary to seek other sources of proof. A thorough investigation of cases may seem like a burdensome task, especially when the short cut of wire tapping can achieve more immediate results. As an officer in India once said, "It is far pleasanter to sit comfortably in the shade rubbing red pepper into a poor devil's eyes than to go out in the sun hunting evidence."

But, even if the situation today demands increased vigilance on the part of the government, restraints on individual rights in the field of individual privacy, morality, and conscience can be a cure worse than the disease. We may be anxious to reduce crime, but we should remember that in our system of justice, the presumption of innocence is prime, and the law cannot apply one rule to Joe who is a good man, and another to John who is a hardened criminal.

The general good Mr. Brownell's proposal is expected to accomplish seems to me to be outweighed by the general harm it may well do.

—Ruth Bader '54

The Cornell Daily Sun

Founded 1880. Incorporated 1905. Published every weekday except Saturday during the college year by The Cornell Daily Sun, Incorporated. Offices, 109 E. State Street. Telephone 3488 or 3489.

An independent newspaper edited by undergraduates of Cornell University. Editorial views do not reflect the official position of the University or necessarily represent the opinion of its student body. Letters to the editor and all other material submitted for publication become the property of this newspaper.

Member of the Associated Collegiate Press

MEMBER OF THE ASSOCIATED PRESS

The Associated Press is exclusively entitled to the use for republication of all news dispatches credited to it, or not otherwise credited in this paper, and also the local news items published herein.

REPRESENTED FOR NATIONAL ADVERTISING BY
National Advertising Service, Inc.
College Publishers Representative
420 Madison Ave. New York, N. Y.
Chicago • Boston • Los Angeles • San Francisco

Five Cents at newstands, Subscriptions, $6.50 per year

Printed by the Ithaca Journal. Entered as second class matter October 3, 1946, at the post office, Ithaca, New York, under the Act of March 3, 1879.

Stuart H. Loory '54 .... Editor-in-Chief
Donald A. Bandman '54 .... Business Manager
Ellen R. Shapiro '54 .... Managing Editor
Ross D. Wetzsteon '54 .... Associate Editor

4

Marty Ginsburg's Favorite Subject

Remarks Introducing Justice Ginsburg (Sept. 25, 2003)

As Marty Ginsburg *recounts in the following piece, it was during her first year at Cornell that Ruth Bader, then seventeen, met the man who would become first her best friend and then her husband and life partner. Marty Ginsburg, eighteen and a sophomore, was handsome, gregarious, brilliant, and brash. He met freshman Ruth on a blind double date orchestrated by Marty's roommate Marc, who was dating a housemate of Ruth's, did not own a car, and wanted Marty to drive all four of them to a formal dance.*

As you will read in Marty's remarks, he was struck by Ruth's beauty from the very beginning. And, as he told us in an interview many years later, he quickly realized that she was more than just attractive. "I did not know she was also smart, but I discovered that when we had a second date and it came through to me that not only was she really smart, [but] unlike most of the smart first-year girls who hadn't yet decided to suppress their intelligence—and there were a few of those—she wasn't glib. I don't remember who said it first, but it's such a wonderful line and so accurate: Ruth is somebody who is simply not afraid of dead air time. If you ask her a question that requires a thought-through answer she will stop, think it through and then answer it. She has done that for the fifty-four years I have known her. She still does it at dinner."[1]

For her part, Ruth called Marty "the first guy ever interested in me because of what was in my head."[2] *Marty was an unusual man for the 1950s: not only was he not threatened by Ruth's intelligence, but he actively encouraged and took pride in her academic and professional pursuits. As Ruth explained, "He's so secure about himself, he never regarded me as any kind of threat to his ego. On the contrary, he took great pride in being married to someone he considered very able."[3] According to Ruth, Marty "always made me feel I was better than I thought I was, that I could accomplish whatever I sought. He had enormous confidence in my ability, more than I had in myself."[4]*

Despite meeting on a blind "date," their relationship remained platonic for some time because Ruth had a boyfriend who attended Columbia Law School and Marty a girlfriend at Smith College. But they soon became best friends, drawn together by shared intellectual interests and abilities, and were delighted to discover that they both loved opera, a passion shared by few of their peers. After Marty gave up his chemistry major because the afternoon science labs interfered with his golf team practice, he and Ruth enrolled in several of the same classes. Taking classes together was a strategic choice for Marty: Not only could he spend more time with Ruth, but he could also rely on her meticulous notes when he cut class.

Having already become such close friends, once Ruth and Marty became romantically involved, it did not take them long to realize that they wanted to marry and spend their lives together. Instead of one "aha" moment, it was more like a steady crescendo. In Marty's words: "When did I decide it would be a sensible idea that Ruth and I should spend the rest of our time together? I don't know, but I can assure you it was long before she did." It was clear to Marty, early on, "that I obviously was going to have a much better and much happier life with Ruth than without her." And when he proposed to Ruth—"I think we were in a car at the time," he recalls—she answered with a resounding "yes."[5] They were married in June 1954, weeks after Ruth graduated from Cornell and Marty finished his first year at Harvard Law School. Decades later, Ruth said, "It was the best decision I ever made."[6]

Introduction by Martin Ginsburg of Ruth Bader Ginsburg
Twentieth Anniversary of Women's Law and Public Policy Fellowship Program
Georgetown University Law Center
September 25, 2003

Well, as you heard, I am involved in tax law and when Wendy Williams and Mary Hartnett asked me to speak at what they said was appropriate length on what they termed my favorite subject naturally I prepared a lengthy discourse addressing the Supreme Court's performance in tax cases. Sadly, Wendy reacted with unexpected hostility and so instead I am going to speak a few minutes only about my life with Honorable Ruth. But you are the losers because, I promise you, the Supreme Court's performance in tax cases is exceedingly funny.

Well, we travel a lot. Our travels, like our life in the District of Columbia, afford memorable moments. In December 2000, just after *Bush v. Gore*, Ruth and I were in New York City to see the play *Proof*. And after the first act intermission, as we walked down the aisle to our seats, what seemed like the entire audience began to applaud, many stood, Ruth beamed. I beamed, too, leaned over, and whispered loudly, "I bet you didn't know there's a convention of tax lawyers in town." Well, without changing her bright smile, Ruth smacked me right in the stomach, but not too hard. And I give you this picture because it fairly captures our nearly fifty-year happy marriage, during which I have offered up an astonishing number of foolish pronouncements with absolute assurance, and Ruth, with only limited rancor, has ignored almost every one.

A few years ago, speaking of Ruth, who in 1972 was his first Columbia Law School tenure hire, Mike Sovern, former dean and president of Columbia, marvelously commented that he had known

Ruth for so long it had begun before either of them was worth cultivating. I'm not sure that was really true about Ruth and Mike but it certainly fits Ruth and me. We met as undergraduates at Cornell University on a blind date in 1950, she newly arrived and I one year ahead. The truth is, it was a blind date only on Ruth's side. I cheated. I asked a classmate to point her out in advance. "Oh she's really cute," I perceptively noticed, and then after a couple of evenings out, I added, "And, boy, she's really, really smart." And of course I was right on both counts.

And in the intervening fifty-three years, nothing changed. I will skip over those intervening years because you are old friends and you know about us, and, indeed, if you are not all old friends, you likely know the essentials, courtesy of an interview our dear daughter, Jane, a serpent's tooth if ever there was, volunteered to the press a decade ago. All smiles, Professor Jane announced she had grown up in a home in which responsibility was equally divided: her father did the cooking, she explained, and her mother did the thinking. It was Jane's press statement that convinced me truth should not be allowed as a defense in defamation actions.

Twenty years ago, in celebrating Ruth's then fiftieth birthday, her D.C. Circuit clerks asked lots of Ruth's friends and acquaintances to write "when-I-think-of-Ruth-Bader-Ginsburg" letters for compilation in a book of warm recollections. Jane, for example, contributed what she described as Mother's extraordinary pot roast recipe. It was horrifyingly accurate and extraordinarily funny. Ruth is no longer permitted in the kitchen. This by the demand of our children, who have taste.

To my mind, however, the very best letter was contributed by Anita Escudero, my wonderful secretary from pre-teaching days when I was a New York City lawyer. Anita, I should explain, was the world's fastest typist. She had been a world-class flamenco dancer in her youth; think about that! In any event, she wrote from what was special personal experience of the impact of Ruth's 1970s efforts to advance gender equality, and because her letter is far better than anything I might write or ever have, I propose to read, in its brief entirety, this previously unpublished grand testimonial to my wife's pre-judicial influence on American life:

> When I think of Ruth Bader Ginsburg, I think of the words *sexual* and *gender*. *Gender-Based Discrimination* was a book I typed for her when I arrived in New York. I had been in New York only a very short time. Born in Arizona, I lived most of my life in Spain and South America. My family needed money and I got a job at a law firm typing in the steno pool. One morning, RBG's husband walked in and handed me 100 pages of handwritten material dealing with sex discrimination, abortion, and so on. I was horrified. The words *female* and *male* loomed out at me. I had never seen or heard them used the way she used them. I had never even thought about those distinctions. I started typing.
>
> Over the next few months in walked this shirtsleeved lawyer with his yellow pad of handwritten notes on this nonsensical subject of sex discrimination. Poverty abounded in great America and I kept typing. One morning the shirtsleeved lawyer announced, "My wife is coming in." I thought, "Good God, here she comes, the weird one." In walked this little five-foot, 100-pound woman with a soft voice wearing a green dashiki and I thought, "It can't be the same woman. She's not supposed to look like that. She's supposed to look like George Sand. Where's the cigar? The fly on her pants?" I kept typing.
>
> I went to Seville, Spain, on vacation with my family, where I have a home. We were invited to a large cocktail party and the room was full of males and females. In walked Anita with her husband. The host presented him: "Don Mario Escudero." Don Mario in turn said, "Esta es mi mujer"—"This is my woman." I threw my chest out and said, "I am not your woman, I am a person! My name is Anita L'Oise Ramos Mosteiro de Escudero!" From the back of the room boomed the host's eighty-year-old grandmother: "¡Viva America!" I had been converted through typing.

Well, whether through typing, reading, listening, [or] arguing, Ruth's work in the 1970s as a teacher and a litigator converted multitudes, including, as we all know, that largest of multitudes, a majority of the Supreme Court. And if Ruth, in 1980, at age forty-seven, retired to a life of TV and bonbons, she would have enjoyed a significant place in twentieth-century history—although with those bonbons a rather fat place.

Well, of course, she did not retire or get fat. She went on to better work. Thirteen years on the D.C. Circuit, where, to take but one example, her efforts on behalf of the ICC's filed rate doctrine will never be forgotten. Rather more important work over the past ten years at the Marble Palace, efforts on behalf of everybody, everyone I guess except the ICC, long departed. In all events, we celebrate this evening a grand performance born of great intelligence, fine judgment, personal warmth, unremittingly hard work, and an advantageous marriage, which is just what I expected after our second date fifty-three years ago. The next decade with only a little luck I am sure will be even better.

I introduce to you the Honorable Ruth Ginsburg.

Ruth and Marty embrace while attending an event.

Ruth and Marty together at Marty's home, following their engagement party, which was held at the Persian Room of the Plaza Hotel in New York City on December 27, 1953.

5

Law and Lawyers in Opera

RUTH GINSBURG'S *fondness for music and especially opera, which she shared with Marty and later, famously, with Justice Antonin Scalia, began at an early age. Ruth played piano in her grade school orchestra, conducted by Miss Murphy. "Others in the orchestra had more talent," she says, "but I tried hard."*[1] *She would ride the subway from her home in Brooklyn to her piano teacher's studio on West 73rd Street in Manhattan for lessons. Ruth's mother and her aunt Cornelia often took Ruth and her cousins to Saturday matinees for children at the Brooklyn Academy, ballet and opera performances at the City Center, and child-friendly hour-long operas conducted and narrated for children by orchestra conductor Dean Dixon. The first opera Ruth ever attended was a Dean Dixon children's version of* La Gioconda, *where she was enthralled by the singing and captivated by the characters: two rivaling beauties; the evil scorned spy; the vengeful betrayed husband; the blind pious mother; and the handsome sea captain, a nobleman in disguise.*

Justice Ginsburg has often said that if she could have chosen any profession she would have loved to be a diva, but she lacked the talent. Despite having to "settle" for her current position as a Supreme Court Justice, she has had the chance to take to the stage, too, in three cameo appearances as a "super" at the Washington National Opera. She debuted in 1994, along with Justice Scalia, in a production of Richard Strauss' Ariadne auf Naxos, *and again when that opera was performed in 2009. She was also onstage in 2003 in Johann Strauss'* Die Fledermaus, *together with Justices Anthony Kennedy and Stephen Breyer: the three black-robed Justices appeared at Prince Orlofsky's ball as specially announced guests, "The Supremes," while Placido Domingo serenaded them. Imagine Justice Ginsburg's delight and surprise when, in 2011, she traveled to Harvard to accept an honorary degree and fellow awardee Plácido Domingo serenaded her as part of the degree conferral.*

Justice Ginsburg is serenaded by opera singer Plácido Domingo while the two receive honorary degrees from Harvard on May 26, 2011.

In the following remarks, Justice Ginsburg reflects on ways in which the law and lawyers have been portrayed in various operas.

Law and Lawyers in Opera
Remarks for WFMT Radio Broadcast*
Chicago, Illinois
September 21, 2015

Truth be told, lawyers do not figure nobly in opera plots. They show up most often as notaries authenticating documents, mainly marriage

---

*Justice Ginsburg has delivered numerous versions of these remarks to various audiences over the years. In this particular broadcast, she was accompanied by young singers from the Chicago Lyric Opera's Ryan Center, who performed several pieces. We have removed specific references to the Ryan Center singers and have edited the remarks for length and to ensure clarity outside the specific context in which they were originally delivered.

contracts, and have few notes to sing. There are bit parts for lawyers in *Fledermaus* and *Porgy and Bess*. Dr. Blind, the lawyer in *Fledermaus*, is so ineffective he gains for his client, Eisenstein, a few extra days in jail. And the lawyer in *Porgy and Bess* offers Bess a divorce for a dollar, then ups the price to $1.50 when Bess tells him she was never really married before.

Law enforcement does figure importantly in many an opera plot. Prisons are a favorite setting for doleful arias and duets that sometimes run on rather long. Regular opera goers will think immediately of *Fidelio*, *Trovatore*, *Don Carlos*, *Faust*, *Tosca*, *Dialogues of the Carmelites*, more recently, *Dead Man Walking*, and scores more.

Law enforcement in Bizet's *Carmen* is in a lighter vein. It involves a jail order, not a prison sentence, and portrays a plea bargain of an unusual sort. In Act I Carmen has assaulted and wounded a coworker in a Seville cigarette factory. To punish her for that infraction, the captain of the brigade orders Don José, the hapless tenor, to cart Carmen off to jail. En route, she negotiates a deal. If Don José allows her to escape, she will sing and dance for him at the cabaret owned by her friend, Lillas Pastia. As the opera progresses, Carmen gets her man, then she does him woefully wrong.

Contracts are prominent in opera plots. The *sturm und drang* in Wagner's *Ring* cycle stem from a breach of contract: Wotan's attempt to renege on his agreement to compensate the giants, Fafner and Fasolt, for building Valhalla, heavenly home of the Gods. The centrality of contract in the *Ring* was brought home to me vividly some years ago when a law clerk applicant submitted as his writing sample an essay titled: "The Significance of Contract, as Played Out in Wagner's *Ring* Cycle." What better illustration of the well-known legal maxim, *pacta sunt servanda*, in plain English, agreements must be kept. I hired that law clerk applicant on the spot.

Trials and inquests abound in grand opera. A select few: a Revolutionary Tribunal condemns the poet Andrea Chenier; in *Aida*, the priests of the immense God Phtah condemn Radames for treason; in *Norma*, the pagan throng lets the high priestess burn for breaking her vow of chastity.

A shipboard court-martial takes place in Benjamin Britten's *Billy Budd*. Some background for the scene. Billy is as good as he is beautiful. He is relentlessly pursued by First Officer John Claggert, who epitomizes evil. Claggert falsely accuses Billy as the ringleader of a planned mutiny. Billy has a tendency to stutter when agitated, and cannot get out words answering the accusation. He strikes Claggert, and the blow results in the officer's death. A drumhead court convened by ship-captain Vere finds Billy guilty, and sentences him to death, to be carried out on deck the following morning. Captain Vere accepts the court-martial's verdict.

But first, let me tell you of the model for Captain Vere. Author of the novella on which the opera is based, Herman Melville, had a father-in-law, Lemuel Shaw, an abolitionist at heart, but also a judge in Massachusetts obliged by his oath to enforce the Fugitive Slave Law implementing the Constitution's Fugitive Slave Clause. A conflict of the same order confronts Captain Vere. He knows Billy is good, and Claggert evil and untrustworthy, yet the law requires that a sailor found guilty of assaulting a superior officer hang from the yardarm. Captain Vere agonizes over his decision to convict, a classic conflict between man's law and divine justice.

Jake Heggie's *Dead Man Walking* portrays a man convicted of murder. Unlike Billy Budd, Joseph DeRocher, the condemned man, has indeed done a terrible thing. But, his mother asks in a moving aria, what does killing him accomplish? Some modern-day context follows.

On June 29, 2015, the last opinion announcement day of the Supreme Court's 2014–15 Term, the Court upheld lethal injection, as currently compounded and administered, as a permissible means of carrying out the death penalty. The vote was 5–4. I joined Justice Breyer's separate dissent, which addressed a more basic question: whether the death penalty, whatever the means employed, is itself unconstitutional. What had experience shown since 1976 when, after a four-year hiatus, the Court allowed states to reinstate the death penalty? Justice Breyer listed four considerations.

First, *reliability* or *accuracy*. Post-1976, more than 100 individuals convicted of capital crimes (and sentenced to death) were later fully exonerated, some of them years after their executions took place.

Second, *arbitrariness*. Factors that should not affect imposition of the death penalty, studies documented, often do, prime among those factors, race and geography.

Third, a matter of time. The average execution occurs some eighteen years after the individual was sentenced to death. Part of the reason for the long delays is the multiple opportunities for appeal available to prisoners sentenced to death. Delay thus might be regarded as a self-inflicted wound. Yet conditions during the wait can be cruel, especially if the waiting time is spent in solitary confinement. What is the alternative to delay? In 2014, a man on death row was exonerated by DNA evidence after spending thirty years on death row. If his sentence had been carried out swiftly, or in ten, even twenty years, he would not have lived to know of his exoneration.

Fourth, perhaps in light of the first three considerations, the incidence of the death penalty has steeply declined. Nineteen states have abolished it, including most recently, Nebraska, by ballot initiative. In 2014, only seven states conducted executions. In forty-three states, there were none. Moreover, the practice is largely confined to a small and diminishing subset of counties.

Ultimately, the considerations Justice Breyer discussed at length may bring us back to the years 1972–76, when no executions took place in the United States.

When must the law be interpreted strictly, and when should there be some elasticity, room for common sense? In the Supreme Court's 2014–15 Term, that dichotomy between literal and purposive reading of the law was evident in some dueling opinions, as it is in diverse operatic scenes. Though they wrote operettas, not grand operas, no team rivals Gilbert and Sullivan in treating law and lawyers satirically. On the distinction between strict and sensible construction of legal texts, *Pirates of Penzance* provides a most apt example.

The operetta's hero, Frederic, when he was a little lad, was, on his father's instruction, to be apprenticed to a pilot. Frederic's nursemaid,

Ruth, was a little hard of hearing, so she apprenticed Frederic to a pirate, instead of to a pilot. The terms of the apprenticeship, Frederic would serve the pirates until his twenty-first birthday. When Frederic has lived twenty-one years, he is released from the pirate band, and promptly undertakes to annihilate his former comrades, in league with his father-in-law to be, a character who is the very model of a modern major general.

But the Pirate King, and hard-of-hearing nursemaid Ruth, now serving as the Piratical Maid of Allworks, pay a visit to Frederic. They know he likes jokes, and have come to tell him of "a most amusing paradox." Frederic was born in a leap year, on the twenty-ninth of February. Strict construction of the text of his bond would make Frederic a lad of five and a little bit over. Purposive interpretation would count his years on earth and acquit him of his obligation to the pirates.

There is a happy ending. It turns out that the pirates were lapsed members of the peerage. They return to their former stations as members of the House of Lords, for above all else, pirates, policemen, and everyone else onstage unite in fidelity to their Queen.

There is a similar reconciliation in a new opera by composer/librettist Derrick Wang, titled *Scalia/Ginsburg*. [*For an excerpt, see p. 43*.] It is a comic opera that had its world premiere at the Castleton, Virginia, festival on July 11, 2015. Composer-librettist Wang wrote a duet for Justice Scalia and me. It is titled "We Are Different, We Are One." Different on questions of major import, but one in our reverence for the institution we serve. Never mind the words of some spicy opinions, we genuinely respect and like each other. Collegiality of that sort is what makes it possible for the Court to do the ever-challenging work the Constitution and Congress assign to us, without the animosity that currently mars the operation of the political branches of our government.

6

Remembering Justice Scalia

JUSTICE GINSBURG *delivered the following remarks at a memorial service held for her close friend "Nino" after his sudden and unexpected death on February 13, 2016. Although very different in temperament, judicial outlook, and political beliefs, the two developed a close friendship, beginning in the 1980s during their service together as judges on the U.S. Court of Appeals for the D.C. Circuit. As Justice Scalia told us in an interview in 2007, "We are two people who are quite different in their core beliefs, but who respect each other's character and ability. There is nobody else I spend every New Year's Eve with."*[1]

Justice Scalia, who had a talent for making the more sober Justice Ginsburg laugh, also was especially struck when he witnessed her tears. "A lot of people," he said, "have this notion that she is a sourpuss, and she is not. She's a pussycat. She's a really nice person. I'll tell you, [*this*] *shows you how tenderhearted—when we were in India together, we went to Agra to see the Taj Mahal and there is a doorway where you first get sight of it, you know the story of it, this guy built it for his deceased wife. She stood there, when we got there, in that doorway—tears were running down her cheek. That emotional. I mean, I was amazed."*[2]

Remembrances of a Treasured Colleague
Remarks at Memorial Service for Justice Antonin Scalia*
Mayflower Hotel, Washington, D.C.
March 1, 2016

The script of John Strand's play, *The Originalist*, opens with two quotations:

1) "[The] Fixed-Meaning Canon: Words must be given the meaning they had when the [legal] text was adopted."
2) "Such is the character of human language, that no word conveys to the mind, in all situations, one single definite idea . . . ."[1]

The first quotation is attributed to Antonin Scalia and Bryan A. Garner, *Reading Law: The Interpretation of Legal Texts*;[2] the second, to Chief Justice John Marshall.[3] Justice Scalia would no doubt stand by the words he and co-author Garner wrote. My view accords with the great Chief Justice's, and I believe Justice Scalia would agree that Marshall had a point. I leave to others discussion of Justice Scalia's provocative jurisprudence and will speak here, instead, of our enduring friendship from the years we served together on the U.S. Court of Appeals for the D.C. Circuit through the nearly twenty-three years we were two of nine Justices on the U.S. Supreme Court.

Among fond memories of Justice Scalia, an early June morning, 1996. I was about to leave the Court to attend the Second Circuit Judicial Conference at Lake George. Justice Scalia entered, opinion draft in hand. Tossing many pages onto my desk, he said: "Ruth, this is the penultimate draft of my dissent in the *VMI* case. It's not yet in shape to circulate to the Court, but the end of the Term is approaching, and I want to give you as much time as I can to answer it."

---

* These remarks have been edited and updated to include additional thoughts and memories that Justice Ginsburg shared in later tributes about Justice Scalia.

On the plane to Albany, I read the dissent. It was a zinger, of the "this wolf comes as a wolf" genre. It took me to task on things large and small. Among the disdainful footnotes: "The Court refers to the University of Virginia at Charlottesville. There is no University of Virginia at Charlottesville, there is only *the* University of Virginia." . . . Thinking about fitting responses consumed my weekend, but I was glad to have the extra days to adjust the Court's opinion. My final draft was more persuasive thanks to Justice Scalia's searing criticism. Indeed, whenever I wrote for the Court and received a Scalia dissent, the majority opinion ultimately released improved on my initial circulation. Justice Scalia homed in on the soft spots, and gave me just the stimulation I needed to strengthen the Court's decision.

Another indelible memory, the day the Court decided *Bush v. Gore*, December 12, 2000, I was in chambers, exhausted after the marathon: review granted Saturday, briefs filed Sunday, oral argument Monday, opinions completed and released Tuesday. No surprise, Justice Scalia and I were on opposite sides. The Court did the right thing, he had no doubt. I disagreed and explained why in a dissenting opinion. Around 9:00 p.m. the telephone, my direct line, rang. It was Justice Scalia. He didn't say "get over it." Instead, he asked, "Ruth, why are you still at the Court? Go home and take a hot bath." Good advice I promptly followed.

Among my favorite Scalia stories, when President Clinton was mulling over his first nomination to the Supreme Court, Justice Scalia was asked a question to this effect: "If you were stranded on a desert island with your new Court colleague, who would you prefer, Larry Tribe or Mario Cuomo?" Scalia answered quickly and distinctly: "Ruth Bader Ginsburg." Within days, the president chose me.

Among Justice Scalia's many talents, he was a discerning shopper. When we were in Agra together in 1994 for a judicial exchange with members of India's Supreme Court, our driver took us to his friend's carpet shop. One rug after another was tossed onto the floor, leaving me without a clue which to choose. Justice Scalia pointed to one he thought his wife, Maureen, would like for their beach house in North Carolina. I picked the same design, in a different color. It has worn very well.

I recall, too, a dark day for me, confined in a hospital in Heraklion, Crete, in the summer of 1999, the beginning of my long bout with colorectal cancer. What brought me to Crete? Justice Scalia's recommendation that I follow him as a teacher in Tulane Law School's summer program there. The first outside call I received was from Justice Scalia. "Ruth," he said, "I am responsible for your days in Crete, so you must get well. Is there anything I can do to help?"

Once asked how we could be friends, given our disagreement on lots of things, Justice Scalia answered: "I attack ideas. I don't attack people. Some very good people have some very bad ideas. And if you can't separate the two, you gotta get another day job. You don't want to be a judge. At least not a judge on a multi-member panel." Example in point, from his first days on the Court, Justice Scalia had great affection for Justice Brennan, as Justice Brennan was drawn to him.

I will miss the challenges and the laughter Justice Scalia provoked, his pungent, eminently quotable opinions, so clearly stated that his words never slipped from the reader's grasp, the roses he brought me on my birthday, the chance to appear with him once more as supernumeraries at the opera.

In his preface to the libretto of the opera buffo *Scalia/Ginsburg*, Justice Scalia described as the peak of his days in D.C. an evening in 2009 at the Opera Ball, at the British Ambassador's Residence, when he joined two Washington National Opera tenors at the piano for a medley of songs. He called it the famous Three Tenors performance. He was, indeed, a magnificent performer. How blessed I was to have a working colleague and dear friend of such captivating brilliance, high spirits, and quick wit. In the words of a duet for tenor Scalia and soprano Ginsburg, we were different, yes, in our interpretation of written texts, yet one in our reverence for the Court and its place in the U.S. system of governance.

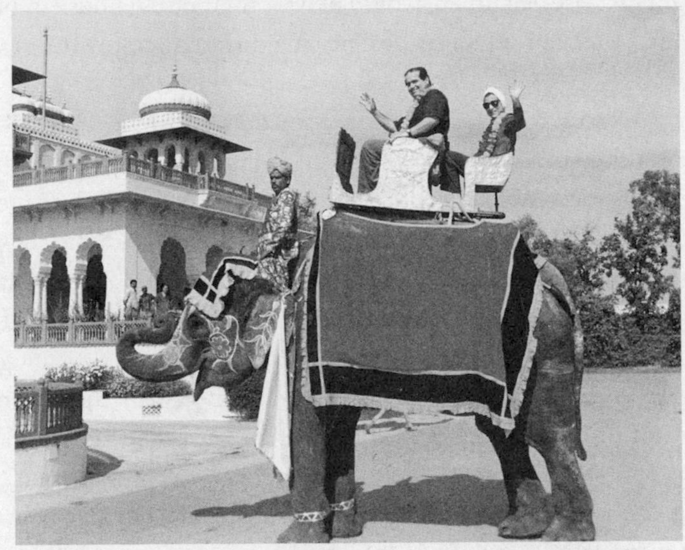

Justice Scalia and Justice Ginsburg pose on an elephant in Rajasthan during their tour of India in 1994.

Justice Ruth Bader Ginsburg (wearing a white dress and holding a fan on the left) and Justice Antonin Scalia (wearing a blue vest and a wig on the right) photographed during a production of Richard Strauss's opera Ariadne auf Naxos. *The Justices appeared as supernumeraries in the Washington National Opera's opening night production at the Kennedy Center in Washington, D.C., on January 7, 1994.*

7

The Scalia/Ginsburg Opera

When Derrick Wang's comic opera Scalia/Ginsburg *was reprinted in the* Columbia Journal of Law and the Arts, *it included prefaces by both Justices. Those prefaces follow, along with excerpts from the opera itself.**

Scalia/Ginsburg:

A (Gentle) Parody of Operatic Proportions

An American comic opera in one act by DERRICK WANG
Libretto by the composer

Inspired by the opinions of U.S. Supreme Court Justices
RUTH BADER GINSBURG and ANTONIN SCALIA

and by the operatic precedent of
HÄNDEL, MOZART, VERDI, BIZET, SULLIVAN, PUCCINI, STRAUSS, ET AL.†

Preface by Justice Ruth Bader Ginsburg

Scalia/Ginsburg is for me a dream come true. If I could choose the talent I would most like to have, it would be a glorious voice. I

*Justice Ginsburg's discussions of judicial philosophy and the value of collegiality, in Part V below, are reflected in the *Scalia/Ginsburg* opera.

† For the full opera, see Derrick Wang, *Scalia/Ginsburg*, 38 *Columbia Journal of Law and Arts* 237 (Winter 2015). The opera had its world premiere at the Castleton Festival in Castleton, Virginia, on July 11, 2015. The excerpt herein is used with the author's permission. Please contact info@derrickwang.com for inquiries regarding the licensing or performance of this opera or any portion thereof. (*Scalia/Ginsburg*, an Opera in one act. Music and Lyrics by Derrick Wang.

would be a great diva, perhaps Renata Tebaldi or Beverly Sills or, in the mezzo range, Marilyn Horne. But my grade school music teacher, with brutal honesty, rated me a sparrow, not a robin. I was told to mouth the words, never to sing them. Even so, I grew up with a passion for opera, though I sing only in the shower, and in my dreams.

One fine day, a young composer, librettist, and pianist named Derrick Wang approached Justice Scalia and me with a request. While studying constitutional law at the University of Maryland Law School, Wang had an operatic idea. The different perspectives of Justices Scalia and Ginsburg on constitutional interpretation, he thought, could be portrayed in song. Wang put his idea to the "will it write" test. He composed a comic opera with an important message brought out in the final duet, "We Are Different, We Are One"—one in our reverence for the Constitution, the U.S. judiciary, and the Court on which we serve.

Would we listen to some excerpts from the opera, Wang asked, and then tell him whether we thought his work worthy of pursuit and performance? Good readers, as you leaf through the libretto, check some of the many footnotes disclosing Wang's sources, and imagine me a dazzling diva, I think you will understand why, in answer to Wang's question, I just said, "Yes."

Preface by Justice Antonin Scalia

While Justice Ginsburg is confident that she has achieved her highest and best use as a Supreme Justice, I, alas, have the nagging doubt that I could have been a contendah—for a divus, or whatever a male diva is called. My father had a good tenor voice, which he trained at the Eastman School of Music. I sang in the Georgetown Glee Club (directed by *Washington Post* music critic Paul Hume, whom President Truman rewarded with a valuable letter for his review of Margaret's singing). I have sung in choirs and choral groups much of my life, up to and including my days on the D.C. Circuit. And the utter peak of my otherwise uneventful judicial career was an evening after the Opera Ball at the British Ambassador's Residence, when I joined two tenors from the Washington Opera singing various songs at the piano—the famous Three Tenors performance.

I suppose, however, that it would be too much to expect the author of *Scalia/Ginsburg* to allow me to play (sing) myself—especially if Ruth refuses to play (sing) herself. Even so, it may be a good show.

Excerpts from the Opera

LIBRETTO

TIME: The present.
SCENE: A chamber, somewhere in the Supreme Court of the United States. A statue is noticeable.

1. Opening (Orchestra)

2. Aria: "The Justices are blind!" (Scalia)

Rage aria, after Händel et al.: Furioso (ma non castrato).

Opening alarum.[1] *Enter JUSTICE SCALIA, in a power suit and high Händelian dudgeon.*

SCALIA:
This court's so changeable[2] —
As if it's never, ever known the law![3]

(Rage aria)[4]
The Justices are blind!
How can they possibly spout this—?
The Constitution says absolutely nothing about this,[5]
This right that they've enshrined[6] —
When did the document sprout this?
The Framers wrote and signed
Words that endured[7] without this;
The Constitution says absolutely nothing about this!

(Reverent)
We all know well what the Framers did say,
And (with certain amendments) their wording will stay,[8]
And these words of our Fathers limit us,
For we are unelected,[9]
And thus, when we interpret them,
Rigor is expected.[10]

(Bewildered)
Oh, Ruth, can you read? You're aware of the text,
Yet so proudly you've failed to derive its true meaning,[11]
And never were so few
Rights made so numerous—
It's almost humorous
What you construe![12]

(With increasing fervor)
Oh, well; oh, well; oh, well; oh, well:
You are the reason I have to rebel![13]

(Aria da capo, with vocal ornamentation)
Though you are all aligned
In your decision to flout this,
The Constitution says absolutely nothing about this—
So, though you have combined,
You would do well not to doubt this:
Since I have not resigned,[14]
I will proceed to shout this:[15]
"The Constitution says absolutely nothing about this!"

. . .

4. Scene: "Ah, there you are, Nino" . . .

Suddenly, the floor bursts open, and JUSTICE GINSBURG, elegantly attired, rises into the chamber.[16]

. . .

GINSBURG:
Ah, yes, the "broccoli horrible."[17]
Well, in my view, the situation is of questionable legality:
You are in a tricky spot.
Then again, if you consider the circumstances in their totality,
Unimaginable evil this is not.[18]
If you might be a bit more flexible—

SCALIA:
"Flexible!"
Like the constant concessions that judges are always demanding.
"Flexible!"
Which goes to show: it is a Constitution you are *expanding*.[19]
"Flexible!"
Just another word for "liberal,"[20]
Always "liberal". . .
What folly! what folly![21]

5. Duettino: "Always 'liberal'" (Scalia, Ginsburg)
Verdi-Mozart mashup. Tempo: Hey, presto![22]

SCALIA (cont'd):
Always "liberal,"[23] these judges:
How they flit from holding to holding . . .

GINSBURG:
Now, wait a minute, Nino,[24]
According to what *we* know,
It isn't only "liberals" who merit your complaint.
(Aside)
(It's not like he's a saint
In matters of restraint.[25])

SCALIA:
How their activism[26] nudges
Us beyond the bounds of the text . . .

GINSBURG:
This Court could very well be
Called "activist"[27] in *Shelby*,[28]
Where Congress's authority to act was at its height[29] —
Yet Congress lost the fight
To judges on the right.[30]

SCALIA:
With their overreaching[31] scolding
And their personal opinions . . .[32]

GINSBURG:
But it isn't overreaching
To oppose discrimination—

SCALIA:
Which, according to your preaching,[33]
Merits proper extirpation?[34]

GINSBURG:
Yes, through proper legislation
That imposes prohibitions—

SCALIA:
Unless we have a situation
Such as race-based admissions![35]

According to your knowledge,[36]
An applicant to college
Can have his fate determined by the color of his skin,
But whether that's a sin
Depends on who gets in.[37]

Is that *not* discrimination
Where the state could be the actor?[38]

GINSBURG:
But that is just a factor,
A factor of a factor,
A "factor of a factor of a factor of a factor."[39]

And people need protection
Against the vile infection[40]
Of rank discrimination in the form of racial caste,[41]
Which looks like it could last
Unless we end it fast.

And saying that our future'll
Be suddenly "race-neutral"
Is acting like an ostrich with its head stuck in the sand—
Because it cannot stand
To see what plagues our land.[42]

SCALIA:
I agree that it is vital
To make whole the wronged *individuals*,
But to reinforce entitle-
Ment will only lead to more harm.[43]

GINSBURG:
What hubris! what hubris![44]

6. Aria & Variations: "You are searching in vain (for a bright-line solution)" (Ginsburg)

After Verdi et al.

GINSBURG (cont'd):
How many times must I tell you,
Dear Mister Justice Scalia:
You'd spare us such pain
If you'd just entertain
This idea . . .
(Then you *might* relax your rigid posture.)[45]

(À la Verdi)[46]
You are searching in vain for a bright-line solution
To a problem that isn't so easy to solve—

But the beautiful thing about our Constitution
Is that, like our society, it can evolve.

For our Founders, of course, were great men with a vision,
But their culture restricted how far they could go,
So, to us, I believe, they bequeath the decision
To allow certain meanings to flourish—
(With a vocal flourish)
—and grow.[47]

(A short cadenza, which evolves via scat solo into a jazz waltz)[48]
Let 'em grow . . .
For the law of the land in that era was grounded
In the notion that justice was just for the few,[49]
But the Founders' assumption was wholly unfounded,
So we've had to subject it to further review.

So we're freeing the people we used to hold captive,[50]
Who deserve to be more than just servants or wives.[51]
If we hadn't been willing to be so adaptive,
Can you honestly say we'd have led better[52] lives?

(A short cadenza, which leads to a gospel-pop ballad)
And we can't wait for slow legislation
To catch up with the lives that we already lead;
We have rights, and they need preservation,
And we have to remember this if we intend to succeed:

Though we won't be afraid of forgiving,
We must not stop in our mission to right every wrong—
Not until We the People and our Constitution are living[53]
In a nation, in a place
That, regardless of station or race,
Is a nation where all of us truly belong![54]

(À la Verdi)
So, until every person is treated as equal
Well beyond what the Founders initially saw,

Let our past and our present be merely the prequel
To a future enlightened by flexible law!

(Roulades in all three styles: opera, jazz and pop)
Law, law, law!

. . .

13. Recitative: "I asked for silence" (Commentator)

. . . An uncomfortably long silence. Then:

COMMENTATOR:
(Eerily calm)
I asked for silence:
Now it is broken.
Justice Scalia,
You who have spoken:
Your precious chance at redemption has vanished:
(Suddenly terrifying)
You have sealed your fate—
And you must be banished!

. . .

This,
This is your fate—
Unless you recant your originalist creed.
That is all you have to do to be freed.
Now, Justice Scalia,
Now, what do you say?

14. Aria: "Structure is destiny" (Scalia)

. . .

SCALIA (cont'd):

I reject your bargain.

. . .

15. Scene: "That won't do" (Ginsburg, Commentator, Scalia)

. . .

GINSBURG:
Banish *me* with him,
For I spoke too.

SCALIA:
Ruth, do not enslave yourself
To my infernal fate . . .

Ruth, leave now and save yourself
Before it is too late . . .

COMMENTATOR:
But what are your grounds?
Justice Ginsburg,
Justify your demand;
Explain this peculiar choice.

GINSBURG:
We serve justice together,
And that means we can speak with one voice.[55]
And here, I choose to join him.[56]

SCALIA:
Ruth, are you sure this is productive?

GINSBURG:
(To the COMMENTATOR, re: SCALIA)
He spoke,
So I spoke.
You may consider *my* speech—constructive.
So banish *me* with him,
For I spoke too.

COMMENTATOR:
But *why* would you do this for your enemy?

GINSBURG, SCALIA:
Enemy?

GINSBURG:
Hardly.

SCALIA:
Sheer applesauce![57]

GINSBURG:
I would not.
But I would do this for my friend.[58]

COMMENTATOR:
Friend?
But you two are so . . . different!

SCALIA, GINSBURG:
Yes:

16. Duet: "We are different. We are one" (Scalia, Ginsburg)

SCALIA, GINSBURG (cont'd):
We are different.
We are one.
The U.S. contradiction—

SCALIA:
The tension we adore:[59]

SCALIA, GINSBURG:
Separate strands unite in friction
To protect our country's core.
This, the strength of our nation,
Thus is our Court's design:

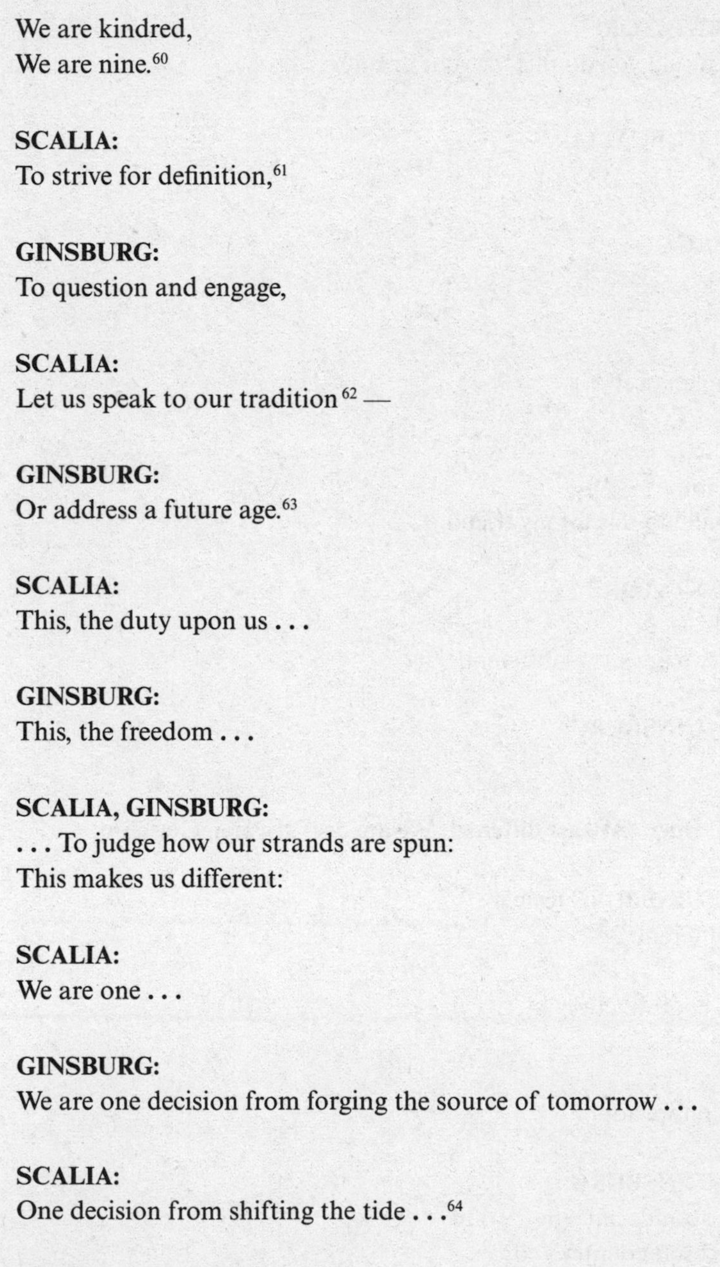

We are kindred,
We are nine.[60]

SCALIA:
To strive for definition,[61]

GINSBURG:
To question and engage,

SCALIA:
Let us speak to our tradition[62] —

GINSBURG:
Or address a future age.[63]

SCALIA:
This, the duty upon us . . .

GINSBURG:
This, the freedom . . .

SCALIA, GINSBURG:
. . . To judge how our strands are spun:
This makes us different:

SCALIA:
We are one . . .

GINSBURG:
We are one decision from forging the source of tomorrow . . .

SCALIA:
One decision from shifting the tide . . .[64]

SCALIA, GINSBURG:
Always one decision from charting the course we will steer . . .[65]

For our future
Is unclear,
But one thing is constant—
The Constitution we revere.[66]
We are stewards of this trust;[67]
We uphold it as we must,
For the work of our Court is just
Begun . . .

And this is why we will see justice done:
We are different;
We are one.

8

The Lighter Side of Life at the Supreme Court

Opera is hardly the only basis for Justice Ginsburg's friendships with her colleagues on the bench. The following speech, given by Justice Ginsburg frequently over the years, discusses the lighter side of life at the Court and highlights customs that have helped encourage collegiality—something Justice Ginsburg values highly and promotes constantly—among the Justices.

Lighter Side of Life at the United States Supreme Court
Remarks Presented to the Association of Business Trial Lawyers*
US Grant Hotel, San Diego, California
February 8, 2013

In these remarks, I will speak not of the heavy lifting done at my workplace, but of the lighter side of life in our Marble Palace, and of certain customs that promote collegiality among the nine Justices.

My first comment concerns our routine gatherings. They begin with handshakes. Before the start of each day in Court, and before each conference discussion, as we enter the Robing Room or the adjacent Conference Room, we shake hands, each Justice with every other. (In

*Justice Ginsburg has delivered numerous versions of these remarks to various audiences over the years. We have edited the remarks for length and to ensure clarity outside the specific context in which they were originally delivered.

total, the mathematically inclined will have computed, handshakes pre-conference or pre-sitting mornings total 36.) Every day the Court hears arguments, and every day we meet to discuss cases, we lunch together in the Justices' Dining Room. The room is elegant, but the lunch is not haute cuisine. It comes from the Court's public cafeteria, the same fare available to anyone who visits the Court.

We lunch together by choice, not by rule, usually six to eight of us, and more than occasionally all nine. When Justice O'Connor (retired since 2006) is in town, she sometimes shares the lunch hour with us and enlivens our conversation with reports of her travels and efforts to promote judicial independence in the United States and around the globe. Also of her project to advance civics education in our nation's grade schools. Justice Stevens, who retired in 2010, also joins us occasionally. Now in his nineties, he is still an avid player of tennis and golf. Justice Souter, retired in 2009, is not fond of city life, Boston excepted. So we seldom see him in D.C., but he sits regularly on First Circuit panels.

What do we talk about at lunch? Perhaps the lawyers' performance in the cases just heard, or a new production in town, for example, at the D.C. Shakespeare Theatre or the Washington National Opera, or the latest exhibition at the Library of Congress, National Gallery, or Phillips Collection. Sometimes Chief Justice Roberts and Justice Alito speak of their children, the older members—Justices Scalia, Kennedy, Breyer, and me—of our grandchildren.

From time to time, we invite a guest to vary the lunch table conversation. Invitees in recent Terms have included: former secretary of state Condoleezza Rice; former president of the Supreme Court of Israel Aharon Barak; former UN secretary general Kofi Annan; retired Justice of the Constitutional Court of South Africa Albie Sachs; and, most recently, Justice Dikgang Moseneke, currently Deputy Chief Justice of the same court. (So far, retired Federal Reserve chairman Alan Greenspan, and former president of the World Bank Jim Wolfensohn, have been our only repeat invitees. Both have an unusual talent. They can engage in lively conversation and eat lunch at the same time.)

We celebrate Justices' birthdays with a pre-lunch toast—a glass of white wine—and a "Happy Birthday" chorus generally led by Justice Scalia, because among us, he is best able to carry a tune. It is traditional, also, when a new Justice comes on board, for the former junior Justice to arrange a welcoming dinner all of us attend.

Other events we host every now and then, mainly for lawyers and judges: We take turns greeting attendees at dinners for newly appointed federal judges, gathered in D.C. for a week of orientation. We also take turns introducing speakers at Supreme Court Historical Society biannual lecture series.

Examples of my ventures for the Historical Society. A few years ago, I participated in a program on the work and days of Belva Lockwood, the first woman ever to gain admission to the Supreme Court's Bar. In 1876, the Justices denied her application for admission, 6–3. But three years later, Congress passed a law requiring the Supreme Court and all federal courts to admit women who possess the necessary qualifications. Not content simply to practice law, Belva Lockwood ran twice for the U.S. presidency, in 1884 and 1888.

Some months later, I presided at a reenactment of arguments before the Court in a famous case decided in 1908, *Muller v. Oregon*. The case involved an Oregon law that limited the hours women could be gainfully employed to ten per day. The defendant, prosecuted for violating the law, was a laundry owner, a man who wanted women employed at the laundry to work twelve hours per day six days a week. The debate involved in the case persists to some extent to this very day: are protective labor laws applicable to women only permissible, or does the equal protection provision in our Constitution require that labor laws protect male and female workers alike?

An annual pleasant pause. Each May, just after hearings are over and before the intense end of May, early June weeks when the Term's remaining opinions must be completed and released, the Court holds a musicale. That tradition was inaugurated in 1988 by Justice Blackmun, who passed the baton to Justice O'Connor when he retired. For the last twelve years, I have attended to arrangements for the musicales. A few years ago, we added a fall recital as well. Among recent performers, Metropolitan Opera stars Renée Fleming, Susan Graham, Joyce DiDonato, Stephanie Blythe, Thomas Hampson, and Bryn Terfel. At our musicale in spring 2012, the principal artist was world-celebrated pianist Leon Fleisher.

Another special event. Every other year the women in the Senate and the women at the Court meet for dinner. The first time, in 1994, there were two Justices and six senators. In 2012, we were three, and seventeen women held Senate seats.

During weeks when the Court is not in session, some of us spend a day or two visiting U.S. universities or law schools, or attending meetings with judges and lawyers across the country. Mid-winter and summer, some of us travel abroad to teach, or to learn what we can about legal systems in other places. For example, in recent recesses, I have taught, lectured, or participated in meetings of jurists in Australia, Austria, China, England, France, India, Ireland, Israel, Italy, Japan, Luxembourg, New Zealand, South Africa, and Sweden. Late January–early February 2012, I visited Egypt and Tunisia to mark the first anniversary of the overthrow of dictatorial regimes in those countries. In September 2013, we will have an exchange in Ottawa with our counterparts on the Supreme Court of Canada, and in February 2014, we will travel to Luxembourg for meetings with members of the European Court of Justice.

Work at the U.S. Supreme Court is ever challenging, enormously time consuming, and tremendously satisfying. We are constantly reading, thinking, and trying to write so that at least lawyers and other judges will understand our rulings.

As you may have noticed, we have sharp differences on certain issues—recent examples include federally mandated health insurance, affirmative action, public school desegregation plans, the Second Amendment right to keep and bear arms, control of corporate spending to elect or defeat candidates for public office, access to court by detainees in Guantanamo Bay, state efforts to apprehend undocumented aliens. But through it all, we remain collegial and, most of the time, we genuinely enjoy each other's company. Ordinarily, our mutual respect is only momentarily touched by our sometimes strong disagreements on what the law is.

All of us appreciate that the institution we serve is far more important than the particular individuals who compose the Court's bench at any given time. And our job, in my view, is the best work a jurist anywhere could have. Our charge is to pursue justice as best we can. The Founding Fathers were wise enough to equip us to do that by according us life tenure (or, as the Constitution says, we hold our offices "during good behavior") and salaries that Congress cannot diminish.

Our former Chief Justice, William H. Rehnquist, spoke of the role of the judge using a metaphor from his favorite sport:

> The Constitution has placed the judiciary in a position similar to that of a referee in a basketball game who is obliged to call a foul against a member of the home team at a critical moment in the game: he will be soundly booed, but he is nonetheless obliged to call it as he saw it, not as the home court crowd wants him to call it.

The day a judge shirks from that responsibility, Chief Justice Rehnquist counseled, is the day he or she should resign from office. I heartily concur in that counsel.

Part Two

Tributes to Waypavers and Pathmarkers

Introduction

AS A YOUNG LAWYER *living in Sweden, Ruth Bader Ginsburg came across the word* vägmärken, *which translates literally as "pathmarker" or "waypaver."*[1] *Many consider the Justice herself to be an exemplary "waypaver" and "pathmarker," blazing the gender equality trail and expanding opportunities for women and men, yet she is also known for giving credit to those who came before her, illuminating little-known historical figures and spotlighting those who helped pave the way for her own opportunities and accomplishments. Even while immersed in her own education and career, she always found time to look back and give credit and thanks to those who came before. She also did this in her earliest Supreme Court briefs, listing as co-counsel predecessors at the American Civil Liberties Union (ACLU) who had helped craft earlier gender equality arguments and noting the contributions of her students to each brief.*

Neither lip service nor window dressing, Justice Ginsburg's tributes involve hours of historical research to discover and then share these stories, including those of early women lawyers and judges, Supreme Court wives, and Jewish Supreme Court Justices. Even now, as arguably the hardest-working Supreme Court Justice, Justice Ginsburg continues to pay tribute to historical figures and colleagues alike. The following tributes are only a small selection from a large and still-growing collection of Justice Ginsburg's dozens of tributes over the years.

1

Belva Lockwood*

Tonight I speak about a woman of courage who would not be put down, a woman who, in 1879, made the U.S. Supreme Court change its ways. Her name, Belva Ann Lockwood, her birth year, 1830. Lockwood was the first woman ever to gain admission to the U.S. Supreme Court's Bar, the first woman to argue a case before the nine Justices, and the first woman to run the full course for president.

Not born to wealth or social advantage, Belva Lockwood grew up on a family farm in Niagara County, New York. Widowed with a child at age twenty-two, after only four years of marriage, she enrolled in college and gained the training needed to become a high school teacher and, later, school principal. In 1866, she moved to Washington, D.C., and remarried two years later. Once settled in the nation's capital city, she became prominent as a suffragist and an ardent advocate for widening employment opportunities for women. In that connection, she embarked on her long-held ambition to become a

---

*Justice Ginsburg has delivered numerous versions of these remarks to various audiences over the years. The version reprinted here was delivered to the Women's Bar Association of Maryland on May 16, 2014, in Baltimore, when Justice Ginsburg received the Rita C. Davidson Award. Justice Ginsburg prefaced these remarks by saying, "Remembering Rita Charmatz Davidson, I am honored to receive this award. Rita was a wise and savvy woman. Keenly intelligent, feisty, funny, persistent, and brave, she used her talent to make things better for those outside the in crowd, and to promote justice, equal and impartial for all." We have edited the remarks for length and to ensure clarity outside the specific context in which they were originally delivered.

lawyer. No easy accomplishment in days when women were not welcomed at the Bar.

Her sister suffragist, Elizabeth Cady Stanton, compared Lockwood to Shakespeare's Portia. Lockwood resembled Shakespeare's character in this respect: Both were individuals of impressive intelligence who demonstrated that women can more than hold their own as advocates for justice. Like Shakespeare's Portia, Lockwood used wit, ingenuity, and sheer force of will to unsettle society's conceptions of women as weak in body and mind. But there was a significant difference. Portia, to accomplish her mission, impersonated a man before revealing who she was. Lockwood, in contrast, used no disguise in tackling the prevailing notion that women and lawyering, no less politics, do not mix. She dressed in the less than comfortable fashion considered proper women's wear in her day.

Unflagging effort marked her path to achievement. In 1869, then a mother of two approaching her thirty-ninth birthday, Lockwood applied for admission to D.C. area law schools. Her applications were rejected on a ground familiar in those not-so-good old days: Her presence, she was told, "would . . . distract the attention of the young men" in the class. Lockwood persevered until the National University Law School (today, the George Washington University Law School) allowed her to matriculate. She encountered yet another impediment when the school refused to confer upon her the diploma she had earned. Men in the class were again the asserted obstacle. Graduating with women, it was feared, would lessen the value of the men's diplomas.

To overcome that roadblock, Lockwood wrote to President Ulysses S. Grant, the university's president ex officio. She wasted no words: "I have passed through the curriculum of study . . . and demand my diploma." Although the president did not directly reply to her, two weeks later, in September 1873, the university's chancellor awarded Lockwood her law degree.

In 1876, having practiced law in the District of Columbia for three years, Lockwood met the experience requirement and sought admission to the U.S. Supreme Court Bar. The Court denied her application, 6 to 3, with this terse explanation:

> By the uniform practice of the Court . . . and by the fair construction of its rules, none but men are permitted to appear before it as attorneys and counselors.

Undaunted, Lockwood relentlessly lobbied Congress to grant her plea. She succeeded less than three years later. In February 1879, Congress decreed that "any woman" possessing the necessary qualifications "shall, on motion, . . . be admitted to practice before the Supreme Court of the United States." (Lockwood's case illustrates the productive dialogue sometimes carried on between the Court and Congress. It shows, too, that Congress sometimes is more in tune with changing times than the Court is. Think of Lilly Ledbetter's case. The Court, five to four, said Ledbetter sued too late. I dissented, saying the Court got it wrong, and Congress should fix it. Congress did, enacting the Lilly Ledbetter Fair Pay Act in record time.)

Twenty-one months after her admission, Lockwood became the first woman to participate in oral argument at the Court. She next and last argued before the Court in 1906. She was then seventy-five. Using the skill she had gained over a thirty-year span in her specialty—pressing money claims against the United States—she helped to secure a five-million-dollar award for Eastern Cherokee Indians whose ancestral lands had been taken from them without just compensation.

Lockwood sought more than suffrage. She urged full political and civil rights for all women. Though she could not vote for president, she twice ran for the office herself, pointing out that nothing in the Constitution barred a woman's candidacy. (She took that bold step 124 years before Hillary Rodham Clinton first became a contender for the Democratic Party's nomination.) Explaining why she entered the race, she wrote in a letter to her future running mate, Marietta Stow: "We shall never have equal rights until we take them, nor equal respect until we command it."

In 1884 and 1888, during her two campaigns as the presidential nominee of the Equal Rights Party, Lockwood cast a spotlight on a range of issues warranting public attention and government action. She advocated, for example, preservation of public lands, citizenship for Native Americans, repeal of the Chinese Exclusion Act, reform of family law to make it less unfair to women, and use of tariff revenues to fund benefits for Civil War veterans. No celestial idealist, Lockwood turned to her advantage the publicity attending the 1884 campaign to launch herself solidly onto the paid lecture circuit. Her fees financed her campaign and she ended up $125 ahead.

Visitors to my chambers will see displayed on a wall, in space occupied by law clerks, a replica of the vote sheet recording the Court's refusal to admit Lockwood. Next to the vote sheet is one of several less than flattering cartoons published during Lockwood's 1884 presidential run against Cleveland and Blaine. Not intimidated by slights and detractors, to the end of her life in 1917, she remained an unflappable optimist.

So much has changed for the better since Belva Lockwood's years in law practice. Admission ceremonies at the Court nowadays include women in sizable numbers. It is no longer cause for special notice when women represent both sides in an argued case. Women today serve as presidents of leading universities and bar associations, law school deans, federal judges, state court judges, elected representatives on the local, state, and federal level, and in high executive posts. Three women sit on the current Supreme Court bench. Even so, there is a need for women of Lockwood's sense and steel to guard against backsliding, and to ensure that our daughters and granddaughters can aspire and achieve, with no artificial barriers blocking their way.

2

Women's Progress at the Bar and on the Bench*

My remarks portray the progress of women at the bar and on the bench in the United States. Remembering the past, I am heartened by the progress. Yet, as the numbers reveal, women in law, even today, are not entering a bias-free profession. Social science research can aid in determining why that is so, and perhaps in solving persistent problems.

In my growing-up years, men of the bench and bar generally held what the French call an *idée fixe*, the unyielding conviction that women and lawyering, no less judging, do not mix. But as ancient texts reveal, it ain't necessarily so.

In Greek mythology, Pallas Athena was celebrated as the goddess of reason and justice.[1] To end the cycle of violence that began with

---

* In these remarks, Justice Ginsburg pays tribute to waypavers including Arabella Mansfield, Lemma Barkaloo, Myra Bradwell, Barbara Nachtrieb Armstrong, Florence Ellinwood Allen, Burnita Shelton Matthews, and Shirley Mount Hufstedler. Justice Ginsburg has delivered numerous versions of these remarks to various audiences over the years. The version reprinted here was delivered at the American Sociological Association Annual Meeting in Montreal on August 11, 2006, at the request of Cynthia Epstein. Justice Ginsburg noted that "[w]hen my dear friend, Cynthia Epstein, asked me to speak at this Meeting, I could hardly resist the invitation. Cynthia's thesis on women in law was a source I mined even before her work became a book in print." Justice Ginsburg's remarks were subsequently published in 30 *Harvard Journal of Law & Gender* 1 (Winter 2007). We have edited the remarks for length and to ensure clarity outside the specific context in which they were originally delivered.

Agamemnon's sacrifice of his daughter, Iphigenia, Athena created a court of justice to try Orestes, thereby installing the rule of law in lieu of the reign of vengeance.[2]

Recall also the biblical Deborah (from the Book of Judges).[3] She was at the same time prophet, judge, and military leader. This triple-headed authority was exercised by only two other Israelites, both men: Moses and Samuel. People came from far and wide to seek Deborah's judgment. According to the rabbis, Deborah was independently wealthy; thus she could afford to work pro bono.[4]

Even if its members knew nothing of Athena and Deborah, the U.S. legal establishment resisted admitting women into its ranks far too long. It was only in 1869 that Iowa's Arabella Mansfield became the first female to gain admission to the practice of law in this country. That same year, the St. Louis Law School became the first in the nation to open its doors to women.[5]

Lemma Barkaloo, among the first women to attend St. Louis, had earlier been turned away by my own alma mater, Columbia. As Cynthia Epstein has related, in 1890, when Columbia denied admission to three more female applicants, a member of the university's Board of Trustees reportedly said: "No woman shall degrade herself by practicing law in New York especially if I can save her. . . . [T]he clack of these possible Portias will never be heard in [our university's] Moot Court."[6] That board member surely lacked Deborah's prophetic powers.

Once granted admission to law schools, women were not greeted by their teachers and classmates with open arms and undiluted zeal. An example from the University of Pennsylvania Law School: In 1911, the student body held a vote on a widely supported resolution to compel members of the freshman class to grow mustaches. A 25 cents per week penalty was to be imposed on each student who failed to show substantial progress in his growth. Thanks to the eleventh-hour plea of a student who remembered the lone woman in the class, the resolution was defeated, but only after a heated debate.[7]

The bar's reluctance to admit women into the club played out in several inglorious cases. In denying Myra Bradwell admission to the bar, the Illinois Supreme Court observed in 1869 that, as a married woman, Bradwell would not be bound by contracts she made.[8] The Illinois court thought it instructive, too, that female attorneys were unknown in the mother country. Concerning English practice, Bradwell wrote:

> According to our . . . English brothers it would be cruel to allow a woman to "embark upon the rough and troubled sea of actual legal practice," but not [beyond the pale] to allow her to govern all England with Canada and other dependencies thrown in. Our brothers will get used to it and then it will not seem any worse to them to have women practicing in the courts than it does now to have a queen rule over them.[9]

(A sense of humor is helpful for those who would advance social change.)

As late as 1968, the law remained largely a male preserve. Textbooks and teachers at that time so confirmed. A widely adopted first-year property casebook published in 1968, for example, made this parenthetical comment: "[F]or, after all, land, like woman, was meant to be possessed."[10]

The few women who braved law school in the 1950s and 1960s, it was generally supposed, presented no real challenge to (or competition for) the men. One distinguished law professor commented at a 1971 Association of American Law Schools meeting, when colleagues expressed misgivings about the rising enrollment of women that coincided with the call-up of men for Vietnam War service: Not to worry, he said. "What were women law students after all, only soft men."[11]

The critical mass achieved in the 1970s contrasts with the transient jump in women's enrollment in law school during World War II. In that earlier era, the president of Harvard was reportedly asked how the law school was faring during the war: "[It's] [n]ot as bad as we thought," he replied. "We have 75 students, and we haven't had to admit any women."[12] (Compare the concern said to have been expressed by the same university's head in Vietnam War days: "We shall be left with the blind, the lame, and the women.")[13]

Why did law schools wait so long before putting out a welcome mat for women? Arguments ranged from the anticipation that women would not put their law degrees to the same full use as men, to the "potty problem," featured in the title of one of Deborah Rhode's recent articles—the absence of adequate bathrooms for women.[14]

Despite the chill air, the depressing signs conveying "No woman wanted here," brave women in law would not be put down. In the early 1960s, women accounted for about 3 percent of the nation's lawyers.[15] Today, their ranks have increased tenfold, to about 30 percent of the U.S. bar.[16]

In the law schools, women filled between 3 and 4.5 percent of the seats each academic year from 1947 until 1967.[17] Today, women are almost 50 percent of all law students,[18] and over 50 percent of the associates at large law firms.[19]

Progress is evident behind the podium, too. In 1919, Barbara Nachtrieb Armstrong was appointed to the Berkeley (Boalt Hall) law faculty.[20] Made an assistant professor in 1923, Armstrong was the first woman ever to gain a tenure-track post at an American Bar Association–approved law school.[21] Over two decades later (1945), only two other women had made their way to the tenure track at schools belonging to the Association of American Law Schools.[22]

When I was appointed to the Rutgers Law School faculty in 1963, women headed for tenure at AALS schools still numbered under twenty.[23] But by 1990, more than 20 percent of law professors were women.[24] Today, women account for roughly 19 percent of law school deans, 25 percent of tenured professors, and about 35 percent of law faculty members overall.[25]

Strides in law practice are similarly marked. Only in Alabama has a woman yet to be elected president of the state bar association. More than 160 women have already served as state bar presidents. Two women have completed terms as president of the American Bar Association, and a third began her term as ABA president this very week. Notably, a woman was chosen to chair the House of Delegates under each female ABA president.[26]

In a November 2005 lecture at the Association of the Bar of the City of New York, Harvard Law School's dean, Elena Kagan, recounted, much as I have just done, the enormous progress women have made at the Bar. But, she added, the news is not all good: "[W]omen lawyers still lag far behind men on most measures of success," she observed.[27] Speaking first of the law school setting, Dean Kagan referred to a student report on women's experiences. The report tracked similar surveys at other top-ranking law schools. Women are less likely to volunteer in class, the report noted, and they gain fewer academic honors. Asked if they consider themselves in the top 20 percent of the class in legal reasoning, 33 percent of the men answered yes, in contrast to 15 percent of the women. Women also rated themselves lower on ability to "think quickly on their feet, argue orally, write briefs, and persuade others."[28] "What's left," Dean Kagan pondered.

Dean Kagan's colleague Lani Guinier, who studied women's situation at the University of Pennsylvania Law School, recorded this comment by a woman studying at that school: "Guys think law school is hard, and we just think we're stupid."[29] (Law schools are hardly unique in this regard. For example, a Brandeis University geneticist, Gregory Petsko, recently observed that, "[a]lmost without exception, the talented women [he had] known have believed they had less ability than they actually had," while "almost without exception, the talented men [he had] known believed they had more.")[30]

Turning to life after law school, Dean Kagan got to the bottom line: *"Women lawyers are not assuming leadership roles in proportion to their numbers."*[31] Although about 30 percent of all lawyers, women account for only some 15 percent of general counsels of Fortune 500 companies and 17 percent of law firm partners.[32]

Another revealing difference. In the Harvard student study, women outnumbered men two to one in reporting that "helping others" was an important consideration in choosing law as a career. On that score, Dean Kagan suggested, shouldn't we be acting affirmatively to encourage men to care more about public service endeavors.[33] Dean Kagan posed these questions: Were women disproportionately interested in public service because they found such work "more personally fulfilling"? Or, is public service employment "more open to [women]—more likely to provide opportunities for advancement and recognition, . . . more flexible regarding leave-taking and reentry"?[34]

There's a problem in this picture of women as law students and lawyers, one that social scientists can help us to fathom. Last September, the *New York Times* did a replay of a story it runs from time to time on what women really want, and why they trail men in professional accomplishment. In a recent survey of female undergraduates at Yale, the *Times* recounted, roughly 60 percent said they would stop, or cut back on, work once they had children.[35] One of the letters to the editor prompted by the piece commented: "I'm glad that the things I declared when I was 19 . . . didn't make front-page news."[36] Dean Kagan countered with a study published in 2005 as a *Harvard Business Review* research report. The study made this notable finding: 93 percent of women in high-caliber employment who have stepped out of the labor force for some time want to return.[37]

Turning to my own line of work, women began to show up on the bench in the twentieth century's middle years. In 1995, I wrote in praise of three door openers in the federal court system: Florence Ellinwood Allen, appointed to the U.S. Court of Appeals for the Sixth Circuit in 1934; Burnita Shelton Matthews, appointed to the U.S. District Court for the District of Columbia in 1949; and Shirley Mount Hufstedler, appointed to the U.S. Court of Appeals for the Ninth Circuit in 1968.[38] To avoid intruding excessively on my copanelists' time, but as a reminder of not-so-long-ago days, I will speak here only of the first of these waypavers, Florence Allen, first woman ever to serve on an Article III federal court.

Before joining the federal bench, Allen achieved many "firsts" in Ohio: first female assistant prosecutor in the country; first woman elected to sit on a court of general jurisdiction; and the nation's first female state supreme court justice.[39] Long tenured on the Sixth Circuit, Allen eventually served as that circuit's chief judge, another first.[40]

It was rumored that Allen might become the first female U.S. Supreme Court Justice. In 1949, two vacancies opened on the Court. President Truman reportedly was not opposed to the idea of filling one of them with a woman.[41] But, as political strategist India Edwards, head of the Women's Division of the Democratic National Committee, recalled, Truman ultimately decided the time was not ripe. Edwards wrote of the brethren's reaction when Truman sought their advice:

> [A] woman as a Justice . . . would make it difficult for [the other Justices] to meet informally with robes, and perhaps shoes, off, shirt collars unbuttoned and discuss their problems and come to decisions. I am certain that the old line about there being no sanitary arrangement for a female Justice was also included in their reasons for not wanting a woman. . . .[42]

(Times have indeed changed: to mark my 1993 appointment to the Supreme Court, my colleagues ordered the installation of a women's bathroom in the Justices' robing room, its size precisely the same as the men's.)

The founding of the National Association of Women Judges in 1978 coincided with, and helped to advance, the end of the days when women appeared on the bench as one-at-a-time curiosities. At the federal level, the administrations of Kennedy, Johnson, Nixon, and Ford combined had appointed just six women to Article III courts.[43] When President Carter took office in 1977, only one woman (Shirley Hufstedler) sat among the 97 judges on the federal courts of appeals and only five among the 399 district court judges.[44] President Carter appointed a barrier-breaking number of women—40—to lifetime federal judgeships.[45]

Once Carter appointed women to the bench in numbers, there was no turning back. President Reagan made history when he appointed the first woman to the Supreme Court, my dear colleague, Justice Sandra Day O'Connor. He also appointed 28 women to other federal courts.[46] The first President Bush, in his single term in office, appointed 36 women.[47] President Clinton appointed a grand total of 104 women, and the current president to date has appointed 52 women.[48]

Today, every federal court of appeals save the First and Eighth Circuits has at least two active women judges. Nine women have served as chief judge of a U.S. court of appeals, including three who currently occupy that post. Forty women have served as chief judge of a U.S. district court, including the seventeen now holding that position. All told, more than 250 women have served as life-tenured federal judges, fifty-eight of them on appellate courts. Yes, there is a way to go, considering that women make up only about one-fourth of the federal judiciary.[49] But what a distance we have come since my 1959 graduation from law school, when Florence Allen remained the sole woman ever to have served on the federal appellate bench.

In the state courts, progress is similarly marked. Every state except Oregon, Indiana, and Kentucky has at least one woman on its court of last resort; 30 percent of the chief justices of those courts are women.

Looking beyond our borders, however, we are not in the lead. For example, the Chief Justice of the Supreme Court of Canada is a woman, as are three of that court's eight other Justices. The Chief Justice of New Zealand is a woman. Four of the sixteen judges on Germany's Federal Constitutional Court are women, and a woman served as president of that court from 1994 to 2002. Currently, five women are members of the European Court of Justice, two as judges and three as advocates-general. Women account for eight out of eighteen judges on the International Criminal Court; one of them serves as that court's first vice president.

At the Court on which I serve, the picture today is not promising. Since Justice O'Connor's retirement effective January 31, 2006, I have been all alone in my corner on the bench.* In the Term just ended, 117 men, but only 26 women, argued cases before the U.S. Supreme Court, and 2,980 men, as opposed to only 1,603 women, elected to become members of the Court's Bar. As Judith Resnik reminds me, no woman, to this date, has ever been appointed by the Court as special master in an original proceeding, i.e., a case in which the Supreme Court is the tribunal of first and last resort. (The Court has original jurisdiction dominantly in cases between states of the United States, or between the United States and one or more states.) Twenty-three men, but only sixteen women served as law clerks last Term. Next Term will set a low for the decade: thirty of the new clerks are men, only seven are women.

A question I am often asked: What does women's participation in numbers on the bench add to our judicial system? It is true, as Jeanne Coyne of Minnesota's Supreme Court famously said: at the end of the day, a wise old man and a wise old woman will reach the same decision.[50] But it is also true that women, like persons of different racial groups and ethnic origins, contribute what the late Fifth Circuit Judge Alvin Rubin described as "a distinctive medley of views influenced by differences in biology, cultural impact, and life experience."[51] Our system of justice is surely richer for the diversity of background and experience of its judges. It was poorer when nearly all of its participants were cut from the same mold.

---

* Since these remarks were delivered, two more female Justices, Sonia Sotomayor and Elena Kagan, have joined the Supreme Court.

3

From Benjamin to Brandeis to Breyer

Is There a Jewish Seat on the United States Supreme Court?*

The man who might have preceded Justice Brandeis by some sixty-three years as first Jewish member of the Supreme Court had a less secure start in life than did Brandeis, and a less saintly character. His name was Judah P. Benjamin. His career path is intriguing.

Born in 1811 in St. Croix in the Virgin Islands, the son of Sephardic Jews, Benjamin grew up in Charleston, South Carolina, and became a celebrated lawyer in antebellum New Orleans. Though his boyhood, unlike Brandeis', was heavily steeped in Jewish tradition, as an adult, he married outside the faith in a Catholic ceremony, and did not keep Jewish laws or celebrate Jewish holidays. Yet he could not escape his Jewish identity. The world in which he lived would not have allowed him to do that.

In 1853, President Millard Fillmore nominated Benjamin to become an Associate Justice of the United States Supreme Court. Chosen the preceding year as one of Louisiana's two U.S. senators, Benjamin declined the High Court nomination. His preference for the Senate suggests that the Supreme Court had not yet become the

---

*Justice Ginsburg has delivered numerous versions of these remarks to various audiences over the years. The version reprinted here was delivered to the Spertus Institute of Jewish Studies on September 13, 2009. We have edited the remarks for length and to ensure clarity outside the specific context in which they were originally delivered.

coequal branch of government it is today. Benjamin was the first acknowledged Jew to hold a U.S. Senate seat; he commenced, in 1858, his second six-year term.

Had Benjamin accepted the Supreme Court post, his service likely would have been brief—certainly far shorter than Brandeis' twenty-three years. In early 1861, in the wake of Louisiana's secession from the Union, Benjamin resigned his Senate seat. He probably would have resigned a seat on the Court had he held one.

Benjamin is perhaps best known in the United States for his stirring orations in the pre–Civil War Senate on behalf of southern interests—orations expressing sentiments with which we would today strongly disagree—and later for his service as attorney general, secretary of war, and finally secretary of state in the Confederate cabinet of Jefferson Davis. Although Judah Benjamin achieved high office, he lived through a time of virulent anti-Semitism in America. Political enemies called him Judas Iscariot Benjamin. He was ridiculed for his Jewishness in the press, by military leaders on both sides (by northern general Ulysses S. Grant, and southern general "Stonewall" Jackson), and by his fellow Confederate politicians.

After the Confederate surrender, Benjamin fled to England; en route, he narrowly survived close encounters with victorious Union troops, rough waters, and storms at sea. Benjamin's political ventures in the U.S. Senate and in the Confederacy of Southern States were bracketed by two discrete but equally remarkable legal careers, the first in New Orleans, the second in Britain.

Having left Yale College after two years, under cloudy circumstances, without completing the requirements for a degree, Benjamin came to New Orleans in 1832 to seek his fortune. He studied and worked hard, and was called to the Bar that same year. Although he struggled initially, his fame and wealth grew large after the publication, in 1834, of a digest of reported decisions of the Supreme Court of Louisiana and of that tribunal's pre-statehood predecessor. Benjamin's book treated comprehensively for the first time Louisiana's uniquely cosmopolitan and complex legal system, derived from

Roman, Spanish, French, and English sources. Benjamin's flourishing practice and the public attention he garnered helped to propel his 1852 election by the Louisiana Legislature to the United States Senate. (Recall that until 1913, when the Seventeenth Amendment became effective, U.S. senators were chosen not directly by the people, but by the legislatures of the several states.)

Benjamin's fortune plummeted with the defeat of the Confederacy. He arrived in England with little money and most of his property lost or confiscated. His Louisiana Creole wife and a daughter reared Catholic had long before settled in Paris; they anticipated continuing support from Benjamin in the comfortable style to which they had grown accustomed. He nevertheless resisted business opportunities in the French capital, preferring the independence of a law practice, this time as a British barrister.

Benjamin opted for a second career at the Bar notwithstanding the requirement that he start over by enrolling as a student at an Inn of Court and serving an apprenticeship. This, Benjamin's contemporaries reported, he undertook cheerfully and with fabulous industry, although he was doubtless relieved when the Inn of Court to which he belonged, Lincoln's Inn, determined to admit him to full membership after six months rather than the usual three years.

Benjamin became a British barrister at age fifty-five. His situation at that mature stage of life closely paralleled conditions of his youth. He was a newly minted lawyer with a struggling practice, but, he wrote to a friend, "as much interested in my profession as when I first commenced as a boy." Repeating his Louisiana progress, Benjamin made his reputation among his new peers by publication. Drawing on the knowledge of civilian systems gained during his practice in Louisiana, Benjamin produced a work in England that came to be known as *Benjamin on Sales*. First published in 1868, the book was a near-instant legal classic. Its author was much praised, and Benjamin passed the remainder of his days as a top-earning, highly esteemed, mainly appellate advocate. He became a Queen's Counsel seven years after his admission to the Bar. His voice was heard in appeals to the House of Lords and the Judicial Committee of the Privy Council in no fewer than 136 reported cases in the ten years between 1872 and 1882.

A biographer of Benjamin tells us that, "[h]owever desperate his case, Benjamin habitually addressed the court as if it were impossible for him to lose." This indomitable cast of mind characterized both Benjamin's courtroom advocacy and his response to fortune's vicissitudes. He rose to the top of the legal profession twice in one lifetime, on two continents, beginning his first ascent as a raw youth and his second as a fugitive minister of a vanquished nation. The London *Times*, in an obituary, described Judah Benjamin as a man with "that elastic resistance to evil fortune which preserved [his] ancestors through a succession of exiles and plunderings."

Louis Dembitz Brandeis, it is well known, was the first Jew to serve on the Supreme Court of the United States. His tenure ran some twenty-three years, from 1916 until 1939. Raised in Louisville, Kentucky, Brandeis graduated from Harvard Law School in 1876 at age twenty, with the highest scholastic average in that law school's history. He maintained close and continuing relationships with his teachers there, and, at age twenty-six, was called back to lecture on the law of evidence. During his years at the Bar, Brandeis was called "the People's Attorney," descriptive of his large part in the social and economic reform movements of the era. He helped to promote the pro bono tradition among lawyers in the United States. Spending at least half his long working days on public causes, Brandeis reimbursed his Boston law firm for the time he devoted to nonpaying matters.

Overcoming his own initial doubts, Brandeis eventually became a staunch supporter of women's suffrage. In this regard, he emphasized the obligations as much as the rights of citizenship. In 1913 he wrote simply and to the point: "We cannot relieve her from the duty of taking part in public affairs." This theme of civic responsibility seems to me Brandeis' leitmotif, first as a lawyer, and later as a judge.

Brandeis made large donations of his wealth from practice to good causes and lived frugally at home. A friend recounted that, whenever he went to the Brandeis home for dinner, he ate before, and afterward.

In 1916, when President Wilson appointed Brandeis to the Court, he was sixty years old, my age in 1993 when President Clinton appointed me to the Court. One of Brandeis' colleagues, James Clark McReynolds, was openly anti-Semitic, as were some detractors at the time of his nomination. When Brandeis spoke in conference, McReynolds would rise and leave the room. No official photograph was taken of the Court in 1924 because McReynolds refused to sit next to Brandeis, where McReynolds, appointed by Wilson two years before Brandeis, belonged on the basis of seniority.

Most people who encountered Brandeis were of a different view. Chief Justice Charles Evans Hughes described him as "master of both microscope and telescope." Commenting on Brandeis' ability to transform the little case before him into a larger truth, Justice Oliver Wendell Holmes said Brandeis had the art of seeing the general in the particular. His opinions are gems, guiding us to this very day. Admirers, both Jewish and Gentile, turned to the scriptures to find words adequate to describe his contributions to U.S. constitutional thought. President Franklin Delano Roosevelt, among others, called Brandeis not "Judas," but "Isaiah."

Brandeis elaborated the canons of judicial restraint more powerfully than any other jurist, cautioning judges to be ever on guard against "erect[ing] our prejudices into legal principles." At the same time, he was an architect—a master builder—of the constitutional right to privacy and of the modern jurisprudence of free speech. He wrote, most famously:

> Those who won our independence believed that the final end of the State was to make men free to develop their faculties; and that in its government the deliberative forces should prevail over the arbitrary. They valued liberty both as an end and as a means. They believed liberty to be the secret of happiness and courage

> to be the secret of liberty. They believed that freedom to think as you will and to speak as you think are means indispensable to the discovery and spread of political truth; that without free speech and assembly discussion would be futile; that with them, discussion affords ordinarily adequate protection against the dissemination of noxious doctrine; that the greatest menace to freedom is an inert people; that public discussion is a political duty; and that this should be a fundamental principle of the American government.

Brandeis was not a participant in religious ceremonies or services, but he was an ardent Zionist, and he encouraged the next two Jewish Justices—Cardozo and Frankfurter—to become members of the Zionist Organization of America. Brandeis scholar Melvin Urofsky commented that Brandeis brought three gifts to American Zionism: organizational talent; an ability to set goals and to lead men and women to achieve them; and above all, an idealism that recast Zionist thought in a way that captivated Jews already well established in the United States. Jews abroad who needed to flee from anti-Semitism, Brandeis urged, would have a home in the land of Israel, a place to build a new society, a fair and open one, he hoped, free from the prejudices that marked much of Europe; Jews comfortably situated in the United States, in a complementary way, would have a mission, an obligation to help their kinsmen build that new land.

When Brandeis retired from the Supreme Court, his colleagues wrote in their farewell letter:

> Your long practical experience and intimate knowledge of affairs, the wide range of your researches and your grasp of the most difficult problems, together with your power of analysis and your thoroughness in exposition, have made your judicial career one of extraordinary distinction and far-reaching influence.

Law as protector of the oppressed, the poor, the minority, the loner, is evident in the life body of work of Justice Brandeis, as it is in the legacies of Justices Cardozo, Frankfurter, Goldberg, and Fortas, the remaining four of the first five Jewish Justices. Frankfurter, once distressed when the Court rejected his view in a case, reminded his brethren, defensively, that he "belong[ed] to the most vilified and persecuted minority in history." I prefer Arthur Goldberg's affirmative comment: "My concern for justice, for peace, for enlightenment," Goldberg said, "stem[s] from my heritage." The other Jewish Justices could have reached the same judgment. Justice Breyer and I are fortunate to be linked to that heritage.

But Justice Breyer's situation and mine is distinct from that of the first five Jewish Justices. I can best explain the difference by recounting a bit of history called to my attention in remarks made some years ago by Seth P. Waxman. Seth served with distinction as solicitor general of the United States from 1997 until January 2001.

Seth spoke of one of his predecessors, Philip Perlman, the first Jewish solicitor general. Perlman successfully urged, in a friend-of-the-court brief, the unconstitutionality of racially restrictive covenants on real property. The case was *Shelley v. Kraemer*, decided in 1948. The brief for the United States was written by four lawyers, all of them Jewish: Philip Elman, Oscar Davis, Hilbert Zarky, and Stanley Silverberg. All the names, save Perlman's, were deleted from the filed brief. The decision to delete the brief drafters' names was made by Arnold Raum, Perlman's principal assistant and himself a Jew. "It's bad enough," Raum said, "that Perlman's name has to be there." It wouldn't do, he thought, to make it so evident that the position of the United States was "put out by a bunch of Jews."

Consider in that light President Clinton's appointments in 1993 and 1994 of the 107th and 108th Justices, first me, then Justice Breyer. Our backgrounds have strong resemblances: we had taught law for several years and served on federal courts of appeals for more years. And we are both Jews. In contrast to Frankfurter, Goldberg, and Fortas, however, no one regarded Ginsburg or Breyer as filling a Jewish seat.* Both of us take pride in and draw strength from our heritage, but our religion simply was not relevant to President Clinton's appointments.

The security I feel is shown by the command from Deuteronomy displayed in artworks, in Hebrew letters, on three walls and a table in my chambers. "Zedek, Zedek, tirdof," "Justice, Justice shalt thou pursue," these artworks proclaim; they are ever-present reminders of what judges must do "that they may thrive." There is also a large silver mezuzah mounted on my door post. It is a gift from super-bright teenage students at the Shulamith School for Girls in Brooklyn, New York, the school one of my dearest law clerks attended.

Jews in the United States, I mean to convey, today face few closed doors and do not fear letting the world know who we are. A question stated in various ways is indicative of large advances made. What is the difference between a New York City garment district bookkeeper and a Supreme Court Justice? One generation my life bears witness, the difference between opportunities open to my mother, a bookkeeper, and those open to me.

---

* Since these remarks were delivered, one more Jewish Justice, Elena Kagan, joined the Supreme Court, becoming the 112th Justice on August 7, 2010. Additionally, on March 16, 2016, President Obama nominated a Jewish judge, Merrick Garland, to the Court. The Senate has not yet acted on his nomination.

4

Three Brave Jewish Women*

I am pleased beyond measure to receive the National Council of Jewish Women's award, because it comes from an organization devoted to the principle of Tikkun Olam, the obligation to improve/fix/better the world carefully and steadily, to do one's part to make our communities, nation, and universe more humane, fairer, more just. There is an age-old connection between social justice and Jewish tradition. The humanity and bravery of Jewish women, in particular, sustain and encourage me when my spirits need lifting. I will mention just three examples.

High on my list of inspirers is Emma Lazarus, cousin to the great jurist Benjamin N. Cardozo. Emma Lazarus was a Zionist before that word came into vogue. She wrote constantly, from her first volume of poetry published in 1866 at age seventeen, until her tragic death from cancer at age thirty-eight. Her love for humankind, and especially for her people, is evident in all her writings. Her poem "The New Colossus," etched on the base of the Statue of Liberty, has welcomed legions of immigrants to the United States.

I draw strength, too, from a diary entry penned decades ago by a girl barely fifteen. These are her words:

---

*These remarks were delivered to the National Council of Jewish Women at the Washington Institute on March 12, 2001. We have edited the remarks for length and to ensure clarity outside the specific context in which they were originally delivered.

One of the many questions that have often bothered me is why women have been, and still are, thought to be so inferior to men. It's easy to say it's unfair, but that's not enough for me; I'd really like to know the reason for this great injustice!

Men presumably dominated women from the very beginning because of their greater physical strength; it's men who earn a living, beget children, [and] do as they please. . . . Until recently, women silently went along with this, which was stupid, since the longer it's kept up, the more deeply entrenched it becomes. Fortunately, education, work and progress have opened women's eyes. In many countries they've been granted equal rights; many people, mainly women, but also men, now realize how wrong it was to tolerate this state of affairs for so long. . . .

Yours,
Anne M. Frank

This insightful comment was one of the last made in her diary. Anne Frank, *Diary* readers in this audience know, was born in the Netherlands in July 1929. She died in 1945, while imprisoned at Bergen-Belsen, three months short of her sixteenth birthday.

My third example comes from Hadassah founder Henrietta Szold, who had seven sisters, but no brother. When Henrietta's mother died, Haym Peretz, no relation, offered to say the Kaddish that, according to ancient custom, could be recited only by men. Henrietta responded in a letter dated September 16, 1916:

It is impossible for me to find words in which to tell you how deeply I was touched by your offer to act as "Kaddish" for my dear mother. . . . What you have offered to do [is beautiful beyond thanks]—I shall never forget it.

You will wonder, then, that I cannot accept your offer. . . . I know well, and appreciate what you say about, the Jewish custom [that only male children recite the prayer, and if there are no male survivors, a male stranger may act as substitute]; and Jewish custom is very dear and sacred to me. [Y]et I cannot ask you to say Kaddish after my mother. The Kaddish means to me that the survivor publicly . . . manifests his . . . intention to assume the relation to the Jewish community which his parent had, [so that] the chain of tradition remains unbroken from generation to generation, each adding its own link. You can do that for the generations of your family, I must do that for the generations of my family. . . .

My mother had eight daughters and no son; and yet never did I hear a word of regret pass the lips of either my mother or my father that one of us was not a son. When my father died, my mother would not permit others to take her daughters' place in saying the Kaddish, and so I am sure I am acting in her spirit when I am moved to decline your offer. But beautiful your offer remains nevertheless, and, I repeat, I know full well that it is much more in consonance with the generally accepted Jewish tradition than is my or my family's conception. You understand me, don't you?

Szold's plea for understanding, for celebration of our common heritage while tolerating—even appreciating—the differences among us on matters of religious practice, is captivating, don't you agree? Can you imagine a more perfect put-down, or words more supportive when a colleague's position seems to betray a certain lack of understanding?

A remark I made at the American Jewish Committee's annual meeting in 1995 holds true today as it will tomorrow. May I close with those words: I am a judge, born, raised, and proud of being a Jew. The demand for justice runs through the entirety of the Jewish tradition. I hope, in all the years I have the good fortune to serve on the bench of the Supreme Court of the United States, I will have the strength and courage to remain steadfast in the service of that demand.

5

Sandra Day O'Connor*

Thanks to the organizers of this event for inviting me to speak, on behalf of my colleagues, in honor of the incomparable Sandra Day O'Connor, first woman ever appointed to the U.S. Supreme Court. During her twenty-five years on the Court's bench and continuing thereafter, she has shown, time and again, that she is a true cowgirl, resourceful, resilient, equipped to cope with whatever fortune brings her way.

Collegiality is key to the effective operation of a multi-member bench. Sandra Day O'Connor has done more to promote collegiality among the Court's members, and with our counterparts abroad, than any other Justice, past or present. Justice Breyer wrote of that quality: "Sandra has a special talent, perhaps a gene, for lighting up the room . . . she enters; for [restoring] good humor in the presence of strong disagreement; for [producing constructive] results; and for [reminding] those at odds today . . . that 'tomorrow is another day.'"[1]

Of all the accolades Justice O'Connor has received, one strikes me as concisely on target. Growing up on the Lazy B Ranch in Arizona, she could brand cattle, drive a tractor, fire a rifle accurately well before

---

*These remarks were delivered at the National Museum of Women and the Arts in Washington, D.C., on April 15, 2015, when Justice Ginsburg, together with Justice Sotomayor and Justice Kagan, attended a ceremony at which retired Justice Sandra Day O'Connor accepted an award from the Seneca Women Global Leadership Forum. We have edited the remarks for length and to ensure clarity outside the specific context in which they were originally delivered.

she reached her teens. One of the hands on the ranch recalled his clear memory of Sandra Day: "She wasn't the rough and rugged type," he said, "but she worked well with us in the canyons—she held her own."[2] Justice O'Connor has done just that at every stage of her professional and family life.

When she joined the Court in 1981, she brought to the Conference table experience others did not possess at all or to the same degree: she grew up female in the 1930s, '40s, and '50s, raised a family, and did all manner of legal work—government service, private practice, successful candidacies for public office, leadership of Arizona's Senate, and state court judicial service, both trial and appellate. Quick and diligent learner that she is, she mastered mysteries of federal law and practice in short order, and held her own from the very start.

Her welcome when I became the junior Justice is characteristic. The Court has customs and habits not recorded in its official rules. Justice O'Connor knew what it was like to learn the ropes on one's own. She told me what I needed to know when I came on board for the Court's 1993 Term—not in an intimidating dose, just enough to enable me to navigate safely my first days and weeks.

At the end of the October 1993 sitting, I anxiously awaited my first opinion assignment, expecting—in keeping with tradition—that the brand-new Justice would be slated for an uncontroversial, unanimous opinion. When the Chief's assignment list came round, I was dismayed. The Chief gave me an intricate, not at all easy, ERISA case, on which the Court had divided 6–3. (ERISA is the acronym for the Employee Retirement Income Security Act, candidate for the most inscrutable legislation Congress has ever passed.) I sought Justice O'Connor's advice. It was simple. "Just do it," she said, "and, if you can, circulate your draft opinion before he makes the next set of assignments. Otherwise, you will risk receiving another tedious case." That advice typifies Justice O'Connor's approach to all things. Waste no time on anger, regret, or resentment, just get the job done.

Justice O'Connor was a dissenter in the ERISA case. As I read the bench announcement summarizing the Court's decision, she gave an attendant a note for me. It read: "This is your first opinion for the Court, it is a fine one, I look forward to many more." (Remembering how good that note made me feel, I sent similar notes to Justices Sotomayor and Kagan when they announced their first opinions for the Court.)

As first woman on the Supreme Court, Justice O'Connor set a pace I could scarcely match. To this day, my mail is filled with requests that run this way: last year (or some years before) Justice O'Connor visited our campus or country, spoke at our bar or civic association, did this or that; next, words politely phrased to this effect—now it's your turn. My secretaries once imagined that Justice O'Connor had a secret twin sister with whom she divided her appearances. The reality is, she has an extraordinary ability to manage her time.

Why has she gone to Des Moines, Belfast, Lithuania, Rwanda, when she might rather fly-fish, ski, play tennis, or golf? In her own words:

> For both men and women the first step in getting power is to become visible to others, and then to put on an impressive show. . . . As women achieve power, the barriers will fall. As society sees what women can do, as *women* see what women can do, there will be more women out there doing things, and we'll all be better off for it.[3]

Of her journeys abroad, her former law clerk, Ruth McGregor, now retired Chief Justice of the Arizona Supreme Court, said: "Justice O'Connor has worked tirelessly to encourage emerging nations [to live under the rule of law]" by "maintain[ing] democratically elected legislatures . . . and independent judiciaries"; at the same time, she has strongly reminded us that "this country could lose the rule of law if we do not act to protect our precious heritage."[4]

There was a time in 1988 when Justice O'Connor's energy flagged, long months in which she coped with rigorous treatment for breast cancer. Though tired and in physical discomfort, she didn't miss a sitting day on the Court that busy Term. Once fully recovered, she spoke of that trying time; her account, carried on public television, gave women battling cancer hope, the courage to continue, to do as she did. She went back to the 8:00 a.m. exercise class she initiated at the Court long before it was predicted she could. "[T]here was a lot I couldn't do," she said, "[b]ut I did a little, I did what I could."[5]

What she could do became evident years later, when the Olympic Women's Basketball Team visited the Court. Justice O'Connor led the team on a tour ending at "the Highest Court in the Land," the full basketball court on the building's top floor. The team practiced some minutes, then one of the players passed the ball to Justice O'Connor. She missed her first shot, but the second went straight through the hoop.

Each case on the Court's docket attracted Justice O'Connor's best effort and she was never shy about stating her views at conference or in follow-on discussions. When she wrote separately, concurring or in dissent, she stated her disagreement directly and professionally. She avoided castigating colleagues' opinions as "Orwellian,"[6] "profoundly misguided,"[7] "not to be taken seriously,"[8] or "a jurisprudential disaster."[9]

In the twelve and a half years we served together, Court watchers have seen that women speak in different voices, and hold different views, just as men do. Even so, some advocates, each Term, revealed that they had not fully adjusted to the presence of two women on the High Court bench. During oral argument, many a distinguished counsel—including a Harvard Law School professor and more than one solicitor general—began his response to my question: "Well, Justice O'Connor . . ." Sometimes when that happened, Sandra would smile and crisply remind counsel: "She's Justice Ginsburg. I'm Justice O'Connor." Anticipating just such confusion, in 1993, my first Term as a member of the Court, the National Association of Women Judges had T-shirts made for us. Justice O'Connor's read, "I'm Sandra, not Ruth," mine, "I'm Ruth, not Sandra."

As a retired Justice, she has taken on an array of "off the bench" activities. Prime among her current undertakings, Sandra created and is promoting the website—www.icivics.org—designed to educate grade school students about the three branches of government. Avidly as well, she has championed judicial independence, urging appointment, rather than election, of judges. She has regularly welcomed foreign jurists visiting the United States, and she has traveled long distances to meet with lawyers and judges abroad, many times at the request of the U.S. State Department.[10]

Some years ago, Justice O'Connor made a surprise one-night appearance in the Shakespeare Theatre's production of *Henry V*. Playing the role of Isabel, Queen of France, and looking regal, she spoke the famous line from the treaty scene: "Hap'ly a woman's voice may do some good."[11] Indeed it may, as Justice O'Connor has constantly demonstrated in her quarter century of service on the Supreme Court, and in all her endeavors.

Justices Sandra Day O'Connor and Ruth Bader Ginsburg hold basketballs that they received as gifts from the United States women's Olympic basketball team during the team's visit to the Court on December 6, 1995.

6

Gloria Steinem*

I have been looking forward to tonight with great joy, for our speaker, Gloria Steinem, is among humans, the least self-regarding, the most caring and giving. I vividly remember the day I opened *New York* magazine and found the first issue of *Ms.* magazine inside. Gloria's bright mind, brave heart, and unflagging energy inspired that venture and so much else that, borrowing words from her friend Marlo Thomas, freed girls and boys to be you and me.

Gloria has been rightly called, now for at least a half century, the face of feminism, the image of the women's liberation movement. Why her face more than any other? Yes, she is uncommonly beautiful. But that is not the reason why. Gail Collins, in a tribute to Gloria at age eighty, identified the trait that distinguishes Gloria from others whose celebrity status draws crowds. It is her gift for empathy: when Gloria is the center of attention, she holds no megaphone; "she's almost always listening."

Like my dear colleague Sandra Day O'Connor, Gloria spends much of her time in the air, traveling to places round the globe that are not the world's best garden spots, places where her voice may do

* These remarks were delivered at the New York City Bar Association on February 2, 2015, when Justice Ginsburg introduced Gloria Steinem, who was about to deliver the Annual Justice Ruth Bader Ginsburg Distinguished Lecture on Women and the Law. We have edited the remarks for length and to ensure clarity outside the specific context in which they were originally delivered.

some good. Sandra is famous for the 8:00 a.m. aerobic class she initiated at the Court to keep fit. Gloria says she stays in shape "just running around airports and cities."

Skilled in the art of persuasion, she captivates audiences by gently leading them her way. One example among thousands. Sometime in the 1970s, Gloria and I attended a Second Circuit Judicial Conference in Buck Hill Falls, Pennsylvania. The topic of our debate with sociologist Lionel Tiger and Fordham Law School professor Whelan: Should we or should we not have an Equal Rights Amendment in our Constitution? The audience was scarcely of one mind at the start. But when Gloria finished, the vote for the ERA would have been nearly unanimous.

For her unrelenting efforts to make our country and world a safer, opportunity-filled, happier place for girls and women, please join me in a rousing "Brava Gloria," and in inviting her to the podium.

7

Remembering Great Ladies

Supreme Court Wives' Stories*

The stately rooms and halls of my workplace, the Supreme Court of the United States, are filled with portraits and busts of great men, 129 portraits in all, including 28 of Chief Justices, and 101 of Associate Justices. Taking a cue from Abigail Adams, I decided it was time to remember the ladies—the women associated with the Court in the nineteenth and early twentieth centuries. Not as Justices, of course—no woman ever served in that capacity until President Reagan's historic appointment of Sandra Day O'Connor in 1981—but as the Justices' partners in life, their wives.

My talk limelights three nineteenth-century ladies whose names even the most diligent students of the Court might not know: from the first part of the nineteenth century, Polly Marshall and Sarah Story; and from the middle of the nineteenth century through the early years of the twentieth century, Malvina Harlan—wives of, respectively, Chief Justice John Marshall (served 1801–35), Justice

---

*Justice Ginsburg has delivered numerous versions of this lecture to various audiences over the years, including at Ventfort Hall in Lenox, Massachusetts, on September 16, 2005. She also coauthored an article on the topic with her 1996 Term law clerk, Laura W. Brill, who initially proposed the idea for the lecture and article. For subsequent additions and revisions to the article, which was ultimately published in 24 *Journal of Supreme Court History* 255 (1999), Justice Ginsburg acknowledges with appreciation the assistance of her law clerks Gillian E. Metzger, Alexandra T. V. Edsall, and Rochelle L. Shoretz. For this compilation, we drew from portions of the Ventfort Hall lecture and the journal article, and edited for length and clarity outside the original context.

Joseph Story (1811–45), and the first Justice John Marshall Harlan (1877–1911) (whose grandson became the second Justice John Marshall Harlan). I will devote principal attention to Malvina Harlan, but will also speak of a dawn of the twentieth-century Court spouse, Helen Herron Taft, called Nellie by family and friends, wife of William Howard Taft, who (as Nellie willed) served first as president, then as Chief Justice (1921–30).

"Behind every great man stands a great woman," so the old saying goes. Yet little attention has been paid to the lives of the women who stood behind the Justices, and one trying to tell the nineteenth-century wives' stories runs up against a large hindrance—the dearth of preserved primary source material penned by the women themselves. A volume titled *My Dearest Polly*, for example, reprints letters Chief Justice John Marshall wrote to his wife. Sadly, according to the compiler of that volume, "while Polly saved [John Marshall's] letters to her," John was not a great saver and "left . . . not one word written by Polly to him."[1]

William Story, son of Joseph and Sarah Story, collected and published a wide range of letters concerning his father's life; not even one of Sarah's letters to Joseph appears in the collection.[2] The index of an otherwise thorough Joseph Story biography contains under Sarah's name only these entries: "marries Story"; "grief at daughter's death"; "as invalid"; and "finds Cotton Mather dull."[3] Surely there was more to Sarah than that.

Malvina Shanklin Harlan, wife of the first Justice John Harlan, did write a work of her own. She described her work and days in an engaging memoir for too long barely noticed, lodged among the Justice's papers in the Library of Congress. I will speak later about the ultimate publication of Malvina's memories and present several samples of her commentary.

Helen Herron Taft, born a quarter century after Malvina Harlan, also told of her life and times. Her manuscript did not languish in a library collection. Her husband and daughter had arranged attractive terms for its publication. They thought work on her life's story would help her overcome post–White House blues. Nellie pored over papers and letters. She reminisced and her daughter, on leave from Bryn Mawr College, did the writing. Helen Taft's *Recollections of Full Years* was published in 1914.[4] The book sold well. By then, the women's suffrage movement had become vibrant in our land. Just this year, HarperCollins published a new biography by Carl Sferrazza Anthony, titled *Nellie Taft: The Unconventional First Lady of the Ragtime Era*.

In the beginning, Washington, D.C., the Federal City, was a swampy, barely built town, a place slept in by many more men than women. Justices of the Supreme Court, in those early days, resided under the same roof, in one boardinghouse or another, whenever the Court sat in the Capital. They left their wives behind.

Wives generally remained at home, too, during the rigorous, sometimes dangerous, circuit rides to U.S. courthouses distant from D.C., arduous journeys that burdened the lives of Supreme Court Justices through most of the nineteenth century.[5] There were notable exceptions; I will mention two. Justice William Cushing, who served from 1789 until 1810, had a carriage specially designed so that Mrs. Cushing could ride circuit with him. Her task was to read aloud to her husband as they jogged along, in weather fair and foul, on unpaved roads.[6] (Julia) Ann Washington also rode circuit with her husband, George Washington's nephew Bushrod, whose Court service ran from 1798 until 1829.[7] Ann Washington's health was poor; to make the bumpy way more tolerable, Bushrod read aloud to *her*.[8] But these instances of togetherness were uncommon. For most couples, circuit riding and D.C. boardinghouse living meant long periods of separation.

If boardinghouse living when the Justices sat in D.C. diminished family life, it served one notable purpose—togetherness day and night helped to secure the institutional authority of the nascent, underfunded Supreme Court. Recent biographies of the great Chief Justice tell how John Marshall used the camaraderie of boardinghouse tables and common rooms, also madeira, to dispel dissent and achieve the one-voiced Opinion of the Court, which he usually composed and delivered himself. The unanimity John Marshall strived to maintain helped the swordless Third Branch fend off attacks from the political branches.[9]

Although Chief Justice Marshall strictly separated his Court and family life, he did not lack affection for his wife. In a letter from Philadelphia in 1797, John Marshall told Polly of his longing. "I like [the big city] well enough for a day or two," he wrote Polly, "but I then begin to require a frugal repast with cool water. I wou[l]d give a great deal to dine with you today on a piece of cold meat with our boys beside us & to see little Mary running backwards & forwards over the floor."[10]

In 1832, a year after Polly's death, Marshall reflected: "Her judgement was so sound & so safe that I have often relied upon it in situations of some perplexity. I do not recall ever to have regretted the adoption of her opinion. I have sometimes regretted its rejection."[11] In truth, however, the marriage, which spanned nearly a half century (forty-nine years),[12] caused John Marshall no little anxiety.

By all accounts, Polly was a frail woman and chronically ill.[13] So acutely noise sensitive was she that John Marshall, to avoid disturbing her, would walk in and around his home without shoes. Richmond, Virginia, officials muffled the town bell so that Polly could sleep undisturbed.[14]

Polly's importance in her husband's life is perhaps best indicated by the simple engraving placed on Marshall's tomb, carrying out a request he made just two days before his death. The engraving records, by names and dates, only three events in Marshall's nearly eighty years on earth: his birth; his marriage to Polly; his departure from this life.

If John Marshall acted as his fragile wife's benevolent protector, the Chief Justice's junior colleague, Joseph Story, thrived in a marriage closer to a joint venture.[15] Joseph Story's first marriage ended tragically with the death of his wife Mary just seven months after their union. His second marriage, to Sarah Waldo Wetmore, proved a happy and enduring match. Joseph's letters to Sarah indicate a relationship of mutual respect. Joseph gave Sarah detailed accounts of the cultural and political life of the capital and of the Court's work, including his impressions of the advocates and their arguments.[16] After delivering an opinion disposing of a well-known will contest, for example, Justice Story wrote, intriguingly, that he would have much to tell Sarah about the case when he got home, for "there are some secrets of private history in it."[17]

In his will, signed in 1843, Story declared his "entire confidence in the sound Discretion of [his] Wife" to provide for the welfare of their children.[18] He bequeathed to Sarah "all the . . . Stock[s] standing in her name, or held by [him] for her use [though purchased] out of her own separate funds."[19] Joseph was of the view that this property fully belonged to Sarah[20] although the Massachusetts legislature had not yet provided that a woman, post-marriage, could hold and manage her own property.[21] He left to her as well all of his copyrights, manuscripts, letters, and other writings.[22] (Story's book royalties, I should add, amounted, annually, to more than twice his judicial salary.) The final statement in Story's will is touching, emblematic of a life partnership, responsive to a question Joseph did not want Sarah to worry over. "I recommend," he wrote, "but do not order, that my wife sell & dispose of all my wines, & all of my Books . . . , which she may not want for her own use, & not . . . keep them merely because they belonged to me, as a memorial of our long & affectionate union."[23]

Joseph Story was the first Justice to break with the Court's brethren-only boardinghouse tradition. Sarah Story accompanied Joseph to Washington, D.C., for the February 1828 Term. Chief Justice Marshall was ambivalent. He told Story it would be fine if Sarah dined with the Justices, whose circle might benefit from a woman's "humanizing influence."[24] On the other hand, there was work to be done. Marshall expressed the hope that Sarah would not "monopolize" her husband.[25] The experiment was not altogether successful. Sarah Story apparently enjoyed Washington society well enough; her digestive system, however, did not take well to boardinghouse fare.[26] And she perhaps grew tired of "waiting in the wings for conferences to cease."[27] She departed town before her husband, and did not return in subsequent years.[28]

But her stay unsettled the boardinghouse culture. Justice John McLean, appointed in 1829, decided he would reside at home in D.C. with his wife and would not board with the brethren. Justice William Johnson, an early dissenter, also stayed away from the group quarters. Chief Justice Marshall was not pleased. The scattering of the Justices, he correctly anticipated, would mean more separate opinions, undermining the unified voice Marshall labored to install.[29]

I turn now to the first wife to tell her own story, Malvina Shanklin Harlan, whose husband, John Marshall Harlan, served on the Court from 1877 until 1911. It was a story known to members of the Harlan family and the Justice's biographer, but until 2001, read by few others. Malvina Shanklin Harlan lived from 1839 until 1916, but she dated her memoir, which she titled *Memories of a Long Life*, from 1854, the year she met John Marshall Harlan, until 1911, the year he died. Malvina's manuscript contained well-told anecdotes and keen insights about the Harlan family, politics in Indiana, Kentucky, and Washington, D.C., in pre– and post–Civil War days, religion, and of course, the Supreme Court.

I was drawn to Malvina's *Memories* as a chronicle of the times, as seen by a brave woman of the era. I thought others would find the manuscript as appealing as I did. For many months, I tried to interest a university or commercial press in Malvina's *Memories*, to no avail. When I was about to give up on the endeavor, the Supreme Court Historical Society rescued the project.

The society devoted the entire summer 2001 issue of its journal to Malvina's *Memories*. Pre-publication in the society's journal, the manuscript was carefully annotated and helpfully introduced by historian and University of Cincinnati law professor Linda Przybyszewski, author of an engaging biography of the Justice titled *The Republic According to John Marshall Harlan*. The historical society acquired, and placed throughout the issue, a number of attractive photographs. On the cover is a portrait of Malvina, age seventeen, and John, age twenty-three, on their wedding day in 1856.

To call attention to the society's publication, I asked the *New York Times* Supreme Court reporter, Linda Greenhouse, if the *Times* might publish a review of the memoir. She said the *Times* was not likely to write a book review of a periodical issue, but added, perhaps something useful might be done. She would think about it. As those who read her *Times* reports know, Linda is a very good thinker.

In August 2001, the *New York Times* ran two feature stories about Malvina's *Memories*. On page one of a Sunday edition, the *Times* ran the wedding photograph and described the memoir. A follow-up story the next week included several quotations from the manuscript. Among them were memories relating to the Civil War.

The first quotation concerned Malvina's decision to marry John, a slave-owning Kentuckian. Malvina, who lived her first seventeen years in Indiana, wrote:

> All my kindred were strongly opposed to Slavery, the "peculiar institution" of the South. Indeed, an uncle on my mother's side, with whom I was a great favourite, was such an out-and-out Abolitionist that I think (before he came to know my husband) he would rather have seen me in my grave than have me marry a Southern man and go to live in the South.

Although Kentucky was a slave state, it remained loyal to the Union. After consulting with Malvina, John Marshall Harlan joined the Union army five years after their marriage, when two children were part of the family. He remained in service throughout the war.

Decades later, in 1903, war stories were still retold. Malvina wrote of a dinner party that year:

> There were perhaps a dozen people at the table. My husband, being in the best of spirits, began to tell the company some of his experiences in the Civil War.
>
> He was describing a hurried march which he and his regiment made through Tennessee and Kentucky in pursuit of the daring

Confederate raider, John Morgan. He came to a point in his story where he and the advance guard of the pursuing Union troops had nearly overtaken the rear-guard of Morgan's men, who had just crossed from the opposite shore.

Suddenly, Judge Lurton [a guest at the dinner] laid down his knife and fork, leaned back in his chair, his face aglow with surprise and wonder, and called out to my husband in a voice of great excitement, "Harlan, is it possible I am just finding out *who* it was that tried to shoot me on that never-to-be-forgotten day?"

In a tone of equal surprise . . . my husband said, "Lurton, do you mean to tell me that *you* were with Morgan on that raid? Now I know *why* I did not catch up with him; and I thank God I didn't hit *you* that day."

The whole company was thrilled by the dramatic sequel to my husband's story, as they realized afresh how completely the wounds of that fratricidal war had been healed; for there were those two men, [one from Kentucky, the other from Tennessee,] fellow citizens of this one and united country, serving together as Judges on the Federal Bench. It was as if there had been no Civil War.

Judge Lurton, at the time of the dinner party, served on the U.S. Court of Appeals for the Sixth Circuit; he was appointed to the Supreme Court seven years later, in 1909, and served his first two years on the Court together with Justice Harlan.

Indicating the power of the press, the *Times* coverage of Malvina's *Memories* garnered the attention of several publishers. Random House made the offer most attractive to Justice Harlan's heirs and the Supreme Court Historical Society. The Modern Library edition was in bookshops in the spring of 2002, in good time for Mother's Day. Malvina's memoir was well received. One reviewer commented that reading it "[was] like engaging with a fine conversationalist," and encountering a "gifted storyteller."

By the time of John Harlan's appointment to the Supreme Court in

1877, boardinghouse days were long over, and a Supreme Court appointment meant a move to Washington, D.C., for all in the Justice's immediate family. It also meant an unpaid job for the Justice's wife.

Malvina Harlan wrote of the "at home" Monday receptions Supreme Court wives were expected to hold. The callers came in numbers. Malvina reported she might receive as many as two hundred to three hundred visitors on an "at home" Monday.[30] These events were more fancy than plain. Tables would be spread with refreshing salads and rich cakes. Musicians were engaged so the young people might dance a waltz or two while the older folk looked on.[31] "At home" Mondays held by Court wives continued into Charles Evans Hughes' Chief Justiceship in the 1930s.[32]

In 1856, when seventeen-year-old Malvina Harlan left her parents' home in Indiana to begin married life in Kentucky, her mother counseled: "You love this man well enough to marry him. Remember, now, that *his* home is YOUR home; *his* people, YOUR people; *his* interests, YOUR interests—you must have *no other*."[33]

Malvina valued that advice, but did not follow it in all respects. She continued to pursue her interest in music[34] and eventually sojourned abroad on her own[35] when her husband returned to the United States to attend the Court's Term. Of her decision to tour Italy with a few friends during that time, she wrote: "This exhibition of independence was so new and surprising to my daughters that they called my Italian trip 'Mother's Revolt.' "

In the main, however, her ambition was her husband's success. She sought to be helpmate to, not independent from, John Marshall Harlan. She took pride in his nickname for her, "Old Woman." She thought it showed "he looked upon [her] as having the judgment and experience that only years can bring."

When John became a Supreme Court Justice, Malvina developed a friendship with First Lady Lucy Hayes, nicknamed "Lemonade Lucy" for her avid temperance.[36] This friendship yielded the Harlans more than occasional invitations to the White House.[37]

At White House evenings, Supreme Court wives did not always

stand solidly, or at least silently, behind their men. Malvina Harlan tells of a dinner at which Chief Justice Waite endured some teasing by his wife and the First Lady for having "squelched" Belva Lockwood's 1870s application to be admitted to practice before the Supreme Court.[38]

Malvina reported an episode, my favorite, showing that Supreme Court wives attended to more than just the social side of their husbands' lives. Justice Harlan was a collector of objects connected with American history.[39] He had retrieved for his collection, from the Supreme Court Marshal's Office, the inkstand Chief Justice Taney used when he penned the 1857 *Dred Scott*[40] decision,[41] which held that no person descended from a slave could ever become a citizen of the United States, and that the majestic Due Process Clause safeguarded one person's right to hold another in bondage. It was a decision with which Harlan, as a Justice, strongly disagreed, an opinion overturned by the Civil War and the Fourteenth Amendment.

Chivalrous gentleman that he was, Harlan promised to deliver the Taney inkstand to a woman he met at a reception, who claimed a family relationship to Chief Justice Taney. Malvina thought the promise unwise, so she hid the inkstand away among her own special things, and Justice Harlan was obliged to report to the purported Taney relative that the item had been mislaid.

In the months immediately following the incident, the Supreme Court heard argument in the so-called *Civil Rights Cases*,[42] which yielded an 1883 judgment striking down the Civil Rights Act of 1875,[43] an act Congress had passed to advance equal treatment without regard to race in various public accommodations. Justice Harlan, alone, resolved to dissent, as he did thirteen years later in *Plessy v. Ferguson*, the 1896 decision that launched the "separate but equal" doctrine. He labored over his dissenting opinion for months, but "his thoughts refused to flow easily." He seemed, Malvina wrote in her memoir, trapped "in a quagmire of logic, precedent, and law."[44]

Malvina, as I earlier mentioned, grew up in a free-state family strongly opposed to slavery.[45] She very much wanted her husband to finish writing that dissent. On a Sunday morning when the Justice was attending church services, Malvina retrieved the Taney inkstand from its hiding place, gave the object "a good cleaning and polishing, and filled it with ink. Then, taking all the other ink-wells from [her husband's] study table, [she] put the historic . . . inkstand directly before his pad of paper."[46] When Justice Harlan came home, Malvina told him he would find "a bit of inspiration on [his] study table."[47] Malvina's memoir next relates:

> The memory of the historic part [t]hat Taney's inkstand had played in the Dred Scott decision, in temporarily tightening the shackles of slavery . . . in the ante-bellum days, seemed, that morning, to act like magic in clarifying my husband's thoughts in regard to the law that had been intended . . . to protect the recently emancipated slaves in the enjoyment of equal civil rights. His pen fairly flew on that day and . . . he soon finished his dissent.[48]

Next time my thoughts on an opinion "refuse to flow easily," I may visit the Marshal's Office in search of a pen in need of absolution, perhaps the one Justice Bradley used to write his now infamous concurring opinion in Myra Bradwell's case, *Bradwell v. Illinois*,[49] an 1873 decision upholding a state's right to exclude women from the practice of law. Justice Bradley wrote in his opinion: "The natural and proper timidity and delicacy which belongs to the female sex evidently unfits it for many of the occupations of civil life. . . ."[50] In his view, women's "domain" did not extend beyond "the domestic sphere." He rooted his opinion in a law higher than the Constitution: "The paramount destiny and mission of woman are to fulfill the noble and benign offices of wife and mother. This is the law of the Creator."[51] (Wouldn't Justice Bradley be amazed to learn that women today are astronauts, commercial pilots, governors, senators and representatives, state and federal judges, and Supreme Court Justices.)

The last of my wives' stories takes us into the twentieth century. I will relate some aspects of the life of Helen ("Nellie") Herron Taft, a woman who wanted the man she married to become president, and actively helped make that dream come true. Sadly, she suffered two strokes during Taft's one-term presidency, the first causing her to become speechless, a disability she struggled to overcome.

Nellie Herron, even as a young woman, did not hide her intelligence, as many marriage-bound women of her generation felt it necessary to do. She pursued university studies in chemistry and German,[52] and until the birth of her first child, taught at a private school for girls.[53] While courting Nellie, William Howard Taft attended Saturday night "salons" Nellie hosted in Cincinnati, at which participants discussed the thoughts of luminaries, including Benjamin Franklin, John Adams, Edmund Burke, Martin Luther, Rousseau, and Voltaire.[54] Taft admired Nellie's "eagerness for knowledge of all kinds," and "her capacity for work."[55] Her credo: "We live to learn."

Shortly before Will and Nellie married in 1886,[56] Nellie visited Washington, D.C. Taft wrote to her: "I wonder, Nellie dear, if you and I will ever be there in an official capacity? Oh yes, I forgot; of course we shall when you become secretary of the treasury."[57] Nellie, according to her father-in-law, was economical and an excellent calculator. Taft wisely entrusted management of the family's finances to her.[58] In 1897, after eleven years of marriage, Taft expressed this sentiment in a letter to Nellie: "You are so much of my life. . . . I am so glad that you don't flatter me and sit at my feet with honey. You are my dearest and best critic and are worth so much to me in stirring me up to best endeavor."[59] Among Nellie's pursuits in the couple's Cincinnati days, she founded and was for several years president of the Cincinnati Symphony Orchestra.

Her eye on the U.S. presidency, Nellie had reservations about her husband's appointment to the U.S. Court of Appeals for the Sixth Circuit in 1892, following his service as solicitor general.[60] She later recalled in her autobiography: "[M]y thinking led me to decide that my husband's appointment on the Bench was not a matter for such warm congratulation. . . . I began even then to fear the narrowing effects of the Bench and to prefer for him . . . an all-round professional development."[61]

Taft left the Court of Appeals in 1901 to become governor of the Philippines.[62] He and Nellie took up residence in Manila. Cholera plagued the island. When President Theodore Roosevelt told Taft that he was in line for a position on the Supreme Court, and eventually, appointment as Chief Justice, Nellie still resisted. "I had always been opposed to a judicial career for him," she wrote, "but at this point I shall have to admit I weakened just a little."[63] Recognizing the grave situation in the Philippines and the importance of his efforts there, Taft, after talking it over with Nellie, declined the Supreme Court appointment.[64]

During their years in the Philippines, Will and Nellie, in contrast to the military leadership, genuinely respected the local culture and sought to pave the way for democratic self-rule. Living to learn, Nellie in those years traveled all over the islands, and also to Japan, Siberia, Russia, and Western Europe.

Taft became a presidential candidate in 1908. The *Washington Post* wrote of Nellie's influence: "There is every reason why she should feel satisfied in her husband's success, for had it not been for her determination to keep him from becoming a Supreme Court Justice he would not have been able to accept the nomination" for the presidency.[65]

As first lady, Nellie fared well in the press. The *Washington Post* commented: "In the matter of mental attainments, she is probably the best fitted woman who ever graced the position she now holds."[66] The *New York Times* put it succinctly: She "has brains and uses them."[67] Among other enterprises, Nellie, with the aid of the mayor of Tokyo, introduced the cherry blossoms that annually adorn the capital city to celebrate the arrival of spring.[68] Among her many "firsts," in 1909, she was the first first lady to ride with the president on Inauguration Day, and the first first lady not only to drive in a car, but to drive one herself.

Taft became Chief Justice of the United States in 1921. It was the post he wanted more than any other. Nellie, whose consuming ambition was to see her husband elected president, did not include in her autobiography a chapter on his tenure at the Court. But we have this information from a letter Taft wrote to his daughter: "She goes without hesitation everywhere, accepts all the invitations that she wishes to accept, goes out at night when there is anything that is attractive to her."[69] Nellie died in 1943, one week shy of her eighty-second birthday.[70] She lived to see all three of her children—her sons Robert and Charles and her daughter Helen, once dean of Bryn Mawr College—gain law degrees.[71]

The life of Supreme Court spouses has changed greatly since the days I have described. Spouses do not receive "at home" callers on Monday, or any day; they pursue careers or interests of their own. Adding "humanizing" variety, two men, so far, count among Supreme Court spouses. Spouses have seats in a special section of the courtroom, and they lunch together three times a year, rotating cooking responsibility. One member favored as a co-caterer is my husband, super-chef Martin D. Ginsburg. The lunches are held in ground-floor space once designated the Ladies Dining Room, but at Justice O'Connor's suggestion, fittingly renamed the Natalie Cornell Rehnquist Dining Room in the 1997 Term. (Nan Rehnquist, who died in 1991, had been the prime mover in renovating the room.)

Chief Justice Rehnquist commented in an address some years ago: "Change is the law of life, and the judiciary will have to change to meet the challenges we will face in the future."[72] Changes are in store for the Court in the Term about to start. But I anticipate that they will be eased by the way the Justices and their partners—at work and in life—relate to, care about, and respect each other.

Part Three

On Gender Equality: Women and the Law

Introduction

NINETEEN-SEVENTY WAS A *watershed year for thirty-seven-year-old Ruth Bader Ginsburg. Inspired by "the awakening consciousness" of her newly activist women law students, the recently tenured Rutgers law professor pivoted the focus of her scholarship and legal analytical skills from the crucially important (but not exactly riveting) principles governing court procedures in the United States and abroad to the equality of the sexes under law. (For the record, Justice Ginsburg herself would dispute our characterization of her earlier scholarly specialty as anything other than riveting. "I love all procedure cases," she told us.*[1] *She loved studying procedure at law school, learning and writing about Swedish procedure in the early sixties, and teaching procedure courses at Rutgers and Columbia law schools. She continues to enjoy crafting procedure opinions as a Justice on the Supreme Court, where Chief Justice Rehnquist indulged her predilection by assigning her more procedure opinions to write than any other Justice.)*

On May 1, Law Day, 1970, Professor Ginsburg chaired a student panel on "women's liberation" at Rutgers Law School in Newark, New Jersey. At year's end, she participated in a panel at the annual meeting of the Association of American Law Schools, held in Chicago, in which she argued that "two jobs merit the immediate attention" of the law schools' academic community: first, "the elimination from law school texts and classroom presentations of attempts at comic relief via stereotyped characterizations of women," and second, "the infusion into standard curricular offerings of material on sex-based discrimination."[2] *In between these events, she was persuaded by her students to teach a course on sex discrimination the following spring and devoted part of her summer to pulling together materials for the course. "In the space of a month," she remembered, "I read every federal decision ever published involving women's legal status, and every law review article. That was no grand feat. There were not many decisions, and not much in the way of commentary."*[3]

In 1971, both of her panel presentations were converted into published law journal articles, becoming her first journal articles on gender equality; these were a precursor to the tsunami of articles about gender and law that flooded law journals over the remainder of the decade.

In the spring of 1971, Professor Ginsburg taught her first seminar on sex discrimination and the law. The course had a practicum component, which involved her students in actual cases that had begun to appear on the docket of the American Civil Liberties Union's New Jersey affiliate. Auspiciously, in the spring and summer of 1971, she also worked on two briefs with the national office of the ACLU. The first brief (which she later designated "the grandmother brief") was for an appeal to the federal Court of Appeals for the Tenth Circuit on behalf of Charles Moritz, a dutiful son of an aging and infirm mother. Moritz challenged a provision of the Internal Revenue Code that provided a tax deduction to employed persons for the cost of providing care to their dependents while they worked—unless they were, like Moritz, single men. The second (or "mother") brief was filed in the United States Supreme Court on behalf of Sally Reed, a bereaved mother who sought to administer the small estate of her deceased teenage son. She was denied appointment, and the boy's father was appointed instead, as the law of Sally's state, Idaho, demanded: it preferred men to women as administrators of the estates of relatives who died without leaving a will.

In the first brief, Professor Ginsburg developed a powerful argument in favor of gender equality under the equal protection component of the Fifth Amendment. The second brief honed and extended that argument, this time under the Fourteenth Amendment's explicit equal protection guarantee. These briefs helped catapult Ginsburg into the role of foremost litigator before the Supreme Court on behalf of equality of the sexes. The case, Reed v. Reed, *decided on November 22, 1971, stands today as an historical landmark: the first time in history that the Supreme Court invalidated a sex-based statute under the Equal Protection Clause. (A few months after* Reed, *the Tenth Circuit similarly struck down the dependent-care gender classification in the tax law, giving Charles Moritz his tax deduction.)*

Just weeks after Reed *was decided, the ACLU voted to establish a Women's Rights Project, which commenced operation in the spring of 1972. Ginsburg agreed to serve as its coordinator. The following year, she was designated one of three general counsel to the ACLU, a position she held until the end of the decade.*

Meanwhile, Columbia University Law School, from which Ginsburg had graduated at the top of the class thirteen years earlier, hired her as the first tenured woman law professor in its 114-year history. (Justice Ginsburg calls 1972 "the year of the woman" in legal academia—law schools around the country were scrambling, under pressure from the Department of Health, Education, and Welfare, to add women to their almost entirely male faculties.) Although she taught standard law school courses such as civil procedure at Columbia, as she had at Rutgers, she also imported the seminar model she had initiated at Rutgers, teaching Columbia law students about gender and law and engaging them in actual litigation and legislation projects relating to gender issues.

Also in 1972, Ginsburg undertook, with Professors Herma Hill Kay of the University of California, Berkeley's law school and Kenneth Davidson of the State University of New York at Buffalo, to produce a casebook (as law-teaching textbooks are known) on sex discrimination and law. That casebook, Sex-Based Discrimination: Text, Cases and Materials, *was published in 1974. The first such work in the United States (and, quite probably, the world), it became an important resource for students and professors in the rapidly proliferating women-and-law courses at law schools across the nation.*

Ginsburg contributed three chapters to the casebook. Chapter 1 addressed women's legal history under the Constitution, the Equal Rights Amendment, and the new direction in which the Supreme Court was heading in its application of equal protection principles in sex discrimination cases (the chapter included the texts of the decisions in Moritz, Reed v. Reed, *and the second of Ginsburg's pathmarking Supreme Court cases,* Frontiero v. Richardson [*1973*]*). Chapter 4 explored the myriad ways women and girls experienced discrimination in educational institutions, from sex-based admissions policies to exclusion from high school sports teams to expulsion of pregnant girls from school. Chapter 6 provided a "comparative side-glance" at the United Nations' declarations on gender equality and the Swedish model for eliminating women's inequality.*

Over the course of the decade, Professor Ginsburg would publish more than twenty-five legal articles chronicling and critiquing the unfolding law, constitutional and otherwise, on gender equality—law that she herself did so much to shape. Under the ACLU's aegis, she would mastermind briefs submitted in twenty-four Supreme Court cases, nine on behalf of litigants and fifteen as friend-of-the-court, or amicus curiae, briefs. On six occasions, she appeared before the Court to present oral argument. She lost just one case. Through her briefs, starting with Reed, *she, more than any other lawyer, shaped the legal arguments reflected in the Court's opinions, earning her the honorific "the Thurgood Marshall of the women's movement." By the time she left teaching and litigation for a judgeship on the federal appeals court for the District of Columbia Circuit in 1980, state and federal law had undergone a revolution.*

But the story of Ruth Ginsburg's contribution to the Supreme Court's equal protection doctrine in gender discrimination cases did not end when she became a judge. In 1996, during her third Term on the Supreme Court of the United States, Justice Ginsburg authored the majority opinion in United States v. Virginia *on behalf of six members of the Court, clarifying and strengthening the approach to gender equality that the Court had developed, under her tutelage, in the 1970s.*

Ginsburg's own words about gender and law in the 1970s—in briefs, articles both scholarly and popular, congressional testimony, and interviews and speeches—could easily fill a large tome. Here, we offer some selections reflecting the scope, substance, and style of those varied communications.

We begin with Professor Ginsburg's "Women and the Law: A Symposium Introduction," because it captures the moment when she entered the legal fray at the beginning of the seventies—back when the subject of human rights for women was nowhere to be found in law casebooks and classrooms, precious few federal courts took sex discrimination seriously, and the feminist legal movement had not begun to barrage the Supreme Court with requests to review gender-based laws and government policies. The second offering, "How the Tenth Circuit Court of Appeals Got My Wife Her Good Job," written by Martin (Marty) Ginsburg—Ruth Ginsburg's "life partner," as she often called him—tells, with his characteristic wit and humor, the story of how those first two cases, Moritz *and* Reed, *came about. Next we offer an example of lawyer Ginsburg's brief-writing on behalf of women's equality—an excerpt from one of her briefs in the* Frontiero *case—followed by a piece titled "The Need for the Equal Rights Amendment," in which she refuted the "three horribles" foretold by the ERA's opponents. Then comes the capstone: the "bench announcement" (an oral précis of Supreme Court opinions for press and public) for* United States v. Virginia, *Justice Ginsburg's most significant opinion on the constitutional equality principle as applied to gender distinctions. The chapter concludes with a 2008 journal article, "The 1970s New Look at the Equality Principle," her reflections on "what that 1970s effort entailed."*

1

Women and the Law

A Symposium Introduction*

> [T]he principle which regulates the existing social relations between the two sexes—the legal subordination of one sex to the other—is wrong in itself, and now one of the chief hindrances to human improvement; . . . it ought to be replaced by a principle of perfect equality, admitting no power or privilege on the one side, nor disability on the other.
>
> —JOHN STUART MILL,[1] *The Subjection of Women* (1869)

As part of its Law Day activities on May 1, 1970, the Student Bar Association of Rutgers Law School organized a panel discussion on women's liberation. . . . As moderator of the panel discussion, and one of then two women law professors at Rutgers, I was asked to furnish an appropriately brief introduction to the symposium. What follows is an updated résumé of my remarks at the Law Day program.

I. Comparative Sideglance

"The family is the most natural form of living for most people in our country. But it should be a togetherness between free and inde-

*This piece was originally published in 25 *Rutgers Law Review* 1 (1971). We have made minor edits based on length and context.

pendent people."[2] Sweden's prime minister, Olof Palme, included these remarks in his response to Swedish housewives who feared "devaluation" as a result of a change in Sweden's system of taxing earned income. The Swedish system resembled the system in effect in the United States: by relating a wife's income to her husband's, it discouraged many wives from working. The new system introduces individual taxation; every person, married or not, will be taxed on earned income separately and under a uniformly applicable graduated rate schedule. Prime Minister Palme explained that the end envisioned, independence and equality for women, was a goal toward which Sweden had already made significant progress through reform of marriage law, in the field of education, on the labor market, and in working out social benefits.

In the United States, in very recent years, appreciation of women's place has reached the nascent state. Activated by feminists of both sexes, courts and legislatures are beginning to recognize the claim of women to full membership in the class *people*, entitled to due process guarantees of life and liberty and equal protection of the laws. But the distance to equal opportunity remains considerable. Some European countries, as slow to accord women the vote, have followed up more rapidly than has the United States that promise of an equal voice in societal affairs.[3] For example, contrast with the Swedish development in income taxation, the recent "reform" in the United States. The Tax Reform Act of 1969 not only perpetuates, but significantly enlarges the "marriage penalty" that has been a feature of United States tax law: when both spouses work and have approximately equal incomes, they will pay substantially larger amounts of income tax than if they were living together unmarried and filing returns as single taxpayers.[4] The "married togetherness" fostered by the 1969 Tax Reform Act is between working husband and stay-at-home wife.[5]

II. New Horizons in Employment and Education: Equal Protection Potential

While it is no longer a popular view that "women . . . are only children of a larger growth,"[6] the notion remains prevalent that women (if they are middle or upper class, and tax disincentives aside) enjoy the best of all possible worlds: the choice between gainful employment and domestic pursuits. Moreover, when women choose gainful employment, they sometimes reap the benefits of special protective legislation. Many men, and perhaps some women, who otherwise see the world without rose-colored glasses still profess belief in the existence of an ideal situation of choice and protection for women.[7]

But . . . choice is channeled during the earliest years.[8] An exceedingly popular and in many respects exemplary television series for preschool children is, according to its director (a woman), "definitely male-oriented."[9] Books for the nursery and kindergarten audience continue to encourage achievement for boys and passivity for girls.[10] Law-sanctioned protection in the labor market, whatever its benefits to women engaged in sweatshop operations at the turn of the century,[11] in more recent times has effectively insulated men from female competition for jobs commanding higher pay.[12] State "protection," and unchecked discrimination by employers (sometimes abetted by male-dominated unions),[13] have stopped many women at the gate, denied promotions to others, and kept great numbers of them at a compensation level appreciably lower than the level assigned to men performing work of the same kind and quality.[14]

Currently, federal legislation and guidelines, and vigorous efforts of women to enforce them, are beginning to rescue the submissive majority[15] from the confinement of old-style state protective laws and the discriminatory practices of employers. Principal measures on the national level are the Equal Pay Act of 1963,[16] Title VII of the Civil Rights Act of 1964,[17] and, most recently, guidelines issued by the Labor Department designed to eliminate discrimination against women in jobs under federal contracts.[18] These developments hold the promise of a new-style protection for society: protection of the equal right of men and women to pursue the employment for which individual talent and capacity best equip them. Illustrative is a recent case in which a federal district court declared inconsistent with Title VII the hours restrictions imposed on women by the Illinois Female Employment Act. Significantly, the plaintiffs were employers who successfully contended that the state "protective" legislation prevented them from promoting or assigning female employees to jobs requiring overtime, and imposed an excess overtime burden on male employees.[19]

While legislative and administrative measures have brightened opportunities for women job seekers, in another key area, education, the judiciary has taken the lead rein. A 1970 decision of a three-judge federal district court, *Kirstein v. University of Virginia*,[20] may well mark the turning point in the long effort to place equal opportunity for women under the aegis of the Federal Constitution.[21] The court held inconsonant with the Fourteenth Amendment's Equal Protection Clause the exclusion of women from the University of Virginia's undergraduate school at Charlottesville; it approved a plan which, after a two-year transition period, requires the admission of women on precisely the same basis as men. Although sixteen years have elapsed since *Brown v. Board of Education*,[22] *Kirstein v. University of Virginia* is the first decision to declare unconstitutional exclusion of women from educational opportunities afforded to men by a state institution.[23]

Significantly, "private" institutions of higher learning that might escape a constitutional prod confined to "state action" are beginning to volunteer similar reforms. For example, Cornell University's College of Arts and Sciences announced during the 1969–70 academic year that it would admit women on the same basis as men and would offer students of both sexes the same options with respect to housing accommodations.[24] New York University's Law School has opened to women once exclusively male scholarship programs and has provided accommodations for single women in a dormitory facility formerly reserved to bachelors and married couples; in response to requests of its women students (now over 15 percent of those enrolled in the J.D. program), it has begun to recruit women for regular faculty positions.[25] Harvard Law School has agreed to provide dormitory accommodations for its women students, to improve medical services for them, and to fund a recruitment program designed to increase the female population of the law school.[26] Dozens of universities and colleges and several law schools have introduced courses relating to sex roles in society.

Of course, the university scene is not yet rosy. Despite the superior performance of the women admitted to undergraduate studies at Yale in 1969–70, the university's president declined to act on a request for increased female enrollment. Apparently in recognition of Yale's dependence upon the support of people who do not believe strongly in coeducation, he stated: "We must not, unless it is absolutely necessary, increase the number of women at Yale at the expense of the number of men."[27] After unsuccessful efforts to persuade the University of Chicago's Law School to exclude from placement office facilities firms that discriminate with respect to the employment of women attorneys, fourteen women law students filed a complaint with the Equal Employment Opportunity Commission charging the school and three Chicago law firms with violations of Title VII.[28] Recently, women's groups have filed complaints with the United States Department of Labor against colleges and universities with federal contracts; these complaints seek investigation of discrimination against women with respect to admissions policies, financial aid, placement of graduates, hiring and promotion for staff and faculty, and salary differentials.[29] A related matter concerning elementary and high school education is now *sub judice*. School desegregation plans tendered in a number of southern communities eliminate race segregation only to substitute in its place sex segregation. No doubt such plans may be challenged as a facade for continued race discrimination. But they also pose the question whether state enforcement of sex segregation is constitutionally permissible at the precollege level.[30]

The decision in *Kirstein v. University of Virginia*[31] points toward a reassessment of the application of the Equal Protection Clause to women in other areas. For example, in *Seidenberg v. McSorley's Old Ale House*,[32] the court declared unconstitutional under the Equal Protection Clause a saloon's 115-year-old practice of catering only to men. At a preliminary stage in the litigation, the court stated: "To adhere to practices supported by ancient chivalristic concepts, when there may no longer exist a need or basis therefor, may only serve to isolate women from the realities of everyday life, and to perpetuate, as a matter of law, economic and sexual exploitation."[33] In its final disposition awarding summary judgment to the plaintiffs, the court concluded that the discrimination was "without foundation in reason."[34]

On the other hand, judicial awakening is hardly universal. Recently, the Idaho Supreme Court found consonant with the Equal Protection Clause a state statute providing: "Of several persons claiming and equally entitled to administer [the estate of a person dying intestate], males must be preferred to females."[35] Decisions of this genre, with formidable United States Supreme Court precedent as a prop,[36] explain why feminists are urging with renewed vigor adoption of the proposed Equal Rights Amendment.[37]

III. Women and the Environment of 1990

In recent months, the mass media have presented frequent, and sometimes misleading, accounts of an activist women's movement. The attention to feminist organizations and activities is not misplaced, however, for in the current decade a less submissive majority seems certain to develop. Those who deride women's liberation, or write off the current feminist appeal as simply a shadow operation in the wake of the civil rights movement, need adjust their sights. Of course, in the United States grand inspiration has come from the organized effort of black people to achieve equal rights. But that model is not close at hand in European countries where women's options are developing more rapidly than in this country. One universal concern is surely a contributing factor: recognition that long-term relief for environmental problems requires increased attention to birth control. For people otherwise indifferent to feminist goals, the prospect of life for women beyond Kinder, Kirche, and Küche takes on a new, attractive dimension. A tolerable future may be anticipated if 220 million rather than 300 million people populate the United States in 1990.[38] This consideration, perhaps more than privacy concerns or the Fourteenth Amendment rights asserted by women,[39] may have influenced the vote of at least some of the legislators and judges who responded affirmatively to demands for repeal or invalidation of abortion laws.

The unfinished business of equality for women is gaining momentum; thought and energy directed to it in the 1970s may contribute significantly to the healthy environment and society universally desired for the decades ahead. Key items on the feminist agenda are vigilantly enforced equality of opportunity in employment and education, generally available quality child care facilities (models presently exist in the Soviet Union and Israel), a tax system that does not penalize a wife for earning as much as her husband but does recognize adequately the business expense entailed in arranging for the care of dependents of working people, and elimination of vestiges of an inferior status still reflected in discriminatory practices in places of public accommodation and housing and in criminal, property, and family law.[40] Pacesetters in the enterprise should be government and universities.[41] Critical to a brighter future is the continued development of activist, but politically acute, feminist organizations—groups dedicated to the principle of equality, but possessing the pragmatism essential to a movement whose ultimate success requires broad popular support.

2

How the Tenth Circuit Court of Appeals Got My Wife Her Good Job

MARTY GINSBURG, *tax lawyer, law professor, and gourmet cook, passed away on June 27, 2010, before he could deliver the speech he had prepared for the Tenth Circuit Court of Appeals' annual conference. Two months later to the day, Justice Ginsburg stood before the conferees in Colorado Springs, Colorado, and began: "My dear husband, who was a great tax lawyer, got an extension for our 2009 tax return, but he had his Tenth Circuit speech all written out and I know he would want you to hear it. So bear with me. My timing won't be like his, but I'll do the best I can." She then read his speech, to laughter and applause, making only one correction to Marty's text (below). When she finished, her audience gave her (and Marty) a standing ovation.*

As you have heard, my field is tax law. When Chief Judge Henry asked me to speak today and hinted it might be on my favorite subject, naturally I prepared a long paper addressing the Supreme Court's performance in tax cases. Sadly, the Chief Judge reacted with surprising hostility and so I am going to speak instead about the only significant thing I have done in my long life with Honorable Ruth. I shall recall for you the one case in which we served as co-counsel. It was also the one occasion either of us was privileged to argue in the Tenth Circuit. Nonetheless, fascinating as you will surely find this reminiscence, all in all you are the losers, for I promise you, the Supreme Court's performance in tax cases is an exceedingly funny subject.

In the 1960s I practiced law, mainly tax law, in New York City, and Ruth began her law teaching career at Rutgers Law School in Newark. One of the courses she taught was Constitutional Law and, toward the end of the decade, she started looking into equal protection issues that might be presented by statutes that differentiate on the basis of sex. A dismal academic undertaking because, back then, the United States Supreme Court had never invalidated any legislative classification that differentiated on the basis of sex.

Then as now, at home Ruth and I worked evenings in adjacent rooms. Her room is bigger. [*Here, Justice Ginsburg interjects: "And I must object—it is just not so! The little room was our bedroom, where I worked; the bigger room was the dining room, where Marty worked, with a large taxbook library shelved around him."*] In my little room one evening in fall 1970, I was reading Tax Court advance sheets and came upon a pro se litigant, one Charles E. Moritz, who, on a stipulated record, was denied a $600 dependent care deduction under old §214 of the Internal Revenue Code, even though, the Tax Court found, the operative facts—save one—fit the statute perfectly. Mr. Moritz was an editor and traveling salesman for a book company. His eighty-nine-year-old dependent mother lived with him. In order to be gainfully employed without neglecting mother or packing her off to an old-age home, Charles paid an unrelated individual at least $600—in fact, a good deal more than that—to take care of his mother when he was away at work.

There was just one small problem, and in the Tax Court, it served to do him in. The statute awarded its up-to-$600 deduction to a taxpayer who was a woman of any classification (divorced, widowed, or single), a married couple, a widowed man, or a divorced man. But not to a single man who had never been married. Mr. Moritz was a single man who had never married. "Deductions are a matter of legislative grace," the Tax Court quoted, and added that if the taxpayer were raising a constitutional objection, forget about it: everyone knows, the Tax Court confidently asserted, that the Internal Revenue Code is immune from constitutional attack.

Let me digress a moment to tell you that in the Tax Court Mr. Moritz, although not a lawyer, had written a brief. It was one page in length and said: "If I were a dutiful daughter instead of a dutiful son, I would have received the deduction. This makes no sense." It was from that brief the Tax Court gleaned the taxpayer might be raising a constitutional objection. Mr. Moritz's one-page submission remains in my mind as the most persuasive brief I ever read.

Well, I went to the big room next door, handed the Tax Court advance sheets to my spouse, and said, "Read this." Ruth replied with a warm and friendly snarl, "I don't read tax cases." I said, "Read this one," and returned to my little room.

No more than five minutes later—it was a short opinion—Ruth stepped into my little room and, with the broadest smile you can imagine, said, "Let's take it!" And we did.

Ruth and I took the *Moritz* appeal pro bono of course, but since the taxpayer was not indigent we needed a pro bono organization. We thought of the American Civil Liberties Union. Mel Wulf, the ACLU's then legal director, naturally wished to review our proposed Tenth Circuit brief, which in truth was 90 percent Ruth's Tenth Circuit brief. When Mel read the brief, he was greatly persuaded.

A few months later, the ACLU had its first sex discrimination/equal protection case in the United States Supreme Court. As many of you will recall, it was titled *Reed v. Reed*. Remembering *Moritz*, Mel asked Ruth if she would take the lead in writing the ACLU's Supreme Court brief on behalf of appellant Sally Reed. Ruth did and, reversing the decision of the Idaho Supreme Court, the U.S. Supreme Court unanimously held for Sally.

Good for Sally Reed and good for Ruth, who decided thereafter to hold down two jobs, one as a tenured professor at Columbia Law School, where she had moved from Rutgers, the other as head of the ACLU's newly created Women's Rights Project.

Now back to *Moritz*. The Tenth Circuit—Judge Holloway writing for the panel—found Mr. Moritz to have been denied the law's equal protection, reversed the Tax Court, and allowed Mr. Moritz his $600 deduction.

Amazingly, the government petitioned for certiorari. The Tenth Circuit's decision, the government asserted, cast a cloud of unconstitutionality over literally hundreds of federal statutes—laws that, like old §214 of the Tax Code, differentiated solely on the basis of sex.

In those pre–personal computer days, there was no easy way for us to test the government's assertion. But Solicitor General Erwin Griswold took care of that by attaching to his cert. petition a list—generated by the Department of Defense's mainframe computer—of those hundreds of suspect federal statutes. Cert. was denied in *Moritz*, and the computer list proved a gift beyond price. Over the balance of the decade, in Congress, the Supreme Court, and many other courts, Ruth successfully urged the unconstitutionality of those statutes.

So our trip to the Tenth Circuit mattered a lot. First, it fueled Ruth's early 1970s career shift from diligent academic to enormously skilled and successful appellate advocate—which in turn led to her next career on the higher side of the bench. Second, with Dean Griswold's help, Mr. Moritz's case furnished the litigation agenda Ruth actively pursued until she joined the D.C. Circuit in 1980.

All in all, great achievements from a tax case with an amount in controversy that totaled exactly $296.70.

As you can see, in bringing those Tax Court advance sheets to Ruth's big room forty years ago, I changed history. For the better. And, I shall claim, thereby rendered a significant service to the nation. I have decided to believe it is the significant service that led to my being invited to speak to you today. And even if you had in mind a topic a little less cosmically significant and substantially more humorous, such as the Supreme Court's performance in tax cases, Ruth and I are truly delighted to be back with you in the Tenth Circuit once again.

After she read Marty Ginsburg's speech, Justice Ginsburg was asked whether she knew what had become of Charles Moritz. Her reply, delivered with a smile, paraphrased the A. A. Milne children's poem about "James James Morrison Morrison Weatherby George Dupree," who "took great care of his mother, though he was only three." "All I know for sure," she said, "is that he took great care of his mother, even when she was ninety-three."

3

The *Frontiero* Reply Brief

In the fall of 1970, Sharron Frontiero was a lieutenant in the U.S. Air Force, stationed at Maxwell Air Force Base in Montgomery, Alabama. Her husband, Joseph Frontiero, was a military veteran and full-time student at Montgomery's Huntingdon College. Under federal law, married members of the military were afforded a supplemental housing allowance and on-base health care for their "dependents"—but the law defined "dependent" more favorably for male than female service members. If Joe had been the service member and Sharron the student, she would automatically have been treated as Joe's dependent without regard to her income, qualifying the family for the statutory benefits. As a servicewoman, however, Sharron was required to prove that her husband relied on her for more than half of his expenses before her family would be deemed eligible. Sharron paid the majority of the family's expenses, but fell a bit short of the required one-half of Joe's support. Sharron filed a lawsuit in federal court against the secretaries of defense and the air force as well as her commanding officer, claiming that the federal law's less generous family benefits for female service members violated her constitutional right to equal protection of the laws.

When the case reached the U.S. Supreme Court, then-Professor Ruth Bader Ginsburg, on behalf of the American Civil Liberties Union, wrote a seventy-page amicus (friend-of-the-court) brief in support of Sharron Frontiero's claim. In it, she laid out the long history of discrimination against women and the Supreme Court's position, unwavering until 1971: legal distinction by sex (what Ginsburg often called "sex-role pigeonholing") was rational and therefore constitutional. She characterized this as "the anything goes" standard of review; it authorized legislators to draw, as the Supreme

Court summed up in 1948, a "sharp line between the sexes." Ginsburg's core contention in the ACLU brief was this: legislative line-drawing based on sex should, like race classifications, be labeled "suspect," so the Court should extend to legal distinctions based on gender the same "strict scrutiny" the Justices, in the early 1970s, reserved (and still give) to race-based legal distinctions. The essential feature of strict scrutiny: a requirement that the state justify its "suspect" classification by proving that it was "necessary to a compelling state interest" and "narrowly tailored" to serve that interest. A legal commentator famously labeled this standard "strict in theory but fatal in fact" because its application so frequently led courts to conclude that racial classifications were unconstitutional.[1]

The attorneys for Sharron Frontiero, who had initially requested the ACLU's assistance with its Supreme Court brief, had declined to make this argument, prompting Ginsburg and the ACLU to submit the argument in their amicus brief. Diplomacy produced a reconciliation, however, and the ACLU and Frontiero's attorneys joined together to submit the final brief, a reply to the government's argument that the federal statute was constitutional. The portion of the reply brief presenting Ginsburg's "sex as suspect" argument is set forth below. This case marked Ginsburg's first personal appearance before the Supreme Court, where she and one of Frontiero's attorneys split the argument time between them, with Ginsburg presenting the "sex as suspect" argument in person to the Justices for the first time.

Excerpt from
Joint Reply Brief of Southern Poverty Law Center, appellants, and the American Civil Liberties Union, Amicus Curiae.
Filed in U.S. Supreme Court, January 12, 1973, in *Frontiero v. Richardson*, 411 U.S. 677 (1973).

Legislative judgments about social roles solely on the basis of sex invoke a suspect criterion.

1. . . . This Court has never to date recognized sex as a "suspect" criterion for legislative distinctions[2] and, according to appellees, it never should. . . . In urging declaration of the sex criterion as suspect in the instant case, appellants merely reiterate what was plain to those who, a decade ago, adverted to the pervasive social, economic, and political effects of sex discrimination in American society: "Equality of rights under the law for all persons, male or female, is so basic to democracy and its commitment to the ultimate value of the individual that it must be reflected in the fundamental law of the land." President's Commission on the Status of Women, *American Women* 44–45 (1963) (statement indicating expectation that this Court would provide "imperative" clarification to remove "ambiguities with respect to the constitutional protection of women's rights").

2. Appellees [in the government brief] concede that a prime ingredient eliciting strict scrutiny is inherent in the sex criterion: "sex, like race and national origin,[3] is a visible and immutable biological characteristic that bears no necessary relation to ability." (Br. Appellees 15.) On the other hand, appellees note that "racial distinctions, unlike sex distinctions, have an especially disfavored status in constitutional history." (Br. Appellees 16.) This proposition is beyond debate. The paramount concern of Congress in the period during which the post–Civil War Amendments were adopted surely did not relate to women,

but neither did it relate to newcomers to our shores. Yet the principle of equal protection, from the start reflected the fundamental notion that legislative distinctions should not be made on the basis of characteristics that bear no necessary relationship to ability and over which persons have no control. In accordance with this notion, in 1971 this Court formally enshrined alienage among the suspect categories. *Graham v. Richardson*, 403 U.S. 365 (1971).[4]

3. Appellees urge, however, that although the sex criterion "bears no necessary relationship to ability," it cannot rank as suspect because women constitute a numerical majority that has not been excluded from the political process. Skipped over is the fact that through most of our nation's history, total political silence was imposed on this numerical majority. *See* E. Flexner, *Century of Struggle* (1959); *Up from the Pedestal* (A. S. Kraditor, ed. 1968); Br. Amicus Curiae 11–18. Even today, in many states, women do not share with men full rights and responsibilities with respect to jury service. *See* Br. Amicus Curiae 41–42. In educational institutions, on the job market, and, most conspicuously, in the political arena, women continue to occupy second-place status.[5] Suggestive of the value that should be assigned to appellees' head count, former Secretary of Labor Hodgson observed in 1970 that discrimination against women in the labor market is "more subtle and more pervasive than against any other minority group."[6]

Women's "political influence" could be characterized as "substantial" [as appellees did in their brief] only by substituting fancy for fact. Not a single woman sits in the United States Senate; only 14 women hold seats in the House of Representatives. Over the past twenty years only one woman has chaired a House committee;[7] no woman has ever chaired a Senate committee. Less than 3 percent of positions in the federal government at and above GS-16 rank are held by women.[8] As of October 31, 1972, women comprised almost one-quarter of the foreign service, but less than 3 percent of the chiefs of missions.[9] At the state level, no woman serves as governor, and less than 6 percent of state legislators are women.[10]

4. Closely related to appellees' head count argument, and as the final reason for denying that the sex criterion is suspect, appellees assert that sex distinctions "do not express an implied legislative judgment of female inferiority." (Br. Appellees 17–19.) No such judgment, according to appellees, is embodied in a statute declaring women unfit for bartending (*Goesaert v. Cleary*, 335 U.S. 464 (1948)); a statute establishing a women's college to equip females to serve as secretaries and homemakers and in other occupations "suitable to their sex" (the state's men's college, by contrast, was established as a military school offering a full range of liberal arts and engineering degrees) (*Williams v. McNair*, 316 F. Supp. 134 (D.S.C. 1970), *aff'd mem.*, 401 U.S. 951 (1971)); a statute presuming that women are preoccupied with home and children and therefore should be spared the bother of serving on juries (*Hoyt v. Florida*, 368 U.S. 57 (1961)); and a statute that has become a major roadblock to women seeking equal opportunities for remuneration and promotions in blue-collar employment (*Muller v. Oregon*, 208 U.S. 412 (1908)).[11]

Legal scholars who have assessed these legislative judgments less perfunctorily than appellees view the matter differently. Each judgment supposed by appellees to imply no "stigma of inferiority" has been exposed as resting upon "unjustified (or at least unsupported) assumptions about individual capacities, interests, goals and social roles solely on the basis of sex." . . .

Legislative judgments "protecting" women from full participation in economic, political, and social life have been labelled "benign" by persons who regard them as marking off for women a "separate but equal" role. Most men and women claim they value qualities traditionally associated with the mother-wife, e.g., selflessness, sensitivity, passivity, non-assertiveness. But investigations of social scientists leave no doubt that traits associated with the male breadwinner, e.g., assertiveness, aggressiveness, independence, are valued more. . . .

Evidence abounds that the "submissive majority" perceives the real judgment underlying "benign" classifications and the "separate but equal" euphemism. Growing up in a society in which virtually all positions of influence and power are held by men, women believe that they belong to the inferior sex. Women's lack of self-esteem and their own belief, shared by men, that it is better to be male than female is reflected, for example, in the fact that male babies are preferred over female babies by both parents. As Matina Horner observed, "It has taken . . . a long time to become aware of the extent to which [the stereotypical] image of woman has actually been internalized, thus acquiring the capacity to exert psychological pressures on [women's] behavior of which [women themselves] are frequently unaware. . . . [S]ocial and, even more importantly, internal psychological barriers rooted in this image really limit the opportunities to men." Horner, *Toward an Understanding of Achievement-Related Conflicts in Women*, 28 J. Social Issues 157, 158 (1972).[12]

5. Women who seek to break out of the traditional pattern face all of the prejudice and hostility encountered by members of a minority group. Worse than being "discrete and insular,"[13] which for other minority groups at least has the advantage of fostering political organizing, women are separated from each other and therefore remain far distant from the political potential appellees ascribe to them. For women who want to exercise options that do not fit within stereotypical notions of what is proper for a female, women who do not want to be "protected" but do want to develop their individual potential without artificial constraints, classifications reinforcing traditional male-female roles are hardly "benign." Where, as in the instant case, a wife and husband deviate from the norm—the wife is the family breadwinner, the husband "dependent" in the sense that the wife supplies more than half the support for the marital unit[14] —"benign" legislative judgments serve as constant reminders that, in the view of predominantly or all-male decision-making bodies, life should not be arranged this way.

Conclusion

In sum, appellants submit that designation of the sex criterion as suspect is overdue, provides the only wholly satisfactory standard for dealing with the claim in this case, and should be the starting point for assessing that claim.

Professor Ginsburg would lose the battle for designating sex as a suspect classification but win the Frontiero *case and, in the years that followed, the larger battle for women's equality in the Supreme Court. Only four of the Justices, in a plurality opinion by Justice Brennan, agreed with her that gender classifications were worthy of strict scrutiny, but four additional Justices, although they declined to label sex classifications suspect, found the statute's gender-specific definitions of dependency unconstitutional nevertheless, citing her 1971* Reed v. Reed *case. Sharron Frontiero had prevailed, eight to one.*

Lacking the essential fifth vote for the proposition that sex, like race, was a "suspect" category, Ginsburg, in subsequent cases, coaxed the Justices into articulating an "intermediate" standard of review for sex discrimination cases. The Court's intermediate standard was first set forth in* Craig v. Boren, *a 1976 case in which Ginsburg and the ACLU had again submitted an amicus brief. In an opinion by Justice Brennan, the Court said:*

> *To withstand constitutional challenge under the equal protection clause of the Fourteenth Amendment, classifications by gender must*

---

*A footnote in the *Frontiero* Reply Brief suggested the direction she would head. There, she quoted from a recent article in the *Harvard Law Review*, written by her former law professor and mentor, Gerald Gunther. Gunther argued that the Supreme Court, without acknowledging it, was already moving toward "a newer equal protection." His evidence included her *Reed* case. Although the Court denied it was changing the standard in *Reed*, Gunther wrote, "It is difficult to understand [*Reed*'s] result without an assumption that some special sensitivity to sex as a classifying factor entered into the analysis. . . . Only by importing some special suspicion of sex-related means . . . can the result be made entirely persuasive."

> *serve important governmental objectives and must be substantially related to achievement of those objectives.*

The new standard—a far cry from the historic "anything goes" approach to sex distinctions in law, but not quite strict scrutiny, the vigorous requirement that the state show its sex-based classifications were narrowly tailored to achieve a "compelling state interest"—proved potent enough to invalidate most of the many federal and state laws that "drew a sharp line" between the sexes. For Ginsburg's culminating chapter in this battle over the proper judicial approach to gendered laws, see by-then-Justice Ginsburg's announcement of the majority opinion in United States v. Virginia *(1996), also known as the* Virginia Military Institute (VMI) *case, at p. 150.*

4

The Need for the Equal Rights Amendment

On March 22, 1972, the United States Senate, as had the House of Representatives five months before, passed the Equal Rights Amendment to the United States Constitution. The proposed amendment then went to the states for ratification. The ERA's basic provision, modeled on the Nineteenth Amendment, which granted women the right to vote, provided simply: "Equality of rights under the law shall not be denied or abridged by the United States or by any State on account of sex."

Frontiero *was decided in May 1973; Ginsburg's article advocating the ERA was published a few months later. It was neither her first nor last word on the subject, but it usefully lays out the history of the amendment and reasons for its ratification, and rebuts the main arguments offered by its opponents. Perhaps speaking out seemed more urgent given that three of the Justices who declined to join Justice Brennan in recognizing sex as a "suspect" classification pointed to the ERA for justification. As Justice Powell wrote for the three:*

> *The Equal Rights Amendment, which if adopted will resolve the substance of this precise question, has been approved by the Congress and submitted for ratification by the States. If this Amendment is duly adopted, it will represent the will of the people accomplished in the manner prescribed by the Constitution. By acting prematurely and unnecessarily, as I view it, the Court has assumed a decisional responsibility at the very time when state legislatures, functioning within the traditional democratic process, are debating the proposed Amendment.*

The Congress that passed the amendment set a deadline for ratification of March 22, 1979. By 1973, a countermovement led by conservative activist Phyllis Schlafly and her STOP ERA organization had emerged and was active in many states. When STOP ERA and associated groups successfully brought ratification to a halt, Congress extended the deadline to mid-1982, but to no avail. On June 21, 1982, the ERA died, three states short of the constitutionally required thirty-eight ratifying states.

Although Justice Ginsburg's own work in the 1970s—and that of many others in the thirty-plus years since the defeat of the ERA—has made the need for a constitutional amendment less urgent than in 1973, she would still like to see the principle of gender equality spelled out in the United States Constitution. In 2014, speaking at the National Press Club in Washington, D.C., she explained why: "I would like my granddaughters, when they pick up the Constitution, to see that notion—that women and men are persons of equal stature—I'd like them to see that is a basic principle of our society."[1]

The Need for the Equal Rights Amendment
American Bar Association Journal, September 1973*

The notion that men and women stand as equals before the law was not the original understanding, nor was it the understanding of the Congress that framed the Civil War amendments. Thomas Jefferson put it this way:

> Were our state a pure democracy there would still be excluded from our deliberations women, who, to prevent depravation of morals and ambiguity of issues, should not mix promiscuously in gatherings of men.[2]

Mid-nineteenth-century feminists, many of them diligent workers in the cause of abolition, looked to Congress after the Civil War for an

---

*This piece was originally published in 59 *American Bar Association Journal* 1013 (September 1973). We have made edits based on length and context.

express guarantee of equal rights for men and women. But the text of the Fourteenth Amendment appalled the proponents of a sex equality guarantee. Their concern centered on the abortive second section of the amendment, which placed in the Constitution for the first time the word *male*. Threefold use of the word *male*, always in conjunction with the term *citizen*, caused concern that the grand phrases of the first section of the Fourteenth Amendment—due process and equal protection of the laws—would have, at best, qualified application to women.[3]

After close to a century's effort, the suffrage amendment was ratified, according to female citizens the right to vote. The most vigorous proponents of that amendment saw it as a beginning, not as a terminal point. Three years after the ratification of the Nineteenth Amendment, the National Woman's Party succeeded in putting before Congress the equal rights amendment that has been reintroduced in every Congress since 1923. On the occasion of the amendment's initial introduction, the executive secretary of the National Woman's Party explained:

> [A]s we were working for the national suffrage amendment . . . it was borne very emphatically in upon us that we were not thereby going to gain full equality for the women of this country, but that we were merely taking a step . . . toward gaining this equality.[4]

Persons unacquainted with the history of the amendment deplore its generality and the absence of investigation concerning its impact. The models of the Due Process and Equal Protection Clauses should suffice to indicate that the wording of the amendment is a thoroughly responsible way of embodying fundamental principle in the Constitution. Before the amendment was proposed, the National Woman's Party, with the aid of a staff of lawyers and expert consultants, tabulated state and federal legislation and court decisions relating to the status of women. Advisory councils were formed, composed of different economic and professional groups of women—industrial workers, homemakers, teachers and students, federal employees. Each council conducted studies of the desirability of equal rights and responsibilities for men and women. Reading debates on the amendment in the law journals of the 1920s is enlightening. The objections still voiced in 1973 were solidly answered then.[5]

Opponents of the amendment suggest the pursuit of alternate routes: particularized statutes through the regular legislative process in Congress and in the states, and test case litigation under the Fourteenth Amendment.[6] Only those who have failed to learn the lessons of the past can accept that counsel.

On the legislative side the cupboard was bare until 1963 when Congress passed the Equal Pay Act. That legislation was hardly innovative. An equal pay requirement was in force during World War II and then quietly retired when there was no longer a need to encourage women to join the labor force.[7] Equal pay was the subject of a 1951 International Labor Organization convention and was mandated by the Rome Treaty that launched the European Economic Community in 1958. Most significantly, mixed motives spurred congressional action. Some congressmen were sold on the bill by this argument: equal pay protects against male unemployment; without access to female labor at bargain prices, employers will prefer to hire men.[8]

The next year sex was included along with race, religion, and national origin in Title VII of the Civil Rights Act of 1964. This was a significant advance, for Title VII is a most potent weapon against employment discrimination. But sex was added to Title VII via the back door. A Southern congressman, steadfast in his opposition to Title VII, introduced the amendment that added sex to the catalogue of prohibited discrimination. His motive was apparent, but his tactic backfired.[9]

In 1972, in Title IX of the Education Amendments of that year, Congress banned federal assistance to educational institutions that discriminate on the basis of sex. Title IX contains several exceptions, for example, admissions to all private and some public undergraduate schools are exempt, and its enforcement mechanism is weak.

These three measures, the Equal Pay Act, Title VII, and Title IX, are the principal congressional contributions. Not an impressive record in view of the job that remains to be done. A recent government computer search, the solicitor general told the Supreme Court this Term, revealed that 876 sections in the United States Code contain sex-based references.[10] Similar searches in some of the states have turned up hundreds of state statutes in need of revision.[11]

Will major legislative revision occur without the impetus of the Equal Rights Amendment? Probably not if past experience is an accurate barometer. Scant state or federal legislative attention focused on the discriminatory statutes identified by the National Woman's Party in the 1920s. After Congress passed the Equal Rights Amendment, it remained unwilling to ban sex discrimination in admissions to undergraduate schools, although the 1971 Newman report informed it that "discrimination against women, in contrast to that against minorities, is still overt and socially acceptable within the academic community." As a graphic illustration, the 1969 profile of the freshman class at a well-known state university cautions: "Admission of women on the freshman level will be restricted to those who are especially qualified."[12] A candid response came from the Air Force Academy this year: We will enroll women in 1975 if the amendment is ratified, the superintendent said. If the amendment is not ratified, women will have to wait a long time before they can expect to enroll.[13]

A preview of the kind of revision that can be expected under the stimulus of the amendment has been provided by legislative analyses in some of the states. These analyses should reassure those who fear intolerable change in the wake of the amendment. They propose extension of desirable protection to both sexes; for example, state minimum wage laws would be extended to men; in no case do they propose depriving either sex of a genuine benefit now enjoyed.[14]

As a sample of laws destined for the scrap heap if the amendment is ratified, consider these: Arizona law stipulates that the governor, secretary of state, and treasurer must be male.[15] In Ohio only men may serve as arbitrators in county court proceedings.[16] In Wisconsin barbers are licensed to cut men's hair and women's hair, but cosmeticians may attend to women only.[17] Georgia law, still faithful to Blackstone, provides:

> The husband is head of the family and the wife is subject to him; her legal civil existence is merged in the husband's, except so far as the law recognizes her separately, either for her own protection, or for her benefit, or for the preservation of public order.[18]

Another embarrassment from the same state reads: "Any charge or intimation against a white female of having sexual intercourse with a person of color is slanderous without proof of special damages."[19] Legislative inertia keeps laws of this kind on the books. Professor Thomas Emerson summarized the situation this way: "It is not a weakness but a strength of the amendment that it will force prompt consideration of changes that are long overdue."[20]

If one turns to the contribution of the judiciary and litigation under the Fourteenth Amendment, Supreme Court decisions that span 1873 to 1961 tell us this. Until the Nineteenth Amendment, women could be denied the right to vote. Of course, they are "persons" within the meaning of the Fourteenth Amendment, but so are children, the Court observed in 1874.[21] The right to serve on juries could be reserved to men,[22] a proposition the Court declined to reexamine in 1971, although Justice Douglas urged his brethren to do so.[23] Women, regardless of individual talent, could be excluded from occupations thought more suitable to men—lawyering and bartending, for example.[24]

Typical of the attitude that prevailed well into the twentieth century is the response of one of our nation's greatest jurists, Harlan Fiske Stone, author of the celebrated *Carolene Products* footnote that supplied the rationale for the suspect classification doctrine. In 1922, when Chief Justice Stone was dean of Columbia Law School, he was asked by a Barnard graduate who wanted to study law, "Why doesn't Columbia admit women?" The venerable scholar replied in a manner most uncharacteristic of him: "We don't because we don't."[25]

A number of "horribles" have been raised in opposition to the amendment. Four of them dominate the literature of amendment opponents.

First horrible. Women will lose the benefit of protective labor laws. Today, challenges to these laws rarely emanate from male employers who wish to overwork women. Since the passage of Title VII, they have come overwhelmingly from blue-collar working women to overcome what they regard as a system that protects them against higher-paying jobs and promotions. In the vast majority of Title VII employment discrimination cases, courts have understood these challenges.[26] Legislatures are beginning to abandon disingenuous protection for women and to extend genuine protection to all workers. Models are ample. In Norway, for example, where opposition to "special protection for women only" came predominantly from women's organizations, a 1956 workers' protective act assures safe and healthy conditions for employees of both sexes. Moreover, extension rather than invalidation of laws that benefit only one sex is a route recently traveled by the Supreme Court. In *Frontiero v. Richardson*, fringe benefits for married male members of the military were extended to married female members. The National Woman's Party put it this way decades ago in 1926:

> [P]rotective legislation that is desirable should be enacted for all workers. . . . Legislation that includes women but exempts men . . . limits the woman worker's scope of activity . . .

> by barring her from economic opportunity. Moreover, restrictive conditions [for women but not for men] fortif[y] the harmful assumption that labor for pay is primarily the prerogative of the male.[27]

Second horrible. Wives will lose the right to support. Only if our legislatures or courts act capriciously, spitefully, without regard for public welfare, and in flagrant disregard of the intent of the amendment's proponents.[28] In a growing number of states the Equal Rights Amendment will occasion no change whatever in current support law. In these states, and under the amendment in all states, either husband or wife can be awarded support depending on the couple's circumstances. Who pays in any particular family will depend upon the division of responsibilities within that family unit. If one spouse is the breadwinner and the other performs uncompensated services at home, the breadwinning spouse will be required to support the spouse who works at home.

Underlying the amendment is the premise that a person who works at home should do so because she, or he, wants to, not because of an unarticulated belief that there is no choice. The essential point, sadly ignored by the amendment's detractors, is this: the Equal Rights Amendment does not force anyone happy as a housewife to relinquish that role. On the contrary, it enhances that role by making it plain that it was chosen, not thrust on her without regard to her preference.

Third horrible. Women will be forced to serve in the military. Only if men are, and assignments would be made on the basis of individual capacity rather than sex. With the draft terminated, it is high time for consideration of the other side of that coin. Women who wish to enlist must meet considerably higher standards than men; women in the service are denied fringe benefits granted men and do not receive equal vocational training opportunities. The reason for higher standards for women was given by an Air Force colonel in a deposition taken in December 1972.[29] He explained: "We have had and we continue to have roughly twice as many women apply[ing] as we are able to . . . take. . . . We don't have an excess of men over what we can take."

Young women's groups uniformly testified during congressional hearings on the amendment that they did not wish exemption from responsibility for service. Conspicuous among these groups was the 200,000-member Intercollegiate Association of Women Students, a group appropriately characterized as "middle American."[30]

In 1948, long before women and the military became an emotion-charged issue in connection with the Equal Rights Amendment, General Dwight D. Eisenhower observed:

> Like most old soldiers I was violently against women soldiers. I thought a tremendous number of difficulties would occur, not only of an administrative nature . . . but others of a more personal type that would get us into trouble. None of that occurred. . . . In the disciplinary field, they were . . . a model for the Army. More than this their influence throughout the whole command was good. I am convinced that in another war they have got to be drafted just like the men.[31]

Final horrible. Restrooms in public places could not be sex separated. Emphatically not so, according to the amendment's proponents in Congress,[32] who were amused at the focus on the "potty problem." Apart from referring to the constitutional regard for personal privacy, they expressed curiosity about the quarter from which objection to current arrangements would come. Did the people who voiced concern suppose that men would want to use women's restrooms or that women would want to use men's? In any event, the clever solution devised by the airlines suggests one way out of the problem.

Some persons have expressed fear of a "flood of litigation" in the wake of the Equal Rights Amendment. But the dramatic increase in sex discrimination litigation under the Fifth and Fourteenth Amendments in the 1970s is indicative that, if anything, ratification of the amendment will stem the tide. The amendment will impel the comprehensive legislative revision that neither Congress nor the states have undertaken to date. The absence of long-overdue statutory revision is generating cases by the hundreds across the country.[33] Legislatures remain quiescent despite the mounting judicial challenges, challenges given further impetus by the Supreme Court's decision in *Frontiero v. Richardson*. Ratification of the amendment, however, would plainly mark as irresponsible any legislature that did not undertake the necessary repairs during the two-year period between ratification and effective date.

To date, three-fifths of the states have ratified the amendment; these thirty states represent a clear majority of the country's population. One state, Nebraska, has attempted to withdraw its ratification. But New Jersey and Ohio took the same action with respect to the Fourteenth Amendment, and New York ratified and then withdrew its ratification of the Fifteenth Amendment. Congress at that time evidently concluded that ratification once accomplished, could not be undone. New Jersey and Ohio were counted to constitute the requisite three-fourths for promulgation of the Fourteenth Amendment. New York was counted among the states that ratified the Fifteenth Amendment.[34]

The Equal Rights Amendment, in sum, would dedicate the nation to a new view of the rights and responsibilities of men and women. It firmly rejects sharp legislative lines between the sexes as constitutionally tolerable. Instead, it looks toward a legal system in which each person will be judged on the basis of individual merit and not on the basis of an unalterable trait of birth that bears no necessary relationship to need or ability. As the Federal Legislation Committee of the Association of the Bar of the City of New York explained:

> [T]he Amendment would eliminate patent discrimination, including all laws which prohibit or discourage women from making full use of their political and economic capabilities on the

strength of notions about the proper "role" for women in society. Any special exceptions or other favorable treatment required by some women because of their physical stature or family roles could be preserved by statutes which utilize those factors—rather than sex—as the basis for distinction.[35]

5

The *VMI* Bench Announcement

On many mornings *during the Supreme Court's Terms, the Justices mount the bench in the ornate courtroom to announce the Court's decisions. To read full opinions of the Court would take many hours (and likely put the audience to sleep), so the Court takes a more practical approach. The author of each majority opinion boils down the decision to its essence and, ideally, reads a succinct, accessible description of what the Court has done and why. Below is Justice Ginsburg's announcement from the bench of the decision in* United States v. Virginia *(known as the* VMI *case), which she has described as one of the most personally satisfying she has delivered in all her years on the bench.*

Worthy of note: the only precedent from which Justice Ginsburg quotes in her bench announcement is Mississippi University for Women v. Hogan *(1982). Those were the words of Justice Sandra Day O'Connor, the first woman to serve on the Supreme Court. Just finishing her first Term, Justice O'Connor wrote for the majority in that 5–4 case holding unconstitutional the exclusion of a man from the university's all-female School of Nursing.*

The full VMI *opinion, in which Ginsburg was joined by five of her colleagues, including Justice O'Connor, is reported at 518 U.S. 515 (1996). Chief Justice Rehnquist filed an opinion concurring in the judgment, which means he signed on to the outcome, although not the reasoning, of the majority opinion. Justice Thomas took no part in the consideration or decision of the case; his son was then attending VMI. Justice Scalia, the lone dissenter, mounted a spirited defense of single-sex education as a legitimate example of diversity in educational options and accused the majority of providing, for sex-based classifications, "a redefinition of intermediate scrutiny that makes it indistinguishable from strict scrutiny." He also accused the Court of "de-*

stroying" VMI, a prediction that proved off base. As Justice Ginsburg has more than once pointed out, in the years since women have been admitted, VMI and its cadets seem to be doing fine, just as she expected they would. (For Justice Ginsburg's reaction to the Scalia dissent, see "Remembrances of a Treasured Colleague," p. 39.)

Bench Announcement

June 26, 1996

***United States v. Virginia*, No. 94–1941**

***Virginia v. United States*, No. 94–2107**

This case concerns an incomparable military college, the Virginia Military Institute (VMI), the sole single-sex school among Virginia's public institutions of higher learning. Since its founding in 1839, VMI has produced civilian and military leaders for the Commonwealth and the Nation. The school's unique program and unparalleled record as a leadership training ground has led some women to seek admission. The United States, on behalf of women capable of all the activities required of VMI cadets, instituted this lawsuit in 1990, maintaining that under the Equal Protection Clause of the Fourteenth Amendment to the U.S. Constitution, Virginia may not reserve exclusively to men the educational opportunities that VMI, and no other Virginia school, affords.

The case has had a long history in court. In the first round, the District Court ruled against the United States, reasoning that the all-male VMI served the State's policy of affording diverse educational programs. The Fourth Circuit vacated that judgment, concluding that a diversity policy serving to "favor one gender" did not constitute equal protection.

In the second round, the lower courts considered, and found satisfactory, the remedy Virginia proposed: a program for women, called the Virginia Women's Institute for Leadership (VWIL) at a private women's college, Mary Baldwin College. A VWIL degree, the Fourth Circuit said, would not carry the historical benefit and prestige of a VMI degree, and the two programs differed markedly in methodology—VMI's is rigorously "adversative," VWIL's would be "cooperative." But overall, the lower courts concluded, the schools were "sufficiently comparable" to meet the demand of equal protection.

We reverse that determination. Our reasoning centers on the essence of the complaint of the United States, and on facts that are undisputed: Some women, at least, can meet the physical standards VMI imposes on men, are capable of all the activities required of VMI cadets, prefer VMI's methodology over VWIL's, could be educated using VMI's methodology, and would want to attend VMI if they had the chance.

With recruitment, the District Court recognized, VMI could "achieve at least 10% female enrollment"—a number, the District Court said, "sufficient . . . to provide female cadets with a positive educational experience." If most women would not choose VMI's adversative method, many men, too, would not want to be educated in VMI's environment. The question before us, however, is not whether women or men should be *forced* to attend VMI. Rather, the question is whether Virginia can constitutionally deny to women who have the will and capacity, the training and attendant opportunities VMI uniquely affords—training and opportunities VWIL does not supply.

To answer that question we must have a measuring rod—what lawyers call a standard of review. In a nutshell, this is the standard our precedent establishes: Defenders of sex-based government action must demonstrate an "exceedingly persuasive justification" for that action. To make that demonstration, the defender of a gender line in the law must show, "at least, that the [challenged] classification serves important governmental objectives and that [any] discriminatory means employed [is] substantially related to the achievement of those objectives." The heightened review standard applicable to sex-based classifications does not make sex a proscribed classification, but it does mark as presumptively invalid—incompatible with equal protection—a law or official policy that denies to women, simply because they are women, equal opportunity to aspire, achieve, participate in, and contribute to society based upon what they can do.

Under this exacting standard, reliance on overbroad generalizations, typically male or typically female "tendencies," estimates about the way most women (or most men) are, will not suffice to deny opportunity to women whose talent and capacity place them outside the average description. As this Court said in *Mississippi University for Women v. Hogan* some 14 years ago, state actors may not close entrance gates based on "fixed notions concerning the roles and abilities of males and females."

A remedial decree must cure the constitutional violation—in this case, the categorical exclusion of women from an extraordinary educational/leadership-development opportunity afforded men. To cure that violation, and to afford genuinely equal protection, women seeking and fit for a VMI-quality education cannot be offered anything less. We therefore reverse the Fourth Circuit's judgment, and remand the case for proceedings consistent with this opinion.

6

Advocating the Elimination of Gender-Based Discrimination

The 1970s New Look at the Equality Principle*

In the 1970s, a revived feminist movement blossomed in the United States. I was in those years a law teacher, general counsel to the American Civil Liberties Union, and a founder of the ACLU's Women's Rights Project. It was my good fortune to be in the right place at the right time, able to participate in the effort to place women's rights permanently on the human rights agenda in the United States. In these remarks, I will recall those now long ago days and describe, from my personal perspective and experience, what that 1970s effort entailed.

Most of the world's nations have rather new constitutions, written since 1970. Newer fundamental instruments of government generally contain a broad equality clause specifically proscribing discrimination on the basis of race, sex, ethnic origin, sexual orientation, religion, and other group characteristics. A few among many examples: Canada's Charter of Rights and Freedoms, adopted in 1982, has such a catalog, as does South Africa's post-apartheid Constitution, and the European Convention on Human Rights.

In contrast to latter-twentieth-century rights declarations, the U.S.

---

*Justice Ginsburg delivered these remarks at Wake Forest Law School's Summer Program in Venice, Italy, in July 2008. We have made edits based on length and context.

Constitution is over 220 years old. It is the oldest written constitution still in force in the world. Except for the Nineteenth Amendment, which gave women the right to vote in 1920, our Constitution contains no express provision regarding discrimination on the basis of gender. Indeed, the Constitution contained no equality prescription at all until after the Civil War. Equal protection jurisprudence in the United States principally involves interpretation of the spare Fourteenth Amendment command that governing authorities shall not deny to any person "the equal protection of the laws."

Those words, inserted into the Constitution in 1868, were once interpreted narrowly, but over time, they proved to have growth potential. In the 1890s, the U.S. Supreme Court said that racial segregation, mandated by state law, was compatible with the Constitution's equal protection principle. By the middle years of the twentieth century, however, the Supreme Court came to recognize how wrong that judgment was. State imposed separation along racial lines, the Court acknowledged in *Brown v. Board of Education*, in 1954, at least in public educational facilities, could never be equal. Yet, until 1971, the Court turned away every woman's complaint that she had been denied equal protection by a state or federal law.

In that year, 1971, the Court turned in a new direction. The Justices began to respond favorably to the arguments of equal rights advocates who urged a more encompassing interpretation of the equality principle, one that would better serve U.S. society as it had evolved since the founding of the nation in the late eighteenth century.

At the ACLU Women's Rights Project, launched early in 1972, and in the law school seminars I conducted first at Rutgers (New Jersey's state university), then at Columbia University, work progressed on three fronts: we sought to advance, simultaneously, public understanding, legislative change, and change in judicial doctrine. I will focus in this class primarily on the litigation endeavors.

In one sense, our mission in the 1970s was easy: the targets were well defined. There was nothing subtle about the way things were. Statute books in the states and nation were riddled with what we then called sex-based differentials. Illustrative laws were set out in an Appendix to a brief the ACLU filed in the Supreme Court in the summer of 1971. The brief was written for the appellant in *Reed v. Reed*, first of the 1970s gender discrimination/equal protection cases to come before the Court. Among many entries, the *Reed* brief Appendix included the domicile rule we inherited from England, a rule once prevalent in the States of the United States and elsewhere in the world, in civil law as well as common law domains. Statutes codifying the rule typically read:

> The husband is the head of the family. He may choose any reasonable place or mode of living and the wife must conform thereto.

On federal legislation in need of repair, the solicitor general of the United States (the Justice Department official who represents the United States in the Supreme Court) provided an important aid, perhaps inadvertently. The solicitor general at the time was former Harvard Law School dean Erwin Griswold. He asked the Supreme Court, in March 1973, to review a decision in a case the ACLU had won at the court of appeals level, *Charles E. Moritz v. Commissioner of Internal Revenue*.

Moritz had encountered undisguised sex discrimination in, of all places, the Internal Revenue Code. He challenged a provision allowing single women, but not single men, a deduction for the cost of caring for an elderly, infirm dependent, in Moritz's case, his aged mother. Congress had prospectively changed the law to eliminate that sex-based differential. With current and future dutiful sons accorded a benefit once reserved for dutiful daughters, there seemed to be no pressing need for High Court review. Take the case nonetheless, the solicitor general urged, for the Court of Appeals decision "casts a cloud of unconstitutionality upon the many federal statutes listed in Appendix E."

What was Appendix E? It was a printout from the Department of

Defense computer (an unexpected release in those ancient pre-PC days). The printout listed, title by title, provisions of the U.S. Code "containing differentiations based upon sex-related criteria." It was a road map for reform efforts. One could use the solicitor general's list to press for curative legislation and, at the same time, bring to courts contests capable of capturing public attention and accelerating the pace of change.

But if our targets were all set out in the law books, our work encountered resistance in this respect. Our starting place was not the same as that of advocates seeking aid from courts in the struggle against race discrimination. Judges and legislators in the 1960s, and at least at the start of the 1970s, regarded laws mandating differential treatment of men and women not as malign, but as operating benignly in women's favor. Legislators and judges, in those years, were overwhelmingly white, well-heeled, and male. Men holding elected and appointed offices generally considered themselves good husbands and fathers. Women, they thought, had the best of all possible worlds. Women could work if they wished; they could stay home if they chose. (Women without husbands earning a good income, of course, never had that choice.) They could avoid jury duty if they were so inclined, or they could serve if they elected to do so. They could escape military duty or they could enlist. So what was there for them to complain about?

Our mission was to educate, along with the public, decisionmakers in the nation's legislatures and courts. We tried to convey to them that something was wrong with their perception of the world. As Justice Brennan wrote in a 1973 Supreme Court plurality opinion, *Frontiero v. Richardson*, decided a year and a half after the Court had begun to listen: "Traditionally, [differential treatment on the basis of sex] was rationalized by an attitude of 'romantic paternalism' which, in practical effect [often] put women, not on a pedestal, but in a cage."

Those with whom I was associated at the ACLU kept firmly in mind the importance of knowing the audience—largely men of a certain age. Speaking to that audience as though addressing one's "home crowd" could be counterproductive. We sought to spark judges' and lawmakers' understanding that their own daughters and granddaughters could be disadvantaged by the way things were. We saw ourselves as teachers appearing before audiences that, on the realities underlying our cases, had not advanced much beyond the third grade.

To trace the story of when, why, and how women began to count in constitutional adjudication, I will start with a prosecution in a Hillsborough County, Florida, courtroom in 1957, a little over half a century ago. Gwendolyn Hoyt stood trial there for murdering her husband; the instrument of destruction, a baseball bat. Gwendolyn Hoyt was what we would today call a battered woman. Her philandering husband had abused and humiliated her to the breaking point. Beside herself with anger and frustration, she administered the blow that ended the couple's altercation and precipitated the murder prosecution.

Florida placed no women on jury rolls in those days, out of paternalistic concern for woman's place at "the center of home and family life." Gwendolyn Hoyt was convicted of second-degree murder by an all-male jury. Her thought was simply this: if women were on the jury, they might have better comprehended her state of mind, casting their ballot, if not for an acquittal, then at least to convict her of the lesser offense of manslaughter.

The Supreme Court, in 1961 (a Court headed by Chief Justice Earl Warren and widely regarded as actively "liberal" in outlook), rejected Gwendolyn Hoyt's plea. The Court did so following an unbroken line of precedent. That precedent reflected the long-prevailing "separate-spheres" mentality, the notion that it was man's lot, because of his nature, to be the breadwinner, the head of household, the representative of the family outside the home; and it was woman's lot, because of her nature, to bear and alone raise children and keep the house in order. Representative of that thinking, a 1948 decision, *Goesaert v. Cleary*, had upheld Michigan's ban on women working as bartenders, unless the woman's husband or father owned the establishment. The consequence, a woman who owned a tavern and her bartending daughter were put out of business.

In 1971, ten years after the decision in Gwendolyn Hoyt's case, the Supreme Court reversed course. So did lower courts all over the United States. The turning point case was *Reed v. Reed*. *Reed* involved a teenage boy from Boise, Idaho, Richard Lynn Reed, who died under tragic circumstances. His parents were long separated, then divorced. Richard's mother, Sally Reed, had unsuccessfully tried to keep the boy totally out of his father's custody. While Richard was staying in his father's house, he died from a bullet shot from one of his father's guns. It was an apparent suicide. Sally Reed, having lost her only child, sought to take charge of her son's few belongings. She applied to the probate court to be appointed administrator of Richard's death estate. The boy's father, Cecil Reed, later applied for the same appointment.

The Idaho probate court rejected Sally Reed's application, although it was first in time, and appointed Cecil Reed under a state statute that read: As between persons equally entitled to administer a decedent's estate, "males must be preferred to females." An intermediate appellate court ruled in Sally's favor, but the Idaho Supreme Court ruled against her.

Sally Reed was not a sophisticated woman. Once a white-collar clerical worker, she later earned her living by caring for elderly and disabled people in her home. She probably did not think of herself as a feminist, but she had the strong sense that her state's law was unjust, and faith that the judiciary could redress her grievance. Ultimately, her faith was vindicated. The Supreme Court unanimously declared Idaho's male preference statute unconstitutional, a plain denial to Sally Reed of the equal protection of the state's law.

Seventeen months after *Reed*, in *Frontiero v. Richardson*, the Court held it unconstitutional to deny female military officers a housing allowance and medical benefits covering their husbands on the same automatic basis as those family benefits were given to married male military officers. Air Force Lieutenant Sharron Frontiero was the successful challenger. Lieutenant Frontiero had this clear view: she saw the laws in question as plain denials of equal pay.

Sharron Frontiero (now Cohen) is not someone you would choose from a crowd as a potential frontrunner. Nor was Sally Reed. Sharron is, and Sally was, an everyday person, uncomfortable with publicity. But they knew they had been shortchanged, they had the courage to complain, and they had faith in the capacity of the judicial system to vindicate their complaints.

Two years after Lieutenant Frontiero's victory, the Court declared unconstitutional an Iowa law allowing a parent to stop supporting a daughter once she reached the age of 18, but requiring parental support for a son until he turned 21. That same year, 1975, the Court decided a case dear to my heart, *Weinberger v. Wiesenfeld*. The case stems from a tragic event in 1972, when Paula Wiesenfeld, a New Jersey public school teacher, died in childbirth. Her husband, Stephen Wiesenfeld, sought to care for the baby personally, but was denied child-in-care Social Security benefits then available only to widowed mothers, not to widowed fathers. Stephen Wiesenfeld won a unanimous judgment in the Supreme Court.

In defense of the sex-based prescription, the government had argued that the classification was entirely rational, because widows, *as a class*, are more in need of financial assistance than are widowers. True in general, the Court acknowledged, but laws reflecting the situation of the *average* woman or the *average* man were no longer good enough even for government work. Many widows in the United States had not been dependent on their husbands' earnings, the Court pointed out, and a still small but growing number of fathers like Stephen Wiesenfeld were ready, willing, and able to care personally for their children. Using sex as a convenient shorthand to indicate financial need or willingness to bring up a baby did not comply with the equal protection principle, as the Court had grown to understand that principle. (As a result of the decision, child care benefits were paid to Stephen Wiesenfeld, who has been an extraordinarily devoted parent. And what was once a widowed mother's benefit became and remains a widowed parent's benefit.)

Next, in 1976, the Court's majority acknowledged that it was applying an elevated standard of review—"heightened scrutiny"—to overt gender-based classifications. The case was *Craig v. Boren*, in which the Court struck down an Oklahoma statute that allowed young women to purchase "near beer," a beverage that contains only 3.2 percent alcohol, at age 18 but required young men to wait until they turned 21 to buy the weak brew. It was a silly law, which the state sought to justify on the ground that boys drive more, drink more, and commit more alcohol-related offenses than girls. One might wish the Court had chosen a less frothy case for announcing the "heightened" review standard. Still, it was a key doctrinal advance.

What caused the Court's understanding to dawn and grow? Judges do read the newspapers and are affected, not by the weather of the day, as distinguished constitutional law professor Paul Freund once said, but by the climate of the era.

The altered conditions accounting for the different outcomes in Gwendolyn Hoyt's case in 1961, and in the 1970s cases of Sally Reed, Sharron Frontiero, Stephen Wiesenfeld, Curtis Craig, and several others, were these. In the years from 1961 to 1971, women's employment outside the home had expanded rapidly. That expansion was attended by a revived feminist movement, fueled in the United States, in part, by the movement of the 1960s for racial justice, but also, as elsewhere in the world, by the force of new thinking both represented and sparked by Simone de Beauvoir's remarkable 1949 publication, *The Second Sex*. Changing patterns of marriage, access to safer methods of controlling birth, longer life spans, and, in significant part, inflation—all contributed to a social dynamic that yielded this new reality: in the 1970s, for the first time in the history of the United States, the "average" woman was experiencing most of her adult years in a household not dominated by child care responsibilities. (That development, a well-known Columbia University economics professor [Eli Ginzberg] said in 1977, might well prove "the single most outstanding phenomenon" of the late twentieth century.)

Congress eventually weighed in, aided by the Department of Justice and a Civil Rights Commission report initially drafted by the ACLU Women's Rights Project working with students in a yearlong seminar I conducted at Columbia. The legislature eliminated most (but not quite all) of the "differentiations based upon sex-related criteria" on Solicitor General Griswold's 1973 list.

In sum, the U.S. Supreme Court in the 1970s, as I see it, effectively carried on in the gender discrimination cases a dialogue with the political branches of government. The Court wrote modestly, it put forth no grand philosophy. But by propelling and reinforcing legislative and executive branch reexamination of sex-based classifications, the Court helped to ensure that laws and regulations would "catch up with a changed world."

Notably, some of the leading cases laying the groundwork for gender equality jurisprudence in the United States were brought by male plaintiffs. Of course, the men were complaining about discrimination rooted in a certain way of thinking about women—as dependents, much like children, subservient to the male head of the household. Cases like Stephen Wiesenfeld's helped judges—who, in those days, were almost uniformly male—to understand that overbroad gender classifications were problematic. Men, too, could be disadvantaged by sex-role stereotyping. And, as Stephen Wiesenfeld's case illustrated, generalizations about the way women and men are may have unhappy consequences for children as well.

Congress, in the late 1970s, continued to play a key part in the dialogue. The legislature had mooted a court case challenging the exclusion of women from the U.S. military academies—West Point, Annapolis, the Air Force Academy. Congress opened the doors of those academies to women. Change in that domain remained incomplete, however, until the Supreme Court, in 1996, decided a case called *United States v. Virginia*. That litigation concerned the Virginia Military Institute (VMI), an all-male state college that had long served as a training ground for people who became prominent in their communities. The state offered no comparable opportunity for women. By the time the *VMI* case was launched, women cadets had graduated from the U.S. military academies for over a decade. The Marine Corps had elevated a career female officer to the rank of three-star general, ironically perhaps, in charge of manpower and planning. Women in service were guarding the Tomb of the Unknown Soldier, flying planes, doing so many things once off-limits to them. The Supreme Court held in *United States v. Virginia* that the state had a choice: it could admit women to VMI, or it could close the school.

Public understanding had advanced so that people comprehended that the *VMI* case was not really about the military. Nor did the Court question the value or viability of single-sex schools. Instead, *VMI* was about a state that invested heavily in a college designed to produce business and civic leaders, that for generations succeeded admirably in the endeavor, and that strictly limited this unparalleled opportunity to men. I regard the *VMI* case as the culmination of the 1970s endeavor to open doors so that women could aspire and achieve without artificial constraints.

One last story from the 1970s: the case of Captain Susan Struck, an Air Force officer serving as a nurse in Vietnam, where, in 1970, she became pregnant. She was offered this choice: have an abortion on base or leave the service. (Captain Struck's case antedated the Supreme Court's 1973 decision in *Roe v. Wade*, which held that women have a constitutionally protected right to control their own reproductive capacity. In those days, several military bases, without fanfare, made abortion available to women service members and dependents of service members.) Captain Struck, a Roman Catholic, would not have an abortion, but she undertook to use no more than her accumulated leave time for the birth, and she had arranged for the baby's adoption immediately after birth. She sued to fend off the discharge Air Force regulations required. She lost in the court of first instance and in the Court of Appeals. But she was well represented by ACLU lawyers in the state of Washington, and each month was able to secure a stay of her discharge.

The Supreme Court agreed to hear her plea. It was an ideal case to argue the sex equality dimension of laws and regulations regarding pregnancy and childbirth. (The Court's later holding, that discrimination on the basis of pregnancy was not sex-based discrimination, might never have occurred had the Court considered and decided Susan Struck's case after full briefing and oral argument.) Solicitor General Erwin Griswold saw loss potential for the government. He recommended that the Air Force waive Captain Struck's discharge and abandon its policy of automatically discharging women for pregnancy. The Air Force did so, and the solicitor general thereupon moved to dismiss the case as moot.

Hoping to keep the case alive, I called Captain Struck and asked if she had been denied anything that could justify our opposition to a mootness dismissal. She was out no pay or allowance, she confirmed. "Isn't there some benefit you wanted and couldn't get because you are a woman?" I inquired. "Of course," she said in our December 1972 conversation. "I'd like to become a pilot, but the Air Force doesn't provide flight training for women." We laughed, agreeing it was hopeless to attack that occupational exclusion then. Today, it would be hopeless, I believe, to endeavor to reserve flight training exclusively for men. That is one measure of what the 1970s litigation/legislation/public education efforts in the United States helped to achieve.

Part Four

A Judge Becomes a Justice

Introduction

William Jefferson Clinton *took office in early January 1993, the first Democrat since the defeat of Jimmy Carter in 1980. Like all presidents, he hoped to appoint one or more Justices to the U.S. Supreme Court, especially as it had been decades since a Democrat had done so. When Justice Byron White announced in March that he would retire at the end of the Court's Term in June, the new president got his wish, and the search for the right candidate began. President Carter had appointed Ruth Bader Ginsburg to the U.S. Court of Appeals for the D.C. Circuit in the waning months of his presidency; now Judge Ginsburg was on President Clinton's list of possible candidates for the Supreme Court.*

The almost three-month-long selection process was meandering and tumultuous, involving numerous "lead" candidates along the way. Among them were New York governor Mario Cuomo, Interior Secretary Bruce Babbitt, and federal judge Stephen Breyer. Even though Judge Ginsburg's name was on the initial "lists," she was not one of the top finalists until very late in the process. In the words of one White House official, "Her pick was only possible because of all the dominoes that had fallen before it."[1] *As Justice Ginsburg somewhat humorously and modestly put it, years later: "I was the last one left standing."*[2]

The final decision wasn't made by the president until Sunday, June 13, after a pivotal meeting at the White House between President Clinton and Judge Ginsburg. The Friday before, she was attending the D.C. Circuit Judicial Conference at the Tidewater Inn in Maryland, with plans to return to D.C. later that day and then fly to Vermont in the evening to attend a wedding. While still at the Judicial Conference, Judge Ginsburg received a call from Joel Klein, a highly regarded attorney who was working closely with the White House on the nomination process. He advised her to stand by for a later call, in which she might be asked to cancel her Vermont plans so that she would be available for a meeting with the president. On her return to D.C., she received another call from Klein, who told her, "It's okay to go to Vermont." The Ginsburgs proceeded to Vermont Friday night and had barely checked into their hotel room when White House Counsel Bernard Nussbaum called, asking Judge Ginsburg to return to Washington as quickly as possible to meet the president. Ruth and Marty stayed for the wedding Saturday evening and flew back to D.C. Sunday morning.

Ruth Ginsburg did not like to get up early, especially on the weekend, but she had no problem waking up early that Sunday morning to catch the first plane back to D.C. It was a beautiful, sunny day when the Ginsburgs arrived back at their home in Watergate South to prepare for the arrival of the White House vetting team and for Judge Ginsburg's meeting with President Clinton at the White House.

Nussbaum and the vetting team arrived and prepared to start work. But first, Marty, an excellent chef, made lunch for them. He recalled serving "a very well-known uncomplicated Tuscan dish of cannellini beans, canned tuna fish, lemon juice, and I make it a little bit differently, but for the better. Fortunately there were scallions in the house and that's all you need, scallions and parsley with that and a few cans, and everyone is amazed."[3]

If the vetters were amazed at the food, they were also quite impressed by how easy the Ginsburgs made the vetting process. "I have vetted a hundred judges," then–Associate White House Counsel Ron Klain told us, "and I never met anyone who was as well prepared as Ruth and Marty. Marty had everything, I mean everything, like, 'Oh, would you like to see Ruth's tax returns back to the year 1946? Here is a list of every person who ever worked in her household and her domestic help, their Social Security numbers, their immigration papers.' If I ever want to get on the Supreme Court, I need to marry someone like Marty."[4] *(The Ginsburgs were amused that everyone assumed tax lawyer Marty was responsible for the thorough and organized records, when in fact it had been Ruth who maintained all of the household financial records over the years.)*

While Marty and the vetting team pored over the Ginsburgs' meticulously kept records and dined on Marty's gourmet fare, Bernie Nussbaum and Judge

Ginsburg headed to the White House to meet the president. To avoid press attention, the president had instructed Nussbaum to avoid the Oval Office and instead usher Judge Ginsburg into the White House through the back door and up into the family's private quarters on the second floor to await his arrival. "We had all this leaking about the process and the candidates," President Clinton told us. "I said, surely to goodness we can get her in on Sunday through the back door without anybody knowing about it. . . . [M]ost of the people that I believe are doing all this leaking, they don't work here on Sunday, just bring her to the back door." (More than two decades later, President Clinton remembered how Judge Ginsburg reacted to her "cloak and dagger" entrance to the White House. "It tickled her that I had to smuggle her into the White House. She liked that, and I liked the fact that she had a sense of humor. I think it's very hard to endure over the long run and have a positive impact on the Court that goes beyond the writing of your opinions if you don't have a sense of humor.")[5]

Judge Ginsburg, who had returned from Vermont wearing slacks and a top and jacket, wanted to change into more formal clothes before heading to the White House, but Nussbaum had assured her there was no need. The president, he said, was coming straight from the golf course and would be dressed casually. But when the president walked in, he was dressed up in a suit and tie. Instead of playing golf, he had decided to go to church that morning and had donned his "Sunday best." Ginsburg leaned over and whispered, "Bernie, what have you done to me?!" Bernie replied, "I don't know what happened, some change in plans. But don't worry, you look very nice."[6]

The president and the judge met for over an hour. Ginsburg felt there was an immediate and strong rapport: "Bill Clinton, whatever his problems were, talks comfortably to women."[7] *They talked about gender equality and church/state cases. The judge was impressed with the president's knowledge of Supreme Court cases and his grasp of constitutional doctrine. She talked with him about her childhood and her work as a women's rights litigator. They discussed the 1957 integration of Little Rock Central High School and how the nine black students enrolled in the school were prevented from entering until President Eisenhower called up the National Guard to escort them in.*

The judge told the president how moved she had been when she visited Central High in 1990 while in Little Rock to give a talk at the University of

Arkansas Law School. She reminded the president that they had in fact met on that very occasion. Then-Governor Clinton and his wife Hillary Rodham Clinton, then head of the American Bar Association Commission on Women, arrived late for Judge Ginsburg's talk, and the three chatted briefly afterward. (Justice Ginsburg later recounted to us that she had called Marty that evening. When she told him that the governor and his wife had come to hear her speak, Marty, ever the comedian, replied: "Well, what else is there to do at night in Little Rock?)"[8]

Ruth Ginsburg left the White House feeling good about her meeting with Bill Clinton. "I really liked him," she told herself, "and I think he liked me."[9] *President Clinton did like Judge Ginsburg: As President Clinton reflected during our interview with him, "We had a wonderful visit and it sort of sealed the deal for me. . . . I felt strongly enough that I trusted myself, the way I felt about her, I wanted to go forward." "Every judge," he told us, "needs to have both the intellectual capacity to deal with the incredible variety and complexity of the issues and an instinctive and immediate understanding of the human implications of the decisions being made. And I just talked to her about her life and her experience, and her family and her work and her judging and that's really what I wanted to know—you know, that it wasn't just stuff that she had written, it was way more than just an intellectual concern of hers. She got the actual human impact of these decisions."*[10]

Bernie Nussbaum wanted the president to call Judge Ginsburg immediately, but the president was having some friends over to watch the third game in the NBA Finals between the Chicago Bulls and the Phoenix Suns. Nussbaum called Ginsburg and told her, "Don't go to sleep, you might get a call."[11] *The basketball game turned out to be one of the longest games in NBA history—three hours and twenty minutes. (The Suns beat the Bulls, 129–121, in triple overtime.) Ruth, not a basketball fan, spent the evening at home with Marty, waiting for the phone to ring.*

When the basketball game finally ended at 11:30 p.m., President Clinton said good night to his guests and went down to the White House kitchen to call Judge Ginsburg. He tried phoning her through the White House switchboard, but there was a problem with the connection. On his first try, he said "Hello, hello," but Ginsburg couldn't hear him. The second time he got through briefly and said "Did I wake you up?" Again, though, there was a problem with the connection. "Hang up," the president said. "I'll call you right back." This time President Clinton dialed the number himself and finally got a good connection. "If I'm going to propose," he joked, "we might as well have a good line." "I'm going to ask you to accept this position tomorrow," he said. "I feel really good about this."[12]

The president went on to tell Ginsburg why he chose her, talked about her work on behalf of women's rights, her outstanding record on the bench, and his belief that as an independent mainstream progressive jurist she could be a real leader on the Court. He also joked about how the selection process bore some resemblance to the suspenseful, marathon basketball game he had just watched. The president ended the call telling his nominee to be at the Rose Garden early the next day with acceptance remarks: "You have a lot of character," he said. "Just speak from your heart and mind tomorrow."[13] *"So I knew," she recalled, that "as high as I was with this great news, I had to settle down and write some remarks that I could deliver the next day."*[14] *But the first order of business after hanging up the phone was a celebratory hug and a kiss from Marty.*

1

Rose Garden Acceptance Speech

June 14, 1993, was a lovely, sun-drenched day in Washington, D.C. Just after 2:00 p.m., President William Jefferson Clinton and Judge Ruth Bader Ginsburg walked out of the White House and into the Rose Garden. They stood side by side on the dais in front of politicians, press, and Ginsburg's family and friends.

President Clinton spoke for about ten minutes, first praising outgoing Justice Byron White before announcing his nomination of Ruth Bader Ginsburg. He chose Judge Ginsburg as his nominee for the Supreme Court, he said, for three reasons: "First, in her years on the bench, she has genuinely distinguished herself as one of our nation's best judges, progressive in outlook, wise in judgment, balanced and fair in her opinions. Second, over the course of a lifetime in her pioneering work on behalf of the women of this country, she has compiled a truly historic record of achievement in the finest traditions of American law and citizenship. And finally, I believe that in the years ahead, she will be able to be a force for consensus-building on the Supreme Court, just as she has been on the Court of Appeals, so that our judges can become an instrument of our common unity in the expression of their fidelity to the Constitution."[1]

After describing Ruth Ginsburg's legal background, the obstacles she had overcome, and her character, he concluded: "Quite simply, what's in her record speaks volumes about what is in her heart. Throughout her life, she has repeatedly stood for the individual, the person less well-off, the outsider in society, and has given those people greater hope by telling them that they have a place in our legal system, by giving them a sense that the Constitution and the laws protect all the American people, not simply the powerful."[2]

President Clinton, most likely hoping to pave the way for a smooth bipartisan confirmation process, made repeated references to Judge Ginsburg as a moderate, calling her a "centrist," a "consensus-builder," a "healer," a judge who "can't be called a liberal or conservative." He went on to speak about the "exhaustive" search process, specifically mentioning Bruce Babbitt and Stephen Breyer as leading candidates who "may well find themselves in that position someday in the future." He concluded his remarks saying, "I am proud to nominate this path-breaking attorney, advocate, and judge, to be the 107th Justice to the United States Supreme Court."[3]

As Judge Ginsburg approached the microphone, the audience stood and applauded. She placed her remarks on the podium, careful to keep her hands on the pages as they fluttered in the summer breeze. There had been no first drafts prepared by White House speechwriters, and no edits from administration officials. Years later she would confide: "One of the nice things about the short amount of time was that I didn't have to run the remarks by anyone on the White House staff, there just wasn't enough time."[4] *She had shown the remarks to the president about fifteen minutes before they stepped out into the Rose Garden.*[5]

President Clinton bent the microphones down so that his diminutive nominee might be heard. Judge Ruth Bader Ginsburg, speaking slowly, and enunciating each word, as is her practice, delivered her acceptance speech.

Nomination Acceptance Speech
White House Rose Garden
Washington, D.C.
June 14, 1993

Mr. President,

I am grateful beyond measure for the confidence you have placed in me. And I will strive, with all that I have, to live up to your expectations in making this appointment. I appreciate, too, the special caring of Senator Daniel Patrick Moynihan. I was born and brought up in New York, the state Senator Moynihan represents, and he was the very first person to call with good wishes when President Carter nominated me, in 1980, to serve on the U.S. Court of Appeals for the

District of Columbia Circuit. Senator Moynihan has offered the same encouragement on this occasion.

May I introduce at this happy moment three people very special to me: my husband, Martin D. Ginsburg; my son-in-law, George T. Spera Jr.; and my son, James Steven Ginsburg.

The announcement the president just made is significant, I believe, because it contributes to the end of the days when women, at least half the talent pool in our society, appear in high places only as one-at-a-time performers. Recall that when President Carter took office in 1977, no woman had ever served on the Supreme Court, and only one woman—Shirley Hufstedler of California—then served at the next federal court level, the United States courts of appeals. Today, Justice Sandra Day O'Connor graces the Supreme Court bench, and twenty-three women serve at the federal court of appeals level, two as Chief Judges. I am confident many more will soon join them.

That seems to me inevitable, given the change in law school enrollment. My law school class in the late 1950s numbered over 500; that class included less than 10 women. As the president said, not a law firm in the entire city of New York bid for my employment as a lawyer when I earned my degree. Today, few law schools have a female enrollment under 40 percent, and several have reached or passed the 50 percent mark. And, thanks to Title VII, no entry doors are barred.

My daughter, Jane, reminded me a few hours ago, in a good-luck call from Australia, of a sign of the change we have had the good fortune to experience. In her high school yearbook on her graduation in 1973, the listing for Jane Ginsburg under "Ambition" was: "To see her mother appointed to the Supreme Court." The next line read: "If necessary, Jane will appoint her." Jane is so pleased, Mr. President, that you did it instead. Her brother James is, too.

I expect to be asked, in some detail, about my views of the work of a good judge on a High Court bench. This afternoon is not the moment for extended remarks on that subject, but I might state a few prime guides. Chief Justice Rehnquist offered one I keep in the front of my mind: a judge is bound to decide each case fairly, in accord with the relevant facts and the applicable law, even when the decision is, as he put it, not the one the home crowd wants.

Next, I know no better summary than the one Justice O'Connor recently provided, drawn from a paper by NYU law professor Burt Neuborne. The remarks concern the enduring influence of Justice Oliver Wendell Holmes. They read:

> When a modern constitutional judge is confronted with a "hard" case, Holmes is at her side with three gentle reminders: (1) intellectual honesty about the available policy choices; (2) disciplined self-restraint in respecting the majority's policy choice; (3) principled commitment to defense of individual autonomy, even in the face of majority action.

To that I can only say, "Amen."

I am indebted to so many for this extraordinary chance and challenge: to a revived women's movement in the 1970s that opened doors for people like me, to the civil rights movement of the 1960s from which the women's movement drew inspiration, to my teaching colleagues at Rutgers and Columbia, and for thirteen years, my D.C. Circuit colleagues, who shaped and heightened my appreciation of the value of collegiality. Most closely, I have been aided by my life partner, Martin D. Ginsburg, who has been since our teenage days my best friend and biggest booster; by my mother-in-law, Evelyn Ginsburg, the most supportive parent a person could have; and by a daughter and son with the taste to appreciate that Daddy cooks ever so much better than Mommy, and so phased me out of the kitchen at a relatively early age.

Finally, I know Hillary Rodham Clinton has encouraged and supported the president's decision to utilize the skills and talents of all the people of the United States. I did not until today know Mrs. Clinton. But, I hasten to add that I am not the first member of my family to stand close to her. There is another I love dearly to whom the first lady is already an old friend—my wonderful granddaughter, Clara. Witness this super, unposed photograph taken last October when Mrs. Clinton visited a nursery school in New York City and led the small people in the toothbrush song. The little one right in front is Clara.

I have a last thank-you. It is to my mother, Celia Amster Bader, the bravest, strongest person I have known, who was taken from me much too soon. I pray that I may be all that she would have been, had she lived in an age when women could aspire and achieve, and daughters are cherished as much as sons.

I look forward to stimulating weeks this summer and, if I am confirmed, to working at a neighboring Court, to the best of my ability, for the advancement of the law in the service of society. Thank you.

President Clinton and Judge Ginsburg at White House Rose Garden announcement of her nomination to the U.S. Supreme Court, June 14, 1993. Judge Ginsburg is holding a photograph showing Hillary Rodham Clinton singing "the toothbrush song" with Ginsburg's granddaughter Clara and her nursery school class.

There were few dry eyes in the Rose Garden when Judge Ginsburg concluded her remarks. The audience immediately rose, applauding. People looked at each other, nodding in approval. The president, obviously moved by her "last thank-you," wiped tears from his eyes and told his nominee in a choked voice, "That was a terrific job."[6]

During our interview with President Clinton in 2014, he reflected back on the Rose Garden event with visible pride. "It was a happy day. God, it was a nice day. She showed up with her family and she was happy as a clam. I remember, you know, she could barely conceal her glee, which is—she's very tight-lipped and disciplined, but I was glad she was happy and not afraid to show it. That meant something to me. I thought it made it likely that she would be not just an intellectual force but a personal force on the Court."[7]

President Clinton added that he was deeply moved by what Judge Ginsburg had said about her mother. "I identified with it," he told us, "because I was influenced by my mother and because . . . her relationship with her mother and what her mother did for her, and how they were, I think had a lot to do with the passion with which she pursued opportunity for the girls and women who might not have had that boost."[8]

Asked how he felt about having nominated Ruth Bader Ginsburg to the Court, President Clinton chuckled and said, "Even better [today] than the day I nominated her. She's been a superb Justice on the Court and off. She's a great role model for women, she's a defender of things I believe are most important in this country. She reads the whole Constitution, doesn't try to rewrite it to fit her political perspectives but understands it. You know, her job is to keep doing what the founders told her to do, which is form a more perfect union."[9]

2

Senate Confirmation Hearing Opening Statement

THE STORY OF *Ruth Bader Ginsburg's transformation from judge to Justice did not, of course, end with her acceptance of the president's nomination. In our constitutional system, the president nominates candidates for the Supreme Court, but the Senate must consent to a president's choice before she can take her place as a life-tenured Justice. The Senate Judiciary Committee held hearings on the nomination of Ruth Bader Ginsburg over a four-day period in late July 1993.*

Senator Joseph Biden, then chair of the Senate Judiciary Committee, opened the session by saying, "Judge Ginsburg welcome, and believe me you are welcome here this morning." He then described his morning train commute from Delaware, and how he had paged through the New York Times *looking for a story about the hearing: "My heart san[g] when I realized it was page 8 or 10 or 12, which was the most wonderful thing that has happened to me since I have been chairman of this committee: that a major hearing warranted the 8th or 9th or 10th page because thus far it has generated so little controversy."*[1]

The atmosphere in the room was relaxed and friendly, more like a graduation or a family reunion than a contentious or combative hearing. Ever since Ginsburg's June 14 nomination, most of Washington's press, pundits, and politicians alike had predicted "smooth sailing" and a "swift confirmation." Perhaps hoping to avoid a repeat of the antagonistic and embarrassing Robert Bork and Clarence Thomas hearings still fresh in the nation's memory, senators on both sides of the aisle seemed to be on their best behavior. As Senator Howell Heflin said in his opening remarks: "What a change in atmosphere from that of the recent past: congeniality prevails over confrontation; back-

slapping has replaced back-stabbing; inquiry is the motivation rather than injury."[2]

After opening statements by Chairman Biden and Orrin Hatch (ranking minority member on the committee), Judge Ginsburg was introduced by her "sponsors": Senators Daniel Patrick Moynihan and Alfonse D'Amato from New York, and Congresswoman Eleanor Holmes Norton from the District of Columbia, after which opening statements were given by the remaining members of the committee. The opening statements were almost uniformly positive. Even the most conservative senators remarked that, although they might differ with Judge Ginsburg on particular issues, they respected her intelligence and ability and thought she was well qualified to be a Supreme Court Justice.

After swearing to give testimony that would be "the whole truth and nothing but the truth," Ginsburg introduced her family and friends, smiling broadly and speaking with unbridled and somewhat uncharacteristic (at least to those who did not know her well) exuberance: "I have such a large family with me today, such an extended family, not just the immediate people behind me who I will introduce, but my friends, my law clerks, my secretaries. My heart is overflowing, because those are the people who have made it possible for me to be here today."[3]

Ruth introduced Marty, who sat behind her beaming and nearly bursting with pride, as "my life's partner for thirty-nine years." She introduced her children and grandchildren, and provoked laughter several times, including when introducing her three-year-old granddaughter, Clara, and relating the story about the White House photographers who tried to get the "sober judge" to smile by telling her to "think of Clara." She then introduced Clara's brother, seven-year-old Paul: "I must tell you that in preparation for these hearings, I have read briefing books, opinion books, law reviews, but there is no book in the world that means as much to me as this one. This is Paul's book. It says 'My Grandma is Very, Very Special.'" Ginsburg showed pages of the book to the senators and the cameras, and the hearing room erupted into laughter as she flipped to the last page, which bore a crayon-drawn map of the United States and Paul's description of his awestruck reaction to hearing the president announce his grandmother's nomination when he was with his mother in Melbourne: "I heard her on the radio all the way from Australia."[4]

Judge Ginsburg then gave her opening statement, reading slowly and clearly from her prepared remarks, taking the time to pause and look up at the senators every few minutes.

Opening Statement
Hearings before the Committee on the Judiciary
United States Senate
July 20, 1993

May I say first how much I appreciate the time committee members took to greet me in the weeks immediately following the president's nomination. It was a particularly busy time for you, and I thank you all the more for your courtesy.

To Senator Moynihan, who has been at my side every step of the way, a thousand thanks could not begin to convey my appreciation. Despite the heavy demands on his time, during trying days of budget reconciliation, he accompanied me on visits to Senate members, he gave over his own desk for my use, he buoyed up my spirits whenever a lift was needed. Last night, he sent me the most beautiful roses. In all, he served as the kindest, wisest counselor a nominee could have.

Senator D'Amato, from my great home state of New York, volunteered to join Senator Moynihan in introducing and sponsoring me, and I am so grateful to him. I have had many enlightening conversations in Senate Chambers since June 14, but my visit with Senator D'Amato was sheer fun. My children decided at an early age that mother's sense of humor needed improvement. They tried to supply that improvement, and kept a book to record their successes. The book was called "Mommy Laughed." My visit with Senator D'Amato would have supplied at least three entries for the "Mommy Laughed" book.

Representative Norton has been a professional colleague and friend since days when we were still young. As an advocate of human rights and fair chances for all people, Eleanor Holmes Norton has been as brave and as vigilant as she is brilliant. I am so pleased that she was among my introducers, and so proud to be one of Eleanor's constituents.

Most of all, the president's confidence in my capacity to serve as a Supreme Court Justice is responsible for the proceedings about to begin. There are no words to tell him what is in my heart. I can say simply this: if confirmed, I will try in every way to justify his faith in me.

I am, as you know from my responses to your questionnaire, a Brooklynite, born and bred—a first-generation American on my father's side, barely second-generation on my mother's. Neither of my parents had the means to attend college, but both taught me to love learning, to care about people, and to work hard for whatever I wanted or believed in. Their parents had the foresight to leave the old country, when Jewish ancestry and faith meant exposure to pogroms and denigration of one's human worth. What has become of me could happen only in America. Like so many others, I owe so much to the entry this nation afforded to people yearning to breathe free.

I have had the great fortune to share life with a partner truly extraordinary for his generation, a man who believed at age eighteen when we met, and who believes today, that a woman's work, whether at home or on the job, is as important as a man's. I attended law school in days when women were not wanted by most members of the legal profession. I became a lawyer because Marty and his parents supported that choice unreservedly.

I have been deeply moved by the outpouring of good wishes received in recent weeks from family, neighbors, camp mates, classmates, students at Rutgers and Columbia, law-teaching colleagues, lawyers with whom I have worked, judges across the country, and many women and men who do not know me. That huge, spirit-lifting collection shows that for many of our people, an individual's sex is no longer remarkable or even unusual with regard to his or her qualifications to serve on the Supreme Court.

Indeed, in my lifetime, I expect to see three, four, perhaps even more women on the High Court bench, women not shaped from the same mold, but of different complexions. Yes, there are miles in front, but what a distance we have traveled from the day President Thomas Jefferson told his secretary of state: "The appointment of women to [public] office is an innovation for which the public is not prepared." "Nor," Jefferson added, "am I."

The increasingly full use of the talent of all of this nation's people holds large promise for the future, but we could not have come to this point—and I surely would not be in this room today—without the determined efforts of men and women who kept dreams of equal citizenship alive in days when few would listen. People like Susan B. Anthony, Elizabeth Cady Stanton, and Harriet Tubman come to mind. I stand on the shoulders of those brave people.

Supreme Court Justices are guardians of the great charter that has served as our nation's fundamental instrument of government for over two hundred years. It is the oldest written constitution still in force in the world. But the Justices do not guard constitutional rights alone. Courts share that profound responsibility with Congress, the president, the states, and the people. Constant realization of a more perfect Union, the Constitution's aspiration, requires the widest, broadest, deepest participation on matters of government and government policy.

One of the world's greatest jurists, Judge Learned Hand, said, as Senator Moseley-Braun reminded us, that the spirit of liberty that imbues our Constitution must lie first and foremost in the hearts of the men and women who compose this great nation. Judge Hand defined that spirit, in a way I fully embrace, as one which is not too sure that it is right, and so seeks to understand the minds of other men and women and to weigh the interests of others alongside its own without bias. The spirit Judge Learned Hand described strives for a community where the least shall be heard and considered side by side with the greatest. I will keep that wisdom in the front of my mind as long as I am capable of judicial service.

Some of you asked me during recent visits why I want to be on the Supreme Court. It is an opportunity beyond any other for one of my training to serve society. The controversies that come to the Supreme Court, as the last judicial resort, touch and concern the health and well-being of our nation and its people. They affect the preservation of liberty to ourselves and our posterity. Serving on this Court is the highest honor, the most awesome trust, that can be placed in a judge. It means working at my craft—working with and for the law—as a way to keep our society both ordered and free.

Let me try to state in a nutshell how I view the work of judging. My approach, I believe, is neither liberal nor conservative. Rather, it is rooted in the place of the judiciary, of judges, in our democratic society. The Constitution's preamble speaks first of "We, the People," and then of their elected representatives. The judiciary is third in line and it is placed apart from the political fray so that its members can judge fairly, impartially, in accordance with the law, and without fear about the animosity of any pressure group.

In Alexander Hamilton's words, the mission of judges is "to secure a steady, upright, and impartial administration of the laws." I would add that the judge should carry out that function without fanfare, but with due care. She should decide the case before her without reaching out to cover cases not yet seen. She should be ever mindful, as Judge and then Justice Benjamin Nathan Cardozo said, "Justice is not to be taken by storm. She is to be wooed by slow advances."

We—this committee and I—are about to embark on many hours of conversation. You have arranged this hearing to aid you in the performance of a vital task, to prepare your Senate colleagues for consideration of my nomination.

The record of the Constitutional Convention shows that the delegates had initially entrusted the power to appoint federal judges, most prominently Supreme Court Justices, not to the president, but to you and your colleagues, to the Senate acting alone. Only in the waning days of the convention did the framers settle on a nomination role for the president and an advice and consent role for the Senate.

The text of the Constitution, as finally formulated, makes no distinction between the appointment process for Supreme Court Justices and the process for other officers of the United States, for example, Cabinet officers. But as history bears out, you and senators past have sensibly considered appointments in relation to the appointee's task.

Federal judges may long outlast the president who appoints them. They may serve as long as they can do the job. As the Constitution says, they may remain in office "during good Behaviour." Supreme Court Justices, most notably, participate in shaping a lasting body of constitutional decisions. They continuously confront matters on which the framers left things unsaid, unsettled, or uncertain. For that reason, when the Senate considers a Supreme Court nomination, the senators are properly concerned about the nominee's capacity to serve the nation, not just for the here and now, but over the long term.

You have been supplied, in the five weeks since the president announced my nomination, with hundreds of pages about me and thousands of pages I have penned—my writings as a law teacher, mainly about procedure; ten years of briefs filed when I was a courtroom advocate of the equal stature of men and women before the law; numerous speeches and articles on that same theme; thirteen years of opinions—counting the unpublished together with the published opinions, well over seven hundred of them—all decisions I made as a member of the U.S. Court of Appeals for the District of Columbia Circuit; several comments on the roles of judges and lawyers in our legal system.

That body of material, I know, has been examined by the committee with care. It is the most tangible, reliable indicator of my attitude, outlook, approach, and style. I hope you will judge my qualifications principally on that written record, a record spanning thirty-four years, and that you will find in that written record assurance that I am prepared to do the hard work and to exercise the informed, independent judgment that Supreme Court decisionmaking entails.

I think of these proceedings much as I do of the division between the written record and briefs, on the one hand, and oral argument on the other hand, in appellate tribunals. The written record is by far the more important component in an appellate court's decision-making, but the oral argument often elicits helpful clarifications and concentrates the judges' minds on the character of the decision they are called upon to make.

There is, of course, this critical difference. You are well aware that I come to this proceeding to be judged as a judge, not as an advocate. Because I am and hope to continue to be a judge, it would be wrong for me to say or to preview in this legislative chamber how I would cast my vote on questions the Supreme Court may be called upon to decide. Were I to rehearse here what I would say and how I would reason on such questions, I would act injudiciously.

Judges in our system are bound to decide concrete cases, not abstract issues. Each case comes to court based on particular facts and its decision should turn on those facts and the governing law, stated and explained in light of the particular arguments the parties or their representatives present. A judge sworn to decide impartially can offer no forecasts, no hints, for that would show not only disregard for the specifics of the particular case, it would display disdain for the entire judicial process.

Similarly, because you are considering my capacity for independent judging, my personal views on how I would vote on a publicly debated issue were I in your shoes—were I a legislator—are not what you will be closely examining. As Justice Oliver Wendell Holmes counseled, "[O]ne of the most sacred duties of a judge is not to read [her] convictions into [the Constitution]." I have tried and I will continue to try to follow the model Justice Holmes set in holding that duty sacred.

I see this hearing, as I know you do, as a grand opportunity once again to reaffirm that civility, courtesy, and mutual respect properly keynote our exchanges. Judges, I am mindful, owe the elected branches—the Congress and the president—respectful consideration of how court opinions affect their responsibilities. And I am heartened by legislative branch reciprocal sensitivity. As one of you said two months ago at a meeting of the Federal Judges Association, "We in Congress must be more thoughtful and more deliberate in order to enable judges to do their job more effectively."

As for my own deportment or, in the Constitution's words, "good Behaviour," I prize advice received on this nomination from a dear friend, Frank Griffin, a recently retired Justice of the Supreme Court of Ireland. Justice Griffin wrote: "Courtesy to and consideration for one's colleagues, the legal profession, and the public are among the greatest attributes a judge can have."

It is fitting, as I conclude this opening statement, to express my deep respect for, and abiding appreciation to Justice Byron R. White for his thirty-one years and more of fine service on the Supreme Court. In acknowledging his colleagues' good wishes on the occasion of his retirement, Justice White wrote that he expects to sit on U.S. courts of appeals from time to time, and so to be a consumer of, instead of a participant in, Supreme Court opinions. He expressed a hope shared by all lower court judges. He hoped "the Supreme Court's mandates will be clear and crisp, leaving as little room as possible for disagreement about their meaning." If confirmed, I will take that counsel to heart and strive to write opinions that both "get it right" and "keep it tight."

Thank you for your patience.

When Judge Ginsburg predicted that during her lifetime she expected to see "three, four, perhaps even more" women on the High Court bench, there was a young attorney sitting directly behind Senator Biden, listening attentively to Ginsburg's remarks and taking copious notes. The then-thirty-three-year-old staffer was Elena Kagan, who served as special counsel to Senator Biden for the Ginsburg confirmation hearings. As she listened to Judge Ginsburg's prediction, Kagan likely had no idea that seventeen years later she would become that fourth woman appointee, and would serve together with Justice Ruth Bader Ginsburg on the High Court bench.

The remainder of the opening day of the hearings, and the next two days, featured thirty-minute question-and-answer periods by individual committee members. The questioning was generally relaxed and friendly, and even when it became serious or contentious the demeanor of the senators was respectful. Several senators, Democrats and Republicans alike, thanked nominee Ginsburg on behalf of their own daughters for her work on gender equality. Ginsburg answered questions patiently and thoroughly, talked about her own experience with gender discrimination, particular cases she had worked on as an advocate, issues she had written about, and opinions she had authored as a judge. And as she had indicated in her opening statement, Judge Ginsburg declined to answer questions about how she would vote on issues that might come before her as a Supreme Court Justice.

There were several funny exchanges, including Judge Ginsburg's response to why she used the term "gender discrimination" instead of "sex discrimination." Everyone laughed when she told the story of when she was at Columbia in the 1970s and her bright secretary Millicent, who typed her briefs, articles, and speeches about sex discrimination, remarked: "I have been typing this word, sex, sex, sex, *over and over. Let me tell you, the audience you are addressing, the men you are addressing . . . the first association of that word is not what you are talking about. So I suggest that you use a grammar-book term. Use the word* gender. *It will ward off distracting associations."*[5]

Thursday, July 22, was the third day of the hearings, and by the day's end the senators had finished their questioning of Ginsburg. The day concluded with highly favorable closing statements from Senators Hatch and Biden. The committee adjourned just before eight in the evening, at which point there were hugs all around, Ginsburg looking elated, exhausted, and exuberant. Linda Campbell from the Chicago Tribune *summed it up well: "She explained. She elaborated. She scolded. She demurred. She even laughed. Ultimately, she conquered."*[6]

With the successful conclusion of Judge Ginsburg's testimony, all that stood between the nominee and the final committee vote was one more day of hearings. The final day consisted first of a closed session with the nominee and the senators, followed by a public session with panels of witnesses who would tes-

tify for or against the nomination. (After the Clarence Thomas hearings, the Judiciary Committee leadership instituted a routine closed session for all Supreme Court nominees, to provide an opportunity to review the nominee's FBI investigative file and any personal allegations that might exist. In Ginsburg's case there were no allegations, and the session lasted less than two hours.)

After the group emerged from the closed session, six panels gave their public testimony for the next three hours, and with few exceptions it was a veritable lovefest in support of Ginsburg's confirmation. The five panels testifying in favor of Judge Ginsburg's nomination included representatives from the American Bar Association (which gave her its highest possible recommendation), leading figures from private practice and academia (including legends in the law Chesterfield Smith, Shirley Hufstedler, Gerald Gunther, and Herma Hill Kay), former colleagues, clerks, and professors, and former client Stephen Wiesenfeld, who talked about how Ginsburg had successfully challenged discriminatory provisions, enabling him to get Social Security benefits after his wife died in childbirth, so that he could stay home and care for their newborn baby boy. After the third panel, Senator Dianne Feinstein remarked: "If Mrs. Ginsburg were of another religion, she might even be canonized at the end of this."[7]

The only panel testifying against Judge Ginsburg's nomination was composed primarily of leaders of pro-life groups who opposed any pro-choice candidate. As one of the panelists said, "As a woman and lawyer, I admire Judge Ginsburg for her achievements over the years and the personal qualities she demonstrated here before this committee. She has been rightly lauded as a pioneer in developing our current laws dealing with equal protection and gender discrimination. Unfortunately, Judge Ginsburg's pioneering efforts appear to be inextricably linked to her view that women must have an unfettered right to abortion."[8] *Representatives from the ultraconservative Eagle Forum and Family Research Council also accused her of being a "radical, doctrinaire feminist" with a "chip-on-the-shoulder radical feminist view."*[9]

Before banging the closing gavel at 2:43 that Friday afternoon, Senator Hatch commended the president for making an excellent choice. Senator Biden then thanked Senator Hatch for being a "gentleman and a scholar," and ended by saying that "next Thursday hopefully we will be able to make that recommendation to the U.S. Senate."[10]

Joel Klein, who had worked closely with the White House both in the nomination process and in helping to prepare Judge Ginsburg for the confirmation hearings, was confident that she would be easily confirmed: "She was seen and respected as a jurist. She was not seen as somebody who was on the far wing of either side of the judicial debate. She was respected by colleagues on both sides. It seemed to me that she brought a story and a lifetime's worth of work that, all things considered, would garner her nine out of ten votes unless something ridiculous happened at the hearings."[11]

As predicted, on July 29, less than a week after the hearings concluded, the committee voted unanimously, 18–0, to endorse Ruth Bader Ginsburg's nomination and send her candidacy to the Senate floor. In its report to the Senate, the Judiciary Committee stated: "The nomination of Judge Ruth Bader Ginsburg is one the committee can enthusiastically recommend for confirmation to the Senate. The committee's recommendation is based on Judge Ginsburg's temperament, character, judicial record, and judicial philosophy. It is made with full confidence."[12]

On August 3, the Senate, by a vote of 96–3, confirmed Ruth Bader Ginsburg for the position of Associate Justice of the United States Supreme Court. Justice Ginsburg was sworn in as the Court's 107th Justice by Chief Justice Rehnquist at ceremonies first at the Supreme Court and then at the White House on August 10, and once more on October 1 at the traditional Supreme Court ceremony attended by the Justices. On the first Monday in October, the opening day of the Supreme Court's 1993 Term, the newest Justice took her seat on the bench alongside seven brethren and the Court's first woman Justice, Sandra Day O'Connor.

Part Five

The Justice on Judging and Justice

Introduction

THIS CHAPTER SAMPLES *Justice Ginsburg's speeches, lectures, and articles on the nature of the Court on which she serves, the job of the Justices, and the standards they do, or in her view should, observe, as they carry out their duty faithfully to apply the provisions of the United States Constitution and interpret the statutes passed by Congress. Striking to us is the way the Justice would give a speech, adapt it to other occasions, use its various points in different contexts, and, in one or more iterations, add footnotes and usher it into print. These varied iterations gave us the latitude to opt for shorter and more widely accessible treatments of the subjects that captured her attention over her years as a Justice. (A similar process was evident in the briefs lawyer Ginsburg wrote for the gender equality cases she brought to the Supreme Court in the 1970s, briefs that organically grew or shrank, changed in emphasis, or altered in their details over the course of years. Husband Marty Ginsburg characterized his spouse's evolutionary process: "In the old days there was 'The Brief,' and now it's 'The Speech.'")*[1]

Ruth Ginsburg is not one given to abstract constructs or dramatic flourishes. Her voice, in public and on paper, is modest and measured, yet her style is distinctive and her point is often captured in a memorable quotation from someone else or a notable and quotable pithy quip of her own. Her legal analyses dig deep into the "real world"—its history and quotidian details, and the way institutions, large and small, public and private, interact with each other and with democracy's people. Always, she pays careful attention to the history and purpose, fairness and effectiveness, of the rules that shape and direct our justice system. Throughout her speeches and writings, she includes "sideglances" at the justice systems of sister democracies for the light they shine on our own and offers homage to the waypavers and the pathmarkers who have improved our world through law. At the heart of the concerns she addresses in the documents selected for this chapter is respect for the dignity and equality of all.

Workways

We begin with Justice Ginsburg's primer on the "workways" of the Supreme Court, invaluable for understanding what she calls the "procedures at my workplace," from how the Justices select the cases they review, to the nature and purpose of oral argument before the Court, to how the Justices reach their decisions and compose and release their written opinions to the public. For anyone from first-year law students to laypeople seeking to understand the Court, there could be no better guide.

(Truth be told, Justice Ginsburg has some rather unusual workways herself. Her ability to go without a normal night's sleep is legendary; her propensity for working until around 4 a.m. and arriving at her chambers in the late morning—earlier when the Court is in session, sitting for oral argument—is known to every clerk and assistant. Her sleeplessness is part of a habit that started in high school and continued in college, where, after her roommates went to bed, she crept away to a quiet place to study into the wee hours. But we digress.)

The second article in this chapter addresses what Justice Ginsburg considers the essential predicate of the work of the Court: judicial independence. Her thesis, supported with historical and current examples: "Essential to the rule of law in any land is an independent judiciary, judges not under the thumb of other branches of Government, and therefore equipped to administer the law impartially. . . . [J]udicial independence, [however,] . . . can be shattered if the society law exists to serve does not take care to ensure its preservation."

Third in this trio comes Justice Ginsburg's tribute to Chief Justice Rehnquist on the occasion of his death in office from cancer in early September 2005. Her tribute gives a human face and personal touch to one who held the august title Chief Justice of the United States for nearly twenty years. Justice Ginsburg's reflections both expand the reader's understanding of any Chief Justice's unique first-among-equals ("primus among the pares") position in the Court's workways and underscore this particular Chief's skillful manage-

ment of the Court and commitment to an independent judiciary. William Hubbs Rehnquist was, she said, "hands down the fairest and most efficient" boss she ever had.

Judging

Just months before President Clinton nominated her to the Supreme Court in the summer of 1993, Judge Ginsburg delivered a lecture-turned-law-review-article, "Speaking in a Judicial Voice," on the appropriate style and substance of judging. The introductory paragraphs reveal her judicial philosophy: where she stands on the spectrum between "originalists"—adherents to what they perceive as the founders' original understanding of the Constitution—and those who espouse "a living Constitution," whose fundamental principles should be interpreted in light of changing circumstances the founders could not have imagined.

Invoking Madison and Hamilton, Ginsburg endorses the concept of a living Constitution. She illustrates her vision with a brief history of the American ideal of equality, a concept limited at the nation's founding by a culture that kept early Americans "from fully perceiving or acting upon ideals of human equality and dignity," but which, she notes, had "growth potential." The story of the Constitution, she says, is "the extension . . . of constitutional rights and protections to once-excluded groups: to people who were once held in bondage, to men without property, to Native Americans, and to women." (For more on this important subject, see the excerpt from the opera Scalia/Ginsburg, *at p. 43, in which the protagonists, Justice Ginsburg [soprano] and Justice Antonin Scalia [tenor], the Court's most outspoken originalist, debate the merits of their opposing theories of constitutional interpretation.)*

After laying this groundwork, Ginsburg turns to the "style and substance" of judging. On style she endorses collegiality between judges and "taking the high ground" in their courtrooms and in their written opinions. Ginsburg advocates this approach not for manners' sake (although, one senses, she believes good manners are generally a good thing), but because collegiality leads to better opinions, and enhances public respect for and confidence in the judiciary. (She includes illustrative "spicy" examples of intemperate language from actual opinions, and even names a few names, albeit in the footnotes.)

On substance, she says: "Measured motions seem to me right, in the main, for constitutional as well as common law adjudication. Doctrinal limbs too swiftly shaped, experience teaches, may prove unstable," thereby "plac[ing] stress on the [judicial] institution." In the Madison Lecture, see p. 228, she offered Roe v. Wade *as a prime example of the Supreme Court doing too much too soon. In Ginsburg's view, the Court's encompassing decision in* Roe *fueled enduring political controversy and failed to home in on a key dimension of the problem: that a woman's ability to control her reproductive life is critical to equality in life and law. In her view, judges are not "platonic guardians" but play an interdependent part in democracy, participating in "a dialogue with other organizations of government, and with the people as well." To Justice Ginsburg, history teaches that the Court should avoid either impeding, or leaping too far ahead of, the political process, instead engaging in "a temperate brand of decisionmaking" that proceeds incrementally, ordinarily deciding what is required by the case before it and leaving further development to later cases.*

Comparative Sideglances and the Equality Ideal

In "A Decent Respect to the Opinions of [Human]kind," Justice Ginsburg, cognizant of congressional controversy in recent years over the Supreme Court's citations to "foreign law"—the rulings of national, multinational, and international courts other than our own—makes the case that "looking beyond our borders" is "altogether fitting and proper for lawyers and judges in the United States." From the earliest days of the Supreme Court to the twenty-first century, she shows, Justices have cited cases decided by the courts of other nations and international bodies. (She notes that even Justice Scalia, a vocal opponent of the practice, had indulged in it on occasion.)

*Indeed, such "comparative sideglances" at the work of legal institutions beyond our shores have been her own practice as lawyer, law teacher, judge, and Justice, and a recurring feature of her articles and speeches. In "*Brown v. Board *in International Context," Justice Ginsburg explores how that decision both reflected and advanced international human rights developments. The international response during the World War II era to the "rank racism" of the Nazis created a dilemma for the United States: how to maintain prestige and moral leadership in the world, given its own policies of racial* *segregation, including the segregation of African-American soldiers fighting and dying in the war against Hitler. The Supreme Court's 1954* Brown *decision, reported around the world, she reflects, "propelled an evolution yet unfinished toward respect, in law and in practice, for the human dignity of all the world's people," and inspired her own work on behalf of women's rights.*

In a brief and poignant follow-up, her "Remarks on Loving v. Virginia,*" delivered a year after the death of Mildred Loving in 2008, describes "one of the most important cases the U.S. Supreme Court has ever decided." In that 1967 case the Court declared Virginia's miscegenation law unconstitutional. Chief Justice Earl Warren wrote for a unanimous court that "restricting the freedom to marry solely because of racial classifications violates the central meaning of the Equal Protection Clause."*

"Remarks on the Value of Diversity," again informed by "comparative sideglances," considers the law and practice of affirmative action, which Ginsburg characterizes as "endeavors to make the equality ideal more than aspirational." Hired as the first woman in a tenured position at Columbia Law School, Justice Ginsburg claims to have been the beneficiary of the Nixon administration's effort to encourage colleges and universities to hire women faculty. (Indeed, she labeled 1972 "the year of the woman" because of the number of women hired that year into all- or nearly all-male institutions.) Her lecture traces the legal status of affirmative action from its origins in the 1960s through its ups and downs in Supreme Court opinions such as Bakke *(1978), and* Gratz *and* Grutter *(2003). (An affirmative action case decided after she gave the Diversity lecture,* Fisher v. University of Texas, *is included among her oral dissents at p. 296.) Justice Ginsburg points to the "attention-riveting line" from a 2007 opinion, which held unconstitutional Seattle's plan to maintain integrated elementary and high schools by taking account of race in assigning children to particular schools: "The way to stop discrimination on the basis of race is to stop discriminating on the basis of race." Ginsburg joined the dissenters in the contrary view: "[There is a] legal and practical difference . . . between the use of race-conscious criteria . . . to keep the races apart, and the use of race-conscious criteria . . . to bring the races together." As she told her audience, it is her belief that "[w]e will all profit from a more diverse, inclusive society, understanding, accommodating, even celebrating our difference, while pulling together for the common good."*

"I Dissent"

Not included in this chapter are any of Justice Ginsburg's majority, concurring, or dissenting opinions (a representative sample of which would fill this entire volume and then some). For the opinions of the Court, readers can go to the Supreme Court website (supremecourt.gov), or to the official United States Reports, available in hard copy in every law library. In their stead, we present some of Ginsburg's most notable legal opinions in their most abbreviated and least technical form—the bench announcement. Bench announcements are the oral summaries of majority opinions—and, much less frequently, dissenting opinions—delivered in the courtroom to waiting press and onlookers when the Court issues newly minted opinions. The bench announcement of her pathmarking majority opinion in United States v. Virginia *is reproduced at p. 150. Several dissents she found important enough to announce from the bench are presented below.*

But first, to prepare you, we bring you a lecture on dissents, delivered by Justice Ginsburg in Paris in 2013. In it, she examines the occasions for and virtues and vices of dissenting opinions, "a subject I have been obliged to think about more than occasionally in recent Terms." The reasons for her heightened attention to dissents are not far to seek: Recent years have brought changes in the composition of the Court and her position within it. Since the appointment of Chief Justice Roberts and Justice Alito, in opinions where the nine Justices split five to four, the five, more often than not, were the Court's conservative members, and the four in dissent, the more liberal Justices. With these appointments, the Court emerged from one of the longest periods in its history without a change in personnel (eleven years), during which Justices Ginsburg and Breyer were at the bottom of the Court's hierarchy, Ginsburg at number 8 and Breyer at number 9. With the retirement of Justices Souter (2009) and Stevens (2010), and the arrival of Justices Sotomayor (2009) and Kagan (2010), Ginsburg became the most senior Justice in the liberal group (and the oldest member of the Court). In 5-to-4 cases with a conservative-liberal split, therefore, she became the one to decide who would write the dissenting opinion. In short, Justice Ginsburg had come into her own.

Characteristically, in this lecture on dissenting opinions, she envisions dissents as part of a conversation among the Justices. As the drafts circulate, the back-and-forth between the author of the majority opinion and the dissenter strengthens the Court's final product. As Justice Ginsburg explains, dissents also speak to the public, to Congress, and to future Courts. She distinguishes between dissents in cases involving interpretation of federal statutes, which "put the ball back in Congress' court," and dissents on constitutional matters, which "appeal to the intelligence of a future day." The selection of her most significant announcements of dissents from the bench, including several she discusses in her lecture on dissents, fill the pages immediately following the lecture.

Highlights of a Year at the Court

The chapter that begins with Justice Ginsburg's description of the workways of the Supreme Court ends with her review of a single Term's work. Every year, in late May or early June, the Justice addresses the annual Judicial Conference for the Second Circuit, presenting the highlights of the Term just ending. She then updates the review when the Term is completed. The completed "Highlights of the 2015–16 Term," hot off the presses as this book went to print, are the Justice's final words in this collection of her work.

1

Workways of the Supreme Court*

I will devote this lecture to procedures at my workplace. Why procedure? For some seventeen years that was my main field as a law school teacher. But much more important, one cannot get a firm grasp on the substance of our decisions without some grounding in the rules, practices, and traditions that frame our decisionmaking. I will begin with the large job the U.S. Constitution and federal laws assign to the Supreme Court of the United States. In the main, the Court serves as last-instance decisionmaker on questions arising under federal law.

The federal law on which we rule may be the Constitution itself. More often, however, we deal not with constitutional questions, but with ordinary laws governing a wide range of areas, for example, statutes governing bankruptcy, federal taxation, intellectual property, environmental protection, pensions, and provision of health care. And we regularly rule not only on laws passed by Congress or by state legislatures, but on the legitimacy of executive actions, including actions of the U.S. president.

The U.S. Supreme Court today is not what jurists call an "error correction" instance. By that I mean the Court will not take up a case

---

*Justice Ginsburg has delivered numerous versions of these remarks to various audiences over the years, including to students in the Wake Forest University School of Law Summer Program in Venice, Italy, in July 2016. We have edited the remarks for length and to ensure clarity outside the context in which they were originally delivered.

simply because a lower court reached an arguably—or even plainly—wrong decision. For correction of errors made in particular cases, we rely largely on the federal courts of appeals, and on the appellate courts (including Supreme Courts) in state judicial systems. (Most of the world's nations have *a* judicial system. The United States has fifty-two systems. In addition to the federal court system, each state and the District of Columbia has its own two- or three-tiered court system.) For the most part, the U.S. Supreme Court will consider for review only cases presenting what we call deep splits—questions of federal law on which other courts (federal courts, state courts, or a mix of both) have strongly disagreed. About 70 percent of the cases we hear fall in that category.

My remarks divide into three parts. I will describe first the Court's highly selective review granting process; next, I will speak of oral argument before the Court; and finally, I will take up the way decisions are reached, and how opinions are composed and released.

1. The Review Granting Process

We start each Term with a long conference one week before the Court Term begins the first Monday in October. At that late September opening conference, the Court disposes of petitions for review accumulated during the summer months—petitions filed from June until the start of September. The opening conference, as all our conferences, takes place behind closed doors and is strictly confidential. No person other than the nine Justices may enter the room when the Court is conferring—no secretary, law clerk, not even a message deliverer. The conferences are not recorded and no laptop is in sight. If there is a knock on the door, or the telephone rings, it is the chore of the junior Justice, now Justice Kagan, to answer. When the conference ends, the junior Justice stays behind to convey actions taken at conference to the administrative personnel whose job it is to inform the public of the Court's dispositions.

While the Term is under way, from October through June, we

confer on review petitions generally at one- or two-week intervals. The number of petitions for review calendared for each standard conference runs in the 100 to 300 range. In all, the Court currently receives between 6,000 and 7,000 requests for review annually.

How do we manage those thousands of pleas for review? Typically, we put less than 15 percent of them to a vote. I will describe, a bit later, just how we reduce the large conference list down to a relatively slim list of cases the Court will actually discuss in conference. First, I will tell you the voting choices we have.

Most often, the vote is simply to grant or deny review. (It takes four votes—one less than a majority—to grant a petition for review.) If review is granted, we schedule the case for full briefing and oral argument. But we have other options. We may decide to hold on to a case—to defer action on the petition temporarily, pending the decision in another case, already granted review, presenting the same or a related issue.

Or, the Court may relist a case for a later conference because one or more of the Justices wants to give further thought to his or her vote, or perhaps wants time to prepare a dissenting opinion disagreeing with the Court's decision to deny review. (It happens sometimes—indeed, it is the definition of success—that a dissent from a denial of review is never published, because the draft dissent, when circulated in-house, produces the very effect the writer seeks: it leads one or more Justices to rethink the matter and supply the vote or votes necessary to grant review. Some of my favorite opinions fall in that category. They are not available for you to read, because they succeeded in changing the public announcement from review denied to review granted.)

In many cases each Term, the Court vacates lower court judgments and remands the case to the court from whence it came, for fresh consideration in light of a recently released Supreme Court decision, one that sets binding precedent bearing on the remanded case. To take a typical example, after deciding, some Terms ago, that the death penalty for a person under age eighteen was unconstitutional, we remanded several other cases presenting the same issue, so that lower courts could apply our decision to those cases. Since then, we have held that juveniles, because of their immaturity, may not be sentenced to life without the possibility of parole, even when convicted of murder.

Occasionally, the Justices invite the views of the solicitor general before voting on a review petition. The solicitor general is the Department of Justice officer responsible for representing the United States in the Supreme Court. When we call for the solicitor's views in a case in which the United States is not a party, the solicitor acts as a true friend of the Court; after consulting with federal executive agencies and officers with relevant information and expertise, the solicitor general offers his views on the importance or unimportance of the question presented to the sound development of federal law. Often, but far from always, we follow the solicitor general's views on whether to grant a petition for review. I would not call the solicitor general, as some legal writers have, the "Tenth Justice." He does not attend our conferences. The Court has no conversation with him that is not on the public record.

About a dozen times a year, the Court finds a case important, yet the answer so clear that we vote to decide it summarily, based on the written petition for review and the brief in opposition to review, without further briefing or oral argument. In the mid-1970s, a colleague and I had that exhilarating experience when we petitioned the U.S. Supreme Court to review a judgment of the Utah Supreme Court. Our clients were gainfully employed women who had been laid off from their jobs because their employer was reducing its workforce. The women sought other paid work, but were unsuccessful in that endeavor. They were some weeks pregnant at the time of their layoff and new job search.

A Utah law in those bygone days absolutely denied unemployment compensation to pregnant women. The Utah Supreme Court upheld the law, declaring that the Constitution's Due Process and Equal Protection Clauses did not rule out denying unemployment compensation to pregnant workers. Once a woman became pregnant, the Utah court apparently supposed, she could not be considered a true member of the labor force. She was, or would soon be, no longer ready, willing, and able to work.

The U.S. Supreme Court found no need for a full-dress presentation. It reversed the Utah judgment unanimously and summarily, holding that Utah's denial of unemployment compensation to able-to-work pregnant women was clearly unconstitutional. Winning that way—without filing detailed briefs or presenting oral argument—is a lawyer's dream come true. (For those who are golfers, it is like getting a hole-in-one on the front nine.)

Returning to how we manage the large numbers of review petitions, a few days before each conference, the Chief Justice circulates a "discussion list" selecting from the many pages of petitions scheduled for conference the dozen or so he thinks worthy of discussion. Any Justice, the next day, may add other cases to this list. Petitions no Justice asks to discuss are denied automatically. That is the fate of some 85 percent of all petitions. Cases placed on the discussion list will be granted review, as I just mentioned, only if at least four Justices so vote.

Every petition for review, no matter how humble, is summarized and explained in a law clerk's memorandum. All of the current Justices, save Justice Alito, participate in a pooling of resources for consideration of petitions for review. Justice Alito and his clerks review all petitions independently, inside the Justice's chambers. The rest of us combine our law clerks (each Justice has four) in a pool and the Chief Justice's administrative aide divides the review petitions evenly among the eight chambers. My law clerks tell me they spend about one-third of their time on petitions for review, more at the beginning of their clerkships, a little less as they become skilled in digesting lower court opinions and review requests.

The Justices, in turn, spend many hours deciding what to decide.

We read the law clerks' memoranda with the judgment one gains from experience with the law and life, and with the Court operating as a collegial body. When necessary, a Justice will personally check the petition for review and the brief in opposition and do whatever other homework she (or he) finds appropriate to determine whether a case is fit for the Court's consideration.

Since 1988, the Court has had almost complete control over its docket. Before then, the Court was obliged to take up cases falling into certain categories—it had little choice in close to 20 percent of the cases set for full briefing and oral argument. Congress, with the Court's enthusiastic endorsement, eliminated most of the "must decide" cases, commencing with the 1988 Term.

Cases we are still obliged to hear are few and far between. They are mainly certain Voting Rights Act cases, and original jurisdiction cases in which the Court serves as the tribunal of first and last instance. (Original jurisdiction cases generally involve controversies between two states—or a state and the United States—often over boundaries, land ownership, or water rights. An example from several years ago, New Jersey and New York crossed swords over ownership of the land-filled portions of Ellis Island, the island that once served as the admissions station for immigrants from Europe to the United States. New Jersey prevailed in that fray.)

With the elimination of most of the Court's mandatory jurisdiction in 1988, and, even more, the Court's clear recognition that it ought not try to serve as an error-correction instance, the controversies the Court calendars for argument have diminished in number from about 140 per Term to between 70 and 80 per Term. With more time, the hope is, one can write better—or at least more comprehensible and hopefully shorter—opinions. (It does take time to write short.)

More time also helps to achieve less division among the Justices. In recent Terms, the Court has ruled unanimously, at least as to the bottom line judgment, in about 40 percent of the argued cases. That is a point the U.S. press little notes—the fact that we agree, without dissent, in a fairly large percentage of the cases we take up. In contrast, the Court divides sharply, 5–4, in fewer than 25 percent of the argued cases.

Press reports on the Supreme Court's actions sometimes exaggerate the significance of an order denying review. I read from time to time that the Court affirmed or upheld Decision X, when the case the report said we affirmed didn't even show up on a conference discussion list. A denial of review, it is important to understand, reveals nothing at all about what the Court would do if it took up the case for review.

We generally await a deep lower court "split"—one unlikely to repair without Supreme Court intervention—not simply to keep our caseload down. Awaiting decisions from several courts can advance our understanding of the importance of an issue, by giving us a sense of the different factual contexts in which the issue arises and the range of lower court opinions on the proper resolution.

A major reason why we resist grants of review when there is no split is the genuine respect we have for the able judges in the federal judiciary—the federal district courts and courts of appeals—and on state benches, too. Those judges are fallible, as all mortals are, but they strive to "get it right" and they generally do. And the Justices of the Supreme Court possess no greater wisdom than do judges on other federal benches. Some of the nation's finest judges missed nomination to the High Court. Luck plays a large part in the selection of the particular nine who sit at any given time. On the Supreme Court's place in the system, Justice Robert H. Jackson (who was a member of the Court from 1941 until his death in 1954, with time out to serve as principal prosecutor at the post–World War II Nuremberg trials) said it best: "We are not final because we are infallible, but we are infallible only because we are final."

I turn now from how we decide what cases to take up for review to "the day in court."

2. The Day in Court

The U.S. Supreme Court, as I have just said, labors long in selecting the cases it will take up for review but, unlike courts of appeals where litigants arrive as of right, the Court spends little time deciding which cases will be set for oral argument (all are, save for the dozen or fewer cases resolved summarily on the basis of the petitions for review and briefs in opposition). Nor do we debate the length of argument time. Cases calendared for argument, no matter how complex, routinely get exactly one half hour per side. When argument time is running out, there is a five-minute-warning light colored white, then a red light. When the red light appears on the lectern, time is up—lawyer and Justice alike must stop talking.

A keen observer of the Court, *New York Times* journalist Anthony Lewis, wrote this description of the current day in Court:

> Oral argument does not play the part in the work of the Supreme Court that it did in the nineteenth century, when Daniel Webster [and other Bar luminaries] would argue a case for days. . . . The modern Supreme Court limits argument severely . . . to half an hour [per side]. But argument still has an important function. It is the one chance the Justices have to . . . grapple directly with the lawyers who represent the clashing interests before them. It is also a rare opportunity for the public to gain insights into the minds of those who actually make the decisions. More than any other officials in Washington, the Justices still do their own work, assisted only by a handful of young law clerks. To observe them as they question counsel in the courtroom is to see an extraordinarily open process, unaffected, human. In a capital puffed up with bureaucracy and public relations, the Court seems old-fashioned, small, personal. For the lawyers, oral argument is a direct opportunity to reach those nine minds—with an idea, a phrase, a fact. Not many cases are won at

> argument, but [a case] can be lost if a lawyer is unable or unwilling to answer a Justice's question [honestly and persuasively].

I agree in full with Anthony Lewis' observation, and could not better describe the role of oral argument.

In the most essential way, oral argument at the Supreme Court is what it generally is in other U.S. appellate tribunals, both federal and state. Oral argument is an occasion not for grand speechmaking, but for a conversation about the case, a dialogue or discussion between knowledgeable counsel and judges who have done their homework, a "hot bench," as appellate advocates say—judges who have read first and foremost the decision we are reviewing, any statutes in point, next, relevant portions of the record, and other judicial decisions bearing on the case. Then we turn to the almost always long briefs filed by the parties and, depending upon their quality, the briefs of supporting, so-called friends of the court, amici curiae.

Some lawyers, I have been told, resent interruption of an oral argument carefully planned as a lecture or oration, and some judges ask few questions. Justice Harry Blackmun, who retired from the Court in 1994, and died in 1999, often recounted advice he was given by Justice Hugo Black in 1970, when Justice Blackmun was appointed to the Court: "Harry," Justice Black cautioned, "never ask many questions from the bench because if you don't ask many questions, you won't ask many foolish [ones]."

But it seems to me a loss of a precious opportunity if an advocate can do no more with her oral argument time than recapitulate the briefing. She will serve her client and cause better, I believe, if she is agile—if she welcomes and responds to questions that may uncover what is in the decisionmakers' minds, while remaining alert to opportunities to use a question as a springboard to advance a key point. So I do not follow Justice Black's advice. And in that, I am hardly alone.

Questions from the bench give counsel a chance to satisfy the Court on matters the questioner, at least, thinks significant, issues the

Court might resolve less satisfactorily without counsel's aid. Sometimes, it is true, a Justice asks a question with persuasion of a colleague in mind, or at least to stimulate the colleague's thinking; at such times, the lawyer may sense she is being talked through, not to. Other times, the questioner may be trying to cue counsel that an argument pursued with zeal is a loser, so counsel had best move on or shift gears. Counsel too intent on adhering to a prepared script or outline may miss the cue.

There is, I appreciate, a difference in the dynamic of a nine-member Court and that of the typical three-judge appellate bench. A conversation accommodating clarifications, interjections, and often interruptions, readily managed among four (counsel and three judges), is less feasible among ten. (The U.S. Supreme Court, you no doubt know, always sits en banc, barring recusals, with all nine Justices participating in every case. We never divide into panels for any purpose.)

Unlike appellate forums in many countries, notably those with a civil law base like Germany or Italy, for example, appellate courts in the United States do not assign a reporting judge to wield the laboring oar in preparing a case for decision. Each of us prepares fully on our own. At oral argument, the Chief does not decide who may speak or when inquiries may be made. Any Justice may ask a question whenever he or she pleases within the allotted argument time.

Though the format is not flawless (some would prefer more time than a half hour per side, and fewer questions), argument at the Court largely succeeds in its mission. It more than occasionally reduces or diminishes confusion and pares down or sharpens the issues in conflict. And it gives counsel an opportunity to face the decisionmakers, a last clear chance to convince the Justices concerning points on which the decision may turn. (In typical civil law courts, in contrast, appellate advocates ordinarily speak with barely any interruption. I would find it hard, as a judge, to listen to lawyers' speeches so passively.)

We do not allow cameras in the courtroom, but we do promptly provide written transcripts and audiotapes of arguments.

I move on, finally, to decisionmaking.

3. Reaching Decisions

To reach decisions, in a typical two-week sitting period, the Court meets each Wednesday afternoon to discuss the preceding Monday's cases, and each Friday, both to dispose of accumulated petitions for review, and to discuss the cases heard the preceding Tuesday and Wednesday. On the second Friday afternoon of a sitting period, the Chief Justice circulates opinion-writing assignments made by him when he is in the majority; and when he is not, he conveys to the full Court the assignments made by the most senior Justice in the majority.

At all Court conferences, the Chief speaks and votes first; the junior Justice speaks and votes last. Our former Chief, Chief Justice Rehnquist, described his disappointment, when he was the junior Justice, that his sage comments at conference were not listened to with rapt attention, because "[dispositive] votes had [already] been cast [higher] up the line." He reported "with newfound clarity," however, having "risen from ninth to seventh to first in seniority," that his idea for "more of a round-table discussion" was academic: "fine in the abstract," he said, but unlikely to "contribute much in practice, and at any rate[,] doomed by the seniority system to which the senior Justices naturally adhere."

Yes, there is sometimes a certain impatience, an expectation of brevity, when the vote comes round to, say Justice Sotomayor, and there is already a clear majority for one side or the other. But last place, now the lot of Justice Kagan, has an occasional suspense-breaking moment, when the ninth vote ends a tie. Justices who speak later do have one advantage. They have an opportunity to adjust their statements to take account of views expressed earlier by others. To do that effectively, one must be both well prepared and a good listener.

Discussion at Supreme Court conferences is often spirited, but seldom protracted. "It will come out in the writing," the Chief Justice is likely to comment, when we have all had our say. And so it does. The conference vote is always tentative. An opinion writer may find that the conference position, in whole or in part, "won't write," so the writer ends up on a different track.

Or, an opinion circulated as a dissent may attract the majority's approval and become the opinion of the Court. (I vividly recall one case several Terms ago in which a dissent for two ended up a majority opinion for six.) The papers of Justices Harry Blackmun and Thurgood Marshall, housed at the Library of Congress and open to the public, show that, in a case I argued before the Court in the mid-1970s, the initial vote at conference was 5–4 against my position. Ultimately, however, after several post-conference exchanges among the Justices, and a few switches, the position I advocated prevailed.

Turning specifically to opinion writing, my colleagues and I have high regard for the label "opinion of the Court." That regard is demonstrated in what I call "Dear Ruth" letters responsive to a circulating opinion. (In all intra-Court correspondence, we use only first names.) "Dear Ruth" letters not uncommonly read: "Please consider adding, deleting, dropping, revising to say [thus and so]," or, more hopefully, "I will join your opinion if you will take out, put in, alter or adjust as follows." I am comforted, at such times, by a comment made by Chief Justice Hughes, who presided from 1930 until 1941. Hughes said that during the many years he served on the Court he always tried to write his opinions logically and clearly, but if another Justice whose vote was necessary to make a majority insisted that particular language be put in, in it went, and let the law schools figure out what it meant!

In truth, much more often than not, my colleagues' comments help me to improve an opinion. And there is nothing better than a good dissent to force one to sharpen her presentation for the Court. (Most appellate courts in civil law–style systems, in contrast, allow no published dissents or separate concurrences; they produce only a nameless, uniform-in-style judgment of the Court.)

I prefer and continue to aim for opinions that both get it right, and keep it tight, without undue digressions or decorations or distracting denunciations of colleagues who hold different views. (But I doubt I will ever match Justice Breyer's discipline and restraint in squelching all temptation to use footnotes.) And it is worth repeating that the Court really does prize collegiality. Yes, in between 20 and 25 percent of the argued cases we have divided 5–4 in recent Terms, but, as I said earlier, our unanimity rate is notable—running in the 40 percent range.

Most impressive, I think, despite sharp differences on certain issues—for example, cases on campaign finance, employment discrimination, affirmative action, access to abortion and contraceptives, prisoners held at Guantanamo Bay, the meaning of the Second Amendment—we remain good friends, people who respect each other, and genuinely enjoy each other's company. Our mutual respect is only momentarily touched, in most instances, by our sometimes strong disagreement on what the law is. The institution we serve is ever so much more important than the particular individuals who compose the Court's bench at any given time. And our job—the job of judging in a U.S. federal court generally—is, in my view, the best work a U.S. lawyer could wish for. We serve no client, our commission is to do what is right—what the law requires and what is just. The guarantees of judicial independence the Founding Fathers were wise enough to place in the U.S. Constitution (including life tenure and no reduction in our salary while we hold office) arm us to do just that. (In many constitutional courts in other lands, a different safeguard of independence is installed: a long, nonrenewable term—9, 12, or 15 years, for example.)

Contrast the security federal judges enjoy with the relative insecurity of state court judges who must stand for periodic elections. In 39 of the 50 states composing the United States, judges, at least at some level in the hierarchy, face elections. One can understand the origins of elections for judicial office in the United States; the practice traces back to the distrust of the king's judges in days when the thirteen original states were British colonies. But, at least in my judgment, elections are a dangerous way to choose or retain judges.

Lady Brenda Hale, the first and still the only woman on the Supreme Court of the United Kingdom, said in a 2003 speech:

> One of the most important tasks of the judiciary is to protect the individual from the power of the state. This includes protecting minorities, often unpopular minorities, from the wrath of the majority. . . . [I]f [the judge] were to have to submit [herself] periodically to election, [she] would find this harder to do.

I concur in that judgment.

2

Judicial Independence*

Essential to the rule of law in any land is an independent judiciary, judges not under the thumb of other branches of government, and therefore equipped to administer the law impartially. As experience in the United States and elsewhere confirms, however, judicial independence is vulnerable to assault; it can be shattered if the society law exists to serve does not take care to ensure its preservation.

My remarks concentrate on judicial independence in the system I know best, the third branch of the U.S. government—the federal courts—and on efforts by the political branches to curtail that independence.

I.

Under the U.S. Constitution, federal judges hold their offices essentially for life, with no compulsory retirement age, and their salaries may not be diminished by Congress.[1] Through these protections, the founders of the United States sought to advance the judiciary's independence from Congress and the president, and thus to safeguard judges' ability to decide cases impartially. Yet I doubt that constitu-

---

*Justice Ginsburg has delivered numerous versions of these remarks to various audiences over the years, including to students in the Wake Forest Law School Summer Program in Venice, Italy, in July 2008. We have edited the remarks for length and to ensure clarity outside the context in which they were originally delivered.

tional insulation would have protected the federal bench if we did not have a culture that frowns on attempts to make the courts over to fit the president's or the Congress' image.

A well-known illustration of that culture. Some seventy years ago, President Franklin Delano Roosevelt announced a proposal to pack the U.S. Supreme Court. The Court of that day had resisted President Roosevelt's New Deal program, holding unconstitutional sixteen pieces of federal social and economic legislation in a thirteen-month span.

Frustrated by his inability to replace the "nine old men" then seated on the Court, President Roosevelt sent to the Senate a bill to overcome the Court's recalcitrance. He proposed adding one Justice for each member of the Court who had served ten years or more, and did not retire within six months after reaching age seventy.[2] FDR's proposal would have immediately swelled the Court's size from 9 to 15 members. (If the 1937 plan were to be applied to the current Court, we would today have a 13-member bench.) Two developments, manifest by the end of 1937, contributed to the defeat of Roosevelt's plan: a groundswell of public opposition to the president's endeavor to capture the Court, and a growing understanding among the Justices that it was appropriate to defer to legislative judgments on matters of social and economic policy. FDR's idea has never been renewed. Those who care about the health and welfare of our system appreciate that packing the Court to suit the mood of the political branches (Congress and the president) would severely erode the status of the judiciary as a co-equal branch of government.

II.

I turn now to some recent threats to the security of U.S. judges who decide cases without regard to what the "home crowd" wants.

A headline-producing case in point. Early in 2005, federal courts sitting in Florida confronted a cause célèbre. On order of the Florida state courts, a hospital had removed the feeding tube from Terri Schiavo, a severely brain-damaged woman whose situation sparked a huge controversy over the right to refuse life support. Congress entered the fray by passing a most unusual statute giving the federal courts jurisdiction to hear the plea of Schiavo's parents, but not altering the governing substantive law.[3] The federal courts read the statute as it was written, and refused to override the Florida courts by ordering restoration of the feeding tube. This was not the outcome wanted by a goodly number of the members of Congress. In angry reaction, the then–House majority leader accused federal judges of "thumb[ing] their nose[s] at Congress and the president."[4] He warned: "[T]he time will come for the men responsible for this to answer for their behavior."[5] "Congress," he said, "for many years has shirked its responsibility to hold the judiciary accountable. No longer."[6]

Similarly unsettling, in the same year, 2005, two episodes of violence against judges shocked the nation. A state court judge was murdered while on the bench in Atlanta, and a federal judge's mother and husband were murdered at the judge's home in Chicago.[7] Shortly thereafter, a prominent senator gave a widely reported speech on the Senate floor. After inveighing against "activist jurists," he suggested there may be "a cause-and-effect connection" between judicial activism and the "recent episodes of courthouse violence in this country."[8]

The blasts from Congress were not merely verbal. In May 2005, the House Judiciary Committee considered creating an "office of inspector general for the federal judiciary."[9] The office would investigate allegations of judicial misconduct and report them to Congress. The committee's chairman said, in announcing the proposal, that judges must "be punished in some capacity for behavior that does not rise to the level of impeachable conduct."[10] If the then-chairman's subsequent action indicated the role he envisioned for the proposed inspector general, judges had good cause for concern. In June 2005, that chairman's office dispatched a letter to a U.S. Court of Appeals, complaining that the court had ordered an unlawfully low sentence for a narcotics-case defendant. The letter called for a "prompt response . . . to rectify" the decision,[11] even though the government sought no further review of the sentence. Never mind that federal law entrusted the decision whether to seek a higher sentence to top-ranking Justice Department officers, not to judges, and certainly not to Congress.

Another troubling congressional initiative: proposals to prohibit federal courts from relying on foreign law.[12] A misunderstanding appears to underlie the opposition to foreign law citations. As Justice Stephen Breyer explained in a recent interview, citations to foreign laws and decisions should not be controversial.[13] "References to cases elsewhere are never binding," Justice Breyer emphasized. We interpret and apply only our own Constitution, our own laws. But it can add to our store of knowledge, Justice Breyer explained, "to look at how other people [with a commitment to democracy similar to our own] solve similar problems." Justice Breyer compared references to the decisions of foreign and international tribunals to references to a treatise or to a professor's work.

Lest I appear to be spreading too much gloom, I should emphasize the vocal defenders of the judiciary, intelligent voices that do not divide along party lines. The *New York Times*, a paper some regard as "liberal," recently editorialized: "The courts will not always be popular; they will not always be right. But if Congress succeeds in curtailing the judiciary's ability to act as a check on the other two branches, the nation will be far less free."[14] Former solicitor general Ted Olson, generally perceived as conservative, published a similar view: "Americans understand," and I hope he is right, "that no system is perfect and no judge immune from error, but also that our society would crumble if we did not respect the judicial process and the judges who make it work."[15]

History suggests that Congress is unlikely to employ the nuclear weapon—impeachment—against judges who decide cases in a way the "home crowd" does not want. In the over 220 years since ratification of the Constitution, the House of Representatives has impeached only thirteen federal judges; in only seven instances did impeachment result in a Senate conviction,[16] and those judges were removed not for wrongly interpreting the law, but for unquestionably illegal behavior, such as extortion, perjury, and waging war against the United States.[17]

Although politically driven impeachment of federal judges is a remote prospect, yet another threat to judicial independence cannot be discounted so easily. In President Clinton's second term, it bears reminding, political hazing of federal judicial nominees was unrelenting. The confirmation process in those years often strayed from examining the qualifications of each nominee into an endeavor to uncover some hidden "liberal" agenda the nominee supposedly harbored. For many Democrats, President Bush's successive terms have been payback time, an opportunity to hold up or reject Bush nominees to the federal judiciary on ideological grounds.

Injecting politics prominently into the nomination or the confirmation process means long delays in filling judicial vacancies. In the face of mounting caseloads, such delays threaten to erode the quality of justice the U.S. federal judiciary can provide. Vacancies in large numbers inevitably sap the energy and depress the spirits of the judges left to cope with heavy dockets shorthanded.

I should mention, too, the host of jurisdiction-curtailing measures placed in the congressional hopper in recent years. One bill would have severely limited the scope of federal habeas corpus review.[18] Another would have removed federal courts' authority to decide any case concerning the Ten Commandments, the Pledge of Allegiance, and the national motto, "In God We Trust."[19] Yet another would have taken away from the federal courts authority to adjudicate free exercise or establishment of religion claims, privacy claims (including those raising "any issue of sexual practices, orientation, or reproduction"), and any claim to equal protection of the laws "based upon the right to marry without regard to sex or sexual orientation."[20]

All these proposals, and other like-minded bills, failed, as students of history could have predicted. Jurisdiction-stripping reactions to disliked decisions have been proposed perennially. In the 1950s, desegregation and domestic security cases were on some legislators' strip lists; in the 1960s, federal court review of certain criminal justice matters; in the 1970s, busing to achieve racial integration in schools; in the 1980s, abortion and school prayer. None of these efforts succeeded, and the more recent endeavors to curb federal court jurisdiction have fared no better. A simple truth has helped to spare the federal judiciary from onslaughts of this character: It is easier to block a bill than to get it enacted.

I note, finally, a Congress-Court confrontation proposed in 2004 and revived the next year. The more recent try, titled the "Congressional Accountability for Judicial Activism Act of 2005," would allow U.S. Supreme Court judgments declaring a federal law unconstitutional to be overturned by a two-thirds vote of the House and Senate.[21] (Canada's Charter of Rights and Freedoms[22] permits legislative override of a Supreme Court decision holding a statute incompatible with a Charter-protected right. But Canada's Parliament has yet to avail itself of that prerogative.)

A Constitution providing for legislative override of Court decisions resolving constitutional questions, author and journalist Anthony Lewis observed, "would be more democratic in the sense that it would remove constraints on majority rule."[23] But, Lewis rightly reminds us, in the words of Aharon Barak, former president of the Supreme Court of Israel: " 'Democracy is not only majority rule. Democracy is also the rule of basic values . . . values upon which the whole democratic structure is built, and which even the majority cannot touch.' "[24] The founders of the United States did not envision a rule of law based on pure majoritarianism,[25] and I see no cause to open the door to a legislative override now.

A note on U.S. state courts. Judges in most states, at least at some levels, are chosen in periodic elections. A question I am often asked when traveling abroad: "Isn't an elected judiciary totally at odds with judicial independence?" How can an elected judge resist doing "what the home crowd wants"? I have no fully satisfactory answers to those questions.

To return to my starting line, when former Chief Justice Rehnquist described an independent judiciary as the United States' hallmark and pride, he was repeating a theme sounded since we became a nation.

It is fitting, I think, to close with the words of two U.S. legal scholars from different ends of the political spectrum—one, Bruce Fein, known for his "conservative perspective," the other, Burt Neuborne, known for his "progressive vision." Though often on opposite sides in debate, they joined together to speak with one voice on the value of judicial independence. Their coauthored essay concludes:

> Judicial independence in the United States strengthens ordered liberty, domestic tranquility, the rule of law, and democratic ideals. . . . It would be folly to squander this priceless constitutional gift to placate the clamors of benighted political partisans.[26]

3

Tribute to Chief Justice Rehnquist*

When my former law clerk, Amanda Tyler, asked me to speak at this program honoring William Hubbs Rehnquist, I looked forward to the Chief's attendance as we celebrated his thirty-three years on the Court, the last nineteen as Chief Justice. Though he fought a dread disease bravely, he was unable to complete the twenty years all of his colleagues hoped he would have at the Court's helm. On September 4, the morning after his death, each of us released statements through the Court's Public Information Office. Mine conveyed that, of all the bosses I have had as a lawyer, law teacher, and judge, Chief Justice Rehnquist was hands down the fairest and most efficient. Presiding over six prime dons and two prima donnas, he kept us all in line and on time. Justice O'Connor, recalling the Chief's mastery of the art of short statement, said: "He led the Court with firm principles but with a light touch." We held him in highest esteem and deep affection, and will try to keep the Court operating with the harmony he successfully endeavored to achieve.

Among his myriad responsibilities, the Chief gave us our homework assignments: at the end of each two-week sitting period, whenever he was in the majority (which he was much more often than not), he decided who would write which opinion. True, there was an

---

*Justice Ginsburg delivered these remarks at George Washington Law School on October 27, 2005, and they were reprinted in 74 *George Washington Law Review* 869 (2006). We have made minor edits to the remarks for length and context.

occasional grumble, for example, from the Justice assigned to write in a sloughy ERISA case. But at the end of each Term there was general agreement that the cases, overall, had been fairly distributed. And when the Chief announced all majority opinions must be in circulation by June 1, all dissents by June 15, no one, in my twelve full Terms at the Court, missed the deadline.

That same talent, to keep the players in line and on time, was evident at oral argument, Court conferences, U.S. Judicial Conferences, Smithsonian Institution meetings, and various other gatherings. Part of the secret of his success, the Chief had an irreverent sense of humor. He could deliver poker-face lines that provoked smiles, sometimes even bursts of laughter.

The Chief was a plain speaker; he had no airs or affectations. A characteristic example. When his nomination as Chief Justice was announced by President Reagan at a June 17, 1986, press briefing, a reporter asked then-Justice Rehnquist: "Do you . . . consider it the culmination of a dream . . . ?" The soon-to-be Chief responded: "I wouldn't call it [that], but it's not every day when you're 61 years old and get a chance to have a new job."

William Hubbs Rehnquist's first job at the Court was as law clerk to Justice Robert H. Jackson, from February 1952 until June 1953. Following that auspicious start, he did just about everything one can do in the legal profession—private practice, service in the executive branch, Supreme Court judging, even, on one occasion, trial court judging. I described that episode a few years ago when I spoke at a Court function. The Chief smiled, so I feel comfortable retelling the story.

While still an Associate Justice, in June 1984, he bravely volunteered to preside over a civil jury case in Richmond. (June, many of you know, is the Supreme Court's busiest time, weeks when all of us labor to produce or refine the opinions that must be released before we recess for the summer.) According to press reports, then-Justice Rehnquist quickly took control of the proceedings, in a captain-like manner. Alas, in the fullness of time, the judgment he entered on the jury verdict was reversed, per curiam, by the Fourth Circuit.

After that encounter with first-instance judging, the Chief remained safely back in his home Court. In accord with Santayana's wisdom, he remembered the past and did not repeat it. And he was mindful of the reality Justice Jackson captured in the famous expression: Supreme Court Justices "are not final because we are infallible, but we are infallible only because we are final."

The Chief was a private person, who did not engage the press (or his colleagues) with stories of his dreams. (If he did have some delectable dreams, they were probably accompanied by tastes of the "mean" hamburgers he himself grilled, or the chocolate chip bars occasionally made for him by son Jim.) Items that might have been on his wish list: to see the paintings of William Hubbs Rehnquist displayed alongside those of Turner and Constable at the National Gallery; to succeed Robert Shaw as leader of glorious chorales; to learn the secret of the aged grandmother in Tchaikovsky's *Pique Dame* (originally Pushkin's *Queen of Spades*) how always to win at cards; to add to his books in print a suspense-packed mystery filled with action in the great outdoors, a book worthy of comparison with Raymond Chandler.

When asked by Senator Laxalt on July 30, 1986, why he believed he was qualified to be the Chief Justice, this is what William Hubbs Rehnquist said:

> I have a very real interest in the Federal judicial system and the American judiciary. . . . I have a very great interest in trying to see improvements made, not just [in the Supreme Court and] in the lower Federal courts, but seeing what might be done through the Center for State Courts, in helping State courts, at least getting financial assistance to them without trying to tell them what to do.

Visitors to the Court in recent years could hardly miss noticing the Chief's self-designed robe, copied from the Lord Chancellor's costume in a local theater company's summer production of Gilbert and Sullivan's *Iolanthe.* The robe has gleaming gold stripes, as does the robe of the United Kingdom's Lord Chancellor, but Chief Justice Rehnquist's version is less regal, resembling the stripes of a master sergeant more than those of a British lord. Why did a man not given to sartorial splendor decide on such a costume? In his own words, he did not wish to be upstaged by the women. (Justice O'Connor has several attractive neckpieces, collars from British gowns, and a frilly French foulard; I wear British and French lace foulards, too, and sometimes a collar of French Canadian design.)

The Chief and I often held different views on important issues. But he sometimes surprised me. Two examples, one from my advocate days, the other from my years on the Court.

Examining then-Justice Rehnquist's first four and a half years on the Court, David Shapiro wrote in a December 1976 *Harvard Law Review* comment: "He has never voted to strike down government action subject to scrutiny under the rational basis test." Even Homer nods. Less than two years earlier, in March 1975, the Court decided the case of a young father, Stephen Wiesenfeld, widowed when his wife died in childbirth. Stephen's wife was a teacher for whom Social Security taxes were regularly paid. When a male wage earner died leaving a child in his wife's sole care, the Social Security law provided monthly child-in-care benefits to the surviving parent. But when the deceased wage earner was female, the law allowed no child-in-care benefits.

The Court reached a unanimous judgment: the gender line was unconstitutional, a violation of the equal protection principle. But the Justices divided over the rationale. The majority viewed the law as discriminating impermissibly against women wage earners, because it provided their families less protection than it provided the families of male wage earners. Counsel had also argued that the law discriminated against men as parents, because it did not afford them the same opportunity as women to care personally for their children. Justice Rehnquist resisted both arguments, but he was satisfied that the baby had been treated arbitrarily. He wrote: "It is irrational to distinguish between mothers and fathers when the sole question is whether a child of a deceased contributing worker should have the opportunity to receive the full-time attention of the only parent remaining to it."

David Shapiro had not missed the *Wiesenfeld* case. As he wrote to me, he had an index card on Justice Rehnquist's atypical opinion. But those were pre-PC days. Professor Shapiro had simply mislaid or overlooked the card when time came to report the results of his research.

Another surprise. In June 1996, I announced the judgment and opinion of the Court in the *Virginia Military Institute* case. Reading the opinions below and the briefs in preparation for oral argument, I feared that the Chief would not share my view of the case. To my delight, he concurred in the judgment, persuaded that Virginia offered a valuable educational opportunity for men and no equivalent opportunity for women. Justice Scalia was the lone dissenter and directed many arrows at the Chief's opinion that might otherwise have elevated the number he aimed in my direction.

Chief Justice Rehnquist regarded an independent judiciary as our country's hallmark and pride. In his annual reports on the state of the federal judiciary, and in his public addresses, he urged Congress to safeguard that independence by resisting measures aimed to curtail Third Branch authority.

A personal note. True to his heritage, the Chief sometimes seemed a model of Nordic cool. But I have seen firsthand his humane qualities. Six years ago, in my yearlong bout with colorectal cancer, he helped allay my anxieties. He kept my assignments light during the most trying weeks and let me decide when I could tackle more challenging cases. Coping with cancer himself last Term, his courage and determination were exemplary, inspiring others battling debilitating diseases to carry on with their lives and work as best they can. His best was awesome. He wrote a fair share of the Court's opinions last Term, and kept as firm control as ever in managing the Court's conferences and operations.

William Hubbs Rehnquist was the sixteenth Chief Justice, and the third Associate Justice to be elevated to the center chair. Describing his office, and the performances of the first fourteen Chief Justices, he said in an April 2002 address:

> The Chief Justice [in contrast to the president] brings to office no one but himself. He takes his seat with eight Associate Justices who are there already, and who are in no way indebted to him. By historic usage, he presides over the Court in open session, presides over the Court's conferences, and assigns the preparation of opinions in cases pending before the Court if he has voted with the majority. He also speaks on behalf of the federal judiciary in matters which pertain to it. . . . Perhaps the best description of the office is to say that the Chief Justice has placed in his hands some of the tools which will enable him to be primus among the pares but his stature will depend on how he uses them.

In his leadership of the U.S. Judicial Conference and his superintendence of the Supreme Court, Chief Justice Rehnquist used to great effect the tools Congress and tradition entrusted to him. In his management of the Third Branch, he earned the enduring appreciation of all who care about the health and welfare of the Federal Courts and the Federal System.

4

The Madison Lecture

Speaking in a Judicial Voice*

Introduction

The Madison Lecture series has exposed and developed two main themes: human rights and the administration of justice, particularly in our nation's federal courts.[1] My remarks touch on both themes; I will speak first about collegiality in style, and next, about moderation in the substance of appellate decisionmaking. My views on these matters reflect experiences over a span of three decades. They have been shaped from my years as a law teacher beginning in the 1960s, through the 1970s when I helped to launch the American Civil Liberties Union's Women's Rights Project, and most recently during the nearly thirteen years I have had the good fortune to serve on the United States Court of Appeals for the District of Columbia Circuit. What I hope to convey about courts, I believe, is in line with the founders'—Madison's and Hamilton's—expectation. As a preface, I will comment on that expectation.

James Madison's forecast still brightens the spirit of federal judges. In his June 1789 speech introducing to Congress the amendments that led to the Bill of Rights, Madison urged:

---

*This article, first published in 67 *New York University Law Review* 1185 (1992), originated as the twenty-fourth James Madison Lecture on Constitutional Law at New York University School of Law on March 9, 1993. Justice Ginsburg acknowledges with appreciation the assistance of her 1992–93 Term law clerks, David Ellen and Malla Pollack, in the preparation of the lecture and this article.

> If [a Bill of Rights is] incorporated into the Constitution, independent tribunals of justice will consider themselves in a peculiar manner the guardians of those rights; they will be an impenetrable bulwark . . . naturally led to resist every encroachment upon rights . . . stipulated for in the Constitution by the declaration of rights.[2]

Today's independent tribunals of justice are faithful to that "original understanding" when they adhere to traditional ways courts have realized the expectation Madison expressed.

In *The Federalist* No. 78, Alexander Hamilton said that federal judges, in order to preserve the people's rights and privileges, must have authority to check legislation and acts of the executive for constitutionality.[3] But he qualified his recognition of that awesome authority. The judiciary, Hamilton wrote, from the very nature of its functions, will always be "the least dangerous" branch of government, for judges hold neither the sword nor the purse of the community; ultimately, they must depend upon the political branches to effectuate their judgments.[4] Mindful of that reality, the effective judge, I believe and will explain why in these remarks, strives to persuade, and not to pontificate. She speaks in "a moderate and restrained" voice,[5] engaging in a dialogue with, not a diatribe against, coequal departments of government, state authorities, and even her own colleagues.

I spoke of the founders' "original understanding" a moment ago, and that expression, as I comprehend it, bears clarification in this preface. In his 1987 foreword to *The Evolving Constitution*, the second collection of Madison Lectures, Norman Dorsen stressed, as Chief Justice John Marshall did in 1819, that our fundamental instrument of government is an evolving document, "an instrument 'intended to endure for ages to come.'"[6] Professor Dorsen quoted Chief Justice Charles Evans Hughes' 1934 rejection of the notion that "the great clauses of the Constitution must be confined to the interpretation which the framers, with the conditions and outlook of their time, would have placed upon them."[7] That understanding, as Professor Dorsen commented, has been and should remain common ground.[8]

In the recent decade and more of bicentennial celebrations, Supreme Court Justice Thurgood Marshall reminded us that while the Constitution's endurance is indeed something to celebrate, the framers had a distinctly limited vision of those who counted among "We the People."[9] Qualified voters when the nation was new bore more than a passing resemblance to the framers: the franchise was confined to property-owning adult white males, people free from dependence on others, and therefore considered trustworthy citizens, not susceptible to influence or control by masters, overlords, or supervisors.[10] In 1787, only five of the thirteen states had abolished slavery, women did not count as part of the franchise-holding, politically active community in any state, and wealth qualifications severely limited voter eligibility even among white males.[11] In correspondence with a friend about the qualifications for voting in his home state of Massachusetts, patriot and second president John Adams elaborated:

> [I]t is dangerous to open so fruitful a source of controversy and altercation as would be opened by attempting to alter the qualifications of voters; there will be no end of it. New claims will arise; women will demand a vote; lads from twelve to twenty-one will think their rights not enough attended to; and every man who has not a farthing, will demand an equal voice with any other, in all acts of state. It tends to confound and destroy all distinctions, and prostrate all ranks to one common level.[12]

Our second president notwithstanding, equalizing voices and destroying rank distinctions have been dominant concerns in recent generations and, as one would expect, the focus of several Madison Lectures.[13] Although the word *equal*, or *equality*, in relation to individual rights does not even appear in the original U.S. Constitution or in the first ten amendments that compose the Bill of Rights,[14] the equal dignity of individuals ideal is part of our constitutional legacy, even of the pre–Civil War original understanding, in this vital sense. The founding fathers rebelled against the patriarchal power of kings and the idea that political authority may legitimately rest on birth status. Their culture held them back from fully perceiving or acting upon ideals of human equality and dignity. Thomas Jefferson, for example, when president, told his secretary of the treasury: "The appointment of a woman to public office is an innovation for which the public is not prepared, nor am I."[15] But the founders stated a commitment in the Declaration of Independence to equality and in the Declaration and the Bill of Rights to individual liberty. Those commitments had growth potential. As historian Richard Morris has written, a prime portion of the history of the U.S. Constitution is the story of the extension (through amendment, judicial interpretation, and practice) of constitutional rights and protections to once-excluded groups: to people who were once held in bondage, to men without property, to Native Americans, and to women.[16]

I. Collegiality in Appellate Decisionmaking

I turn now to the first of the two topics this lecture addresses—the style of judging appropriate for appellate judges whose mission it is, in Hamilton's words, "to secure a steady, upright, and impartial administration of the laws."[17] Integrity, knowledge, and, most essentially, judgment are the qualities Hamilton ascribed to the judiciary.[18] How is that essential quality, judgment, conveyed in the opinions appellate judges write? What role should moderation, restraint, and collegiality play in the formulation of judicial decisions? As background, I will describe three distinct patterns of appellate opinion-casting: individual, institutional, and in-between.[19]

The individual judging pattern has been characteristic of the Law Lords, who serve as Great Britain's Supreme Court. The Lords sit in panels of five and, traditionally, have delivered opinions seriatim, each panel member, in turn, announcing his individual judgment and the reasons for it.[20]

In contrast to the British tradition of opinions separately rendered by each judge as an individual, the continental or civil law traditions typified and spread abroad by France and Germany call for collective, corporate judgments. In dispositions of that genre, disagreement is not disclosed. Neither dissent nor separate concurrence is published. Cases are decided with a single, per curiam opinion generally following a uniform, anonymous style.[21]

Our Supreme Court, when John Marshall became Chief Justice, made a start in the institutional opinion direction. Marshall is credited with establishing the practice of announcing judgments in a single opinion for the Court.[22] The Marshall Court, and certainly its leader, had a strong sense of institutional mission, a mission well served by unanimity. Marshall was criticized, in those early days, for suppressing dissent. Thomas Jefferson complained: "An opinion is huddled up in conclave, perhaps by a majority of one, delivered as if unanimous, and with the silent acquiescence of lazy or timid associates, by a crafty chief judge, who sophisticates the law to his own mind, by the turn of his own reasoning."[23]

But even Marshall, during his long tenure as Chief Justice, ultimately dissented on several occasions and once concurred with a separate opinion.[24] We continue in that middle way today. Our appellate courts generally produce a judgment or opinion for the court. In that respect, we bear some resemblance to the highly institution-minded civil law judges, although our judges individually claim authorship of most of the opinions they publish. In tune with the British or common law tradition, however, we place no formal limit on the prerogative of each judge to speak out separately.

To point up the difference between individual and institutional modes of judging, I have drawn upon a 1989 letter from a civilian jurist.[25] The letter came from a member of the Conseil d'Etat, the illustrious body created by Napoleon that still serves, among other functions, as Supreme Administrative Court for France. The conseiller who wrote to me had observed, together with several of his colleagues, an appellate argument in the District of Columbia Circuit.

1
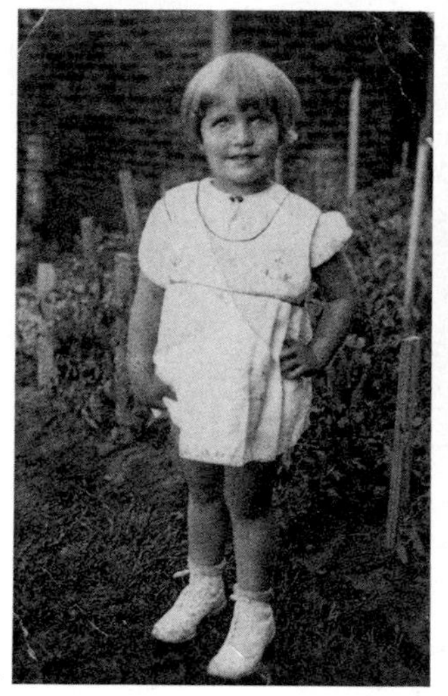

Photograph of Ruth Bader taken when she was two years old.

2

Ruth Bader walks down the aisle as the maid of honor at the wedding of her cousin Seymour "Si" Bessen and Roslyn Bessen, October, 1951.

3

Teenage cousins Ruth and Richard Bader skiing at Balfour Lake Lodge in the Adirondacks, circa 1946.

4

Professional bridal photograph of Ruth Bader taken in June 1954.

5

Columbia Law Professor Ruth Bader Ginsburg, photographed in the spring of 1980 shortly after President Carter nominated her for the U.S. Court of Appeals for the District of Columbia Circuit.

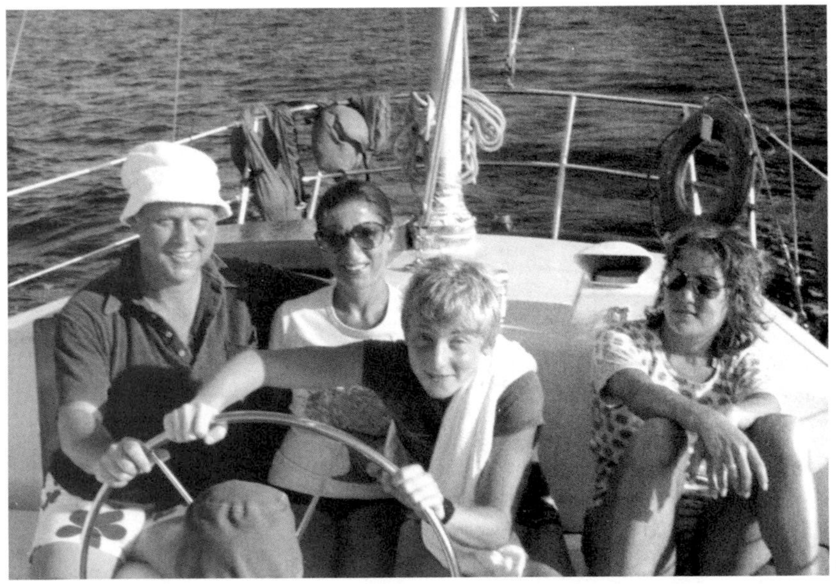

6

Ruth Bader Ginsburg, her husband, Martin Ginsburg, and their children, James and Jane, off the shore of St. Thomas in the Virgin Islands, December 1979.

7

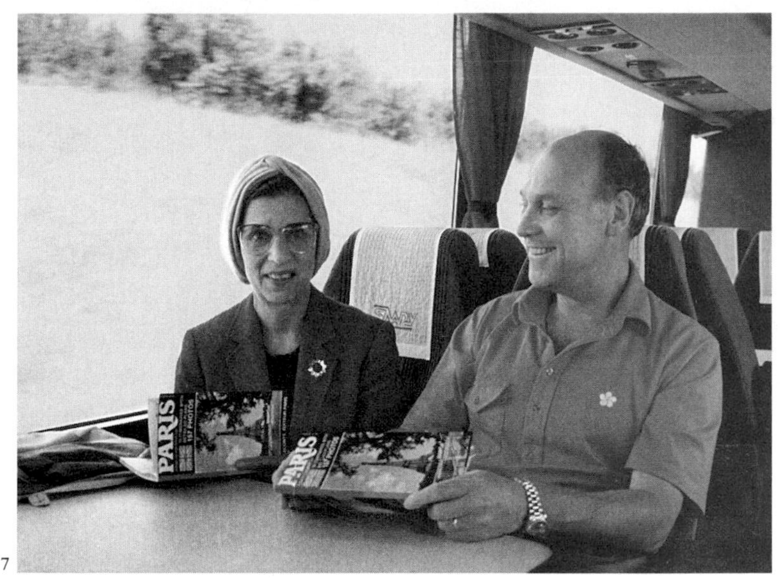

Ruth Bader Ginsburg and Marty Ginsburg travel by bus from Charles de Gaulle Airport to downtown Paris, circa 1988.

8

Marty Ginsburg in his office at Fried, Frank law firm in Washington, D.C., in August 2004.

9

Ruth Bader Ginsburg on the steps of the Supreme Court on November 1, 1978, following the oral arguments for *Duren v. Missouri*, the last case she argued before the Court. Son James Ginsburg is on the right, and brother-in-law and nephew Ed and David Stiepleman are on the left.

10

Official informal group photograph of the Supreme Court as composed under Chief Justice William H. Rehnquist, taken in the West Conference Room on December 3, 1993. Seated in the chair on the left is Justice John Paul Stevens and in the chair on the right is Justice Harry A. Blackmun. Standing from left to right are Justices Clarence Thomas, Antonin Scalia, Chief Justice Rehnquist, and Justices Sandra Day O'Connor, Anthony M. Kennedy, David Souter and Ruth Bader Ginsburg.

President Obama and Justice Ginsburg hug one another at the State of the Union Address, February 24, 2009. 11

12 Justice Ginsburg with President Barack Obama and First Lady Michelle Obama at the White House.

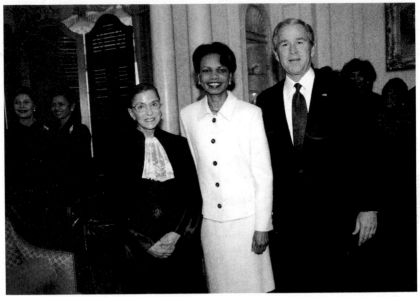

12

Justice Ginsburg with President George W. Bush and Secretary of State Condoleezza Rice at the Department of State on January 28, 2005, the day Justice Ginsburg swore Rice in as Secretary of State.

13

Justice Ginsburg meets with a Buddhist abbot at the Lingyin Temple in Hangzhou, Zhejiang Province, during a 2005 trip to China.

14

Formal group photograph of the Supreme Court as comprised from 2010 until Justice Scalia's death on February 13, 2016. The Justices are posed in front of red velvet drapes and arranged by seniority, with five seated and four standing. Seated from left are Justices Clarence Thomas and Antonin Scalia, Chief Justice John G. Roberts, Jr., and Justices Anthony M. Kennedy and Ruth Bader Ginsburg. Standing from left are Justices Sonia Sotomayor, Stephen G. Breyer, Samuel A. Alito, and Elena Kagan.

15

A photograph of Justice Ginsburg's family taken in the East Conference Room of the Supreme Court following the wedding ceremony of her son, James Ginsburg to Patrice Michaels. Standing, from left to right: George Spera, Clara Spera, Paul Spera, Jane Ginsburg. Seated, from left to right: Satinder Bedi, Justice Ginsburg, James Ginsburg, Patrice Michaels, Harjinder Bedi. Seated on the floor, from left to right: Abigail Ginsburg, Miranda Ginsburg.

16

The only women who have become Supreme Court Justices pose in the Justices' Conference Room on October 1, 2010, the day of Justice Elena Kagan's investiture. Standing, from left to right, are retired Justice Sandra Day O'Connor and Justices Sonia Sotomayor, Ruth Bader Ginsburg, and Elena Kagan.

The appeal was from a criminal conviction; the prime issue concerned the Fifth Amendment's double jeopardy ban.[26] When the case was decided, I sent our French visitors copies of the slip sheet. It contained the panel's judgment, and three opinions, one per judge. I paraphrase the conseiller's reaction:

> The way the decision is given is surprising for us according to our standards. The discussion of theory and of the meaning of precedents is remarkable. But the divided opinions seem to me very far from the way a judgment should issue, particularly in a criminal case. The judgment of a court should be precise and concise, not a discourse among professors, but the order of people charged to speak in the name of the law, and therefore written with simplicity and clarity, presenting short explanations. A judgment that is too long indicates uncertainty.
>
> At the same time, it is very impressive for me to see members of a court give to the litigants and to the readers the content of their hesitations and doubts, without diminishing the credibility of justice, in which the American is so confident.[27]

The conseiller seems at first distressed, even appalled, at our readiness to admit that legal judgments (including constitutional rulings) are not always clear and certain. In his second thought, however, the conseiller appears impressed, touched with envy or admiration, that our system of justice is so secure, we can tolerate open displays of disagreement among judges about what the law is.[28]

But overindulgence in separate opinion writing may undermine both the reputation of the judiciary for judgment and the respect accorded court dispositions. Rule of law virtues of consistency, predictability, clarity, and stability may be slighted when a court routinely fails to act as a collegial body.[29] Dangers to the system are posed by two tendencies: too frequent resort to separate opinions and the immoderate tone of statements diverging from the position of the court's majority.

Regarding the first danger, recall that "the Great Dissenter," Justice Oliver Wendell Holmes, in fact dissented less often than most of his colleagues.[30] Chief Justice Harlan F. Stone once wrote to Karl Llewellyn (both gentlemen were public defenders of the right to dissent): "You know, if I should write in every case where I do not agree with some of the views expressed in the opinions, you and all my other friends would stop reading my separate opinions."[31] In matters of statutory interpretation, Justice Louis D. Brandeis repeatedly cautioned: "It is more important that the applicable rule of law be settled than that it be settled right." "This is commonly true," Brandeis continued, "even where the error is a matter of serious concern, provided correction can be had by legislation."[32] Revered constitutional scholar Paul A. Freund, who clerked for Justice Brandeis, recalled Justice Cardozo's readiness to suppress his dissent in common law cases (the Supreme Court had more of those in pre-*Erie*[33] days), so that an opinion would come down unanimous.[34]

Separate concurrences and dissents characterize Supreme Court decisions to a much greater extent than they do court of appeals three-judge panel decisions. In the District of Columbia Circuit, for example, for the statistical year ending June 1992, the court rendered 405 judgments in cases not disposed of summarily; over 86 percent of those decisions were unanimous.[35] During that same period, the Supreme Court decided 114 cases with full opinions; only 21.9 percent of the decisions were unanimous.[36] A reality not highlighted by a press fond of separating Carter from Reagan/Bush appointees[37] accounts in considerable measure for this difference: the character of cases heard by courts of appeals combines with our modus operandi to tug us strongly toward the middle, toward moderation and away from notably creative or excessively rigid positions.[38] (The tug is not so strong, however, as to make a proposal I recently advanced acceptable. At a meeting of U.S. court of appeals judges in February 1993, I suggested that when panels are unanimous, the standard practice should be to issue the decision per curiam, without disclosing the opinion writer. That would encourage brevity, I thought, and might speed up dispositions. Few of the judges in attendance found the idea appealing.)

Concerning the character of federal cases, unlike the Supreme Court, courts of appeals deal far less frequently with grand constitutional questions than with less cosmic questions of statutory interpretation or the rationality of agency or district court decisions. In most matters of that variety, as Justice Brandeis indicated, it is best that the matter be definitively settled,[39] preferably with one opinion. Furthermore, lower court judges are bound more tightly by Supreme Court precedent than is the High Court itself.

Turning to the way we operate, I note first that no three-judge panel in a circuit is at liberty to depart from the published decision of a prior panel; law of the circuit may be altered only by the court en banc.[40] To ensure that each panel knows what the others are doing, the District of Columbia Circuit, and several other federal circuit courts of appeals, circulate opinions to the full court, once approved by a panel, at least a week in advance of release.[41]

Second, in contrast to district judges, who are the real power holders in the federal court system—lords of their individual fiefdoms from case filing to first instance final judgment—no single court of appeals judge can carry the day in any case. To attract a second vote and establish durable law for the circuit, a judge may find it necessary to moderate her own position, sometimes to be less bold, other times to be less clear.[42] We can listen to and persuade each other in groups of three more effectively than can a larger panel.

On the few occasions each year when we sit en banc—in the District of Columbia Circuit, all twelve of us when we are full strength—I can appreciate why unanimity is so much harder to achieve in Supreme Court judgments. Not only do the Justices deal much more often with constitutional questions, where, in many cases, only overruling or constitutional amendment can correct a mistake. In addition, one becomes weary after going round the table on a first ballot. It is ever so much easier to have a conversation—and an exchange of views on opinion drafts—among three than among nine or twelve.[43]

In writing for the court, one must be sensitive to the sensibilities and mind-sets of one's colleagues, which may mean avoiding certain arguments and authorities, even certain words.[44] Should institutional concerns affect the tone of separate opinions, when a judge finds it necessary to write one?

I emphasize first that dissents and separate concurrences are not consummations devoutly to be avoided. As Justice William J. Brennan said in thoughtful defense of dissents: "None of us, lawyer or layman, teacher or student, in our society must ever feel that to express a conviction, honestly and sincerely maintained, is to violate some unwritten law of manners or decorum."[45] I question, however, resort to expressions in separate opinions that generate more heat than light. Consider this sample from an April 1991 District of Columbia Circuit decision. The dissenter led off: "Running headlong from the questions briefed and argued before us, my colleagues seek refuge in a theory as novel as it is questionable. Unsupported by precedent, undeveloped by the court, and unresponsive to the facts of this case, the . . . theory announced today has an inauspicious birth."[46] That spicy statement, by the way, opposed an en banc opinion in which all of the judges concurred, except the lone dissenter.

It is "not good for public respect for courts and law and the administration of justice," Roscoe Pound decades ago observed, for an appellate judge to burden an opinion with "intemperate denunciation of [the writer's] colleagues, violent invective, attributi[on]s of bad motives to the majority of the court, and insinuations of incompetence, negligence, prejudice, or obtuseness of [other judges]."[47] Yet one has only to thumb through the pages of current volumes of United States Reports and Federal Reporter Second to come upon condemnations by the score of a court or colleague's opinion or assertion as, for example, "folly,"[48] "ludicrous,"[49] "outrageous,"[50] one that "cannot be taken seriously,"[51] "inexplicable,"[52] "the quintessence of inequity,"[53] a "blow against the People,"[54] "naked analytical bootstrapping,"[55] "reminiscent . . . of Sherman's march through Georgia,"[56] and "Orwellian."[57]

"[L]anguage impugning the motives of a colleague," Senior Third Circuit Judge Collins J. Seitz recently commented, may give momentary satisfaction to the separate opinion writer, but "does nothing to further cordial relationships on the court."[58] Judge Seitz counseled "waiting a day"—I would suggest even a week or two—"before deciding whether to send a biting response."[59]

The most effective dissent, I am convinced, "stand[s] on its own legal footing";[60] it spells out differences without jeopardizing collegiality or public respect for and confidence in the judiciary. I try to write my few separate opinions each year as I once did briefs for appellees—as affirmative statements of my reasons, drafted before receiving the court's opinion, and later adjusted, as needed, to meet the majority's presentation. Among pathmarking models, one can look to Justice Curtis' classic dissent in the *Dred Scott* case,[61] and, closer to our time, separate opinions by the second Justice John Marshall Harlan.[62]

Taking a comparative sideglance, I find instructive the March 5, 1992, judgment of the Supreme Court of Ireland in the case of *Attorney General v. X.*[63] The case involved a fourteen-year-old girl who, it was alleged, had been raped by the father of a school friend and had become pregnant. She and her parents had gone to England to secure an abortion. But they promptly returned home when notified that the attorney general had obtained an order from the High Court (the court of first instance) in Ireland enjoining their travel and its purpose. At issue was a clause of the Constitution of Ireland that read: "The State acknowledges the right to life of the unborn and, with due regard to the equal right to life of the mother, guarantees in its laws to respect, and, as far as practicable, by its laws to defend and vindicate that right."[64]

In fact, no implementing laws had been passed, so the courts were called upon to interpret the Constitution directly. The Supreme Court, composed of five judges, voted four to one to set aside the High Court's February 17, 1992, injunction.[65] Each judge spoke separately, but the majority agreed that, in view of the documented "real and substantial" risk that the girl would take her own life, termination of her pregnancy was permissible, even in Ireland itself. In so ruling, the Chief Justice referred to precedent calling upon judges to bring to bear on their judgments the instruction in the Constitution's preamble that the fundamental instrument of government was adopted by the people "to promote the common good, with due observance of prudence, justice and charity so that the dignity and freedom of the individual might be assured."[66] Those concepts and judicial interpretations of them, the Chief Justice said, "may gradually change or develop as society changes and develops."[67]

The dissenting Justice spent no energy characterizing his colleagues' opinions as "activist" or "imperial."[68] He simply stated affirmatively his view that the evidence did not justify overturning the injunction.[69] "Suicide threats," he reasoned, "can be contained."[70] "The choice," he said, was "between the certain death of the unborn life and a feared substantial danger . . . but no degree of certainty of the mother's death by way of self-destruction."[71] The Constitution's "equal right" provision, he concluded, required the judiciary to prevent the certain death, not the one that could be guarded against.

I did not select this example as a springboard to comparison of positions on access to abortion under constitutional prescriptions and legal regimes here and abroad.[72] I chose *Attorney General v. X* only to demonstrate that even in the most emotion-laden, politically sensitive case, effective opinion writing does not require a judge to upbraid colleagues for failing to see the light or to get it right.[73]

Concerned about the erosion of civility in the legal profession, the Seventh Circuit, commencing in the fall of 1989, conducted a "study and investigation into litigation practices and the attending relationships among lawyers, among judges, and between lawyers and judges."[74] The Final Report of the committee in charge of the study, released in June 1992, urges judges to set a good example by staying on the high ground. Specifically, the report calls on judges to avoid "disparaging personal remarks or criticisms, or sarcastic or demeaning comments about another judge," and instead to "be courteous, respectful, and civil in opinions, ever mindful that a position articulated by another judge generally is the result of that judge's earnest effort to interpret the law and the facts correctly."[75] To that good advice, one can say "amen."

II. Measured Motions in Third Branch Decisionmaking

Moving from the style to the substance of Third Branch decisionmaking, I will stress in the remainder of these remarks that judges play an interdependent part in our democracy. They do not alone shape legal doctrine but, as I suggested at the outset, they participate in a dialogue with other organs of government, and with the people as well.[76] "Judges do and must legislate," Justice Holmes "recognized without hesitation," but "they can do so," he cautioned, "only interstitially; they are confined from molar to molecular motions."[77] Measured motions seem to me right, in the main, for constitutional as well as common law adjudication. Doctrinal limbs too swiftly shaped, experience teaches, may prove unstable.[78] The most prominent example in recent decades is *Roe v. Wade.*[79] To illustrate my point, I have contrasted that breathtaking 1973 decision with the Court's more cautious dispositions, contemporaneous with *Roe*, in cases involving explicitly sex-based classifications,[80] and will further develop that comparison here.

The seven-to-two judgment in *Roe v. Wade*[81] declared "violative of the Due Process Clause of the Fourteenth Amendment" a Texas criminal abortion statute that intolerably shackled a woman's autonomy; the Texas law "excepted from criminality only a *life-saving* procedure on behalf of the pregnant woman."[82] Suppose the Court had stopped there, rightly declaring unconstitutional the most extreme brand of law in the nation, and had not gone on, as the Court did in *Roe*, to fashion a regime blanketing the subject, a set of rules that displaced virtually every state law then in force.[83] Would there have been the twenty-year controversy we have witnessed, reflected most recently in the Supreme Court's splintered decision in *Planned Parenthood v. Casey*?[84] A less encompassing *Roe*, one that merely struck down the extreme Texas law and went no further on that day, I believe and will summarize why, might have served to reduce rather than to fuel controversy.

In the 1992 *Planned Parenthood* decision, the three controlling Justices accepted as constitutional several restrictions on access to abortion that could not have survived strict adherence to *Roe.*[85] While those Justices did not closely consider the plight of women without means to overcome the restrictions, they added an important strand to the Court's opinions on abortion—they acknowledged the intimate connection between a woman's "ability to control her reproductive life" and her "ability . . . to participate equally in the economic and social life of the Nation."[86] The idea of the woman in control of her destiny and her place in society[87] was less prominent in the *Roe* decision itself, which coupled with the rights of the pregnant woman the free exercise of her physician's medical judgment.[88] The *Roe* decision might have been less of a storm center[89] had it both homed in more precisely on the women's equality dimension of the issue and, correspondingly, attempted nothing more bold at that time than the mode of decisionmaking the Court employed in the 1970s gender classification cases.

In fact, the very Term *Roe* was decided, the Supreme Court had on its calendar a case that could have served as a bridge, linking reproductive choice to disadvantageous treatment of women on the basis of their sex. The case was *Struck v. Secretary of Defense*;[90] it involved a captain the Air Force sought to discharge in Vietnam War days. Perhaps it is indulgence in wishful thinking, but the *Struck* case, I believe, would have proved extraordinarily educational for the Court and had large potential for advancing public understanding. Captain Susan Struck was a career officer. According to her commanding officer, her performance as a manager and nurse was exemplary.[91] Captain Struck had avoided the drugs and the alcohol that hooked many service members in the late 1960s and early 1970s,[92] but she did become pregnant while stationed in Vietnam. She undertook to use, and in fact used, only her accumulated leave time for childbirth. She declared her intention to place, and in fact placed, her child for adoption immediately after birth. Her religious faith precluded recourse to abortion.[93]

Two features of Captain Struck's case are particularly noteworthy. First, the rule she challenged was unequivocal and typical of the time. It provided: "A woman officer will be discharged from the service with the least practicable delay when a determination is made by a medical officer that she is pregnant."[94] To cover any oversight, the Air Force had a backup rule: "The commission of any woman officer will be terminated with the least practicable delay when it is established that she . . . has given birth to a living child while in a commissioned officer status."[95]

A second striking element of Captain Struck's case was the escape route available to her, which she chose not to take. Air Force regulations current at the start of the 1970s provided: "The Air Force Medical Service is not subject to State laws in the performance of its functions. When medically indicated or for reasons involving medical health, pregnancies may be terminated in Air Force hospitals . . . ideally before 20 weeks gestation."[96]

Captain Struck argued that the unwanted discharge she faced unjustifiably restricted her personal autonomy and dignity; principally, however, she maintained that the regulation mandating her discharge violated the equal protection of the laws guarantee implicit in the Fifth Amendment's Due Process Clause.[97] She urged that the Air Force regime differentiated invidiously by allowing males who became fathers, but not females who became mothers, to remain in service and by allowing women who had undergone abortions, but not women who delivered infants, to continue their military careers.[98] Her pleas were unsuccessful in the lower courts, but on October 24, 1972, less than three months before the *Roe* decision, the Supreme Court granted her petition for certiorari.[99]

At that point the Air Force decided it would rather switch than fight. At the end of November 1972, it granted Captain Struck a waiver of the once-unwaivable regulation and permitted her to continue her service as an Air Force officer. The solicitor general promptly and successfully suggested that the case had become moot.[100]

Given the parade of cases on the Court's full calendar, it is doubtful that the Justices trained further attention on the *Struck* scenario. With more time and space for reflection, however, and perhaps a female presence on the Court, might the Justices have gained at least these two insights? First, if even the military, an institution not known for avant-garde policy, had taken to providing facilities for abortion, then was not a decision of *Roe*'s muscularity unnecessary? Second, confronted with Captain Struck's unwanted discharge, might the Court have comprehended an argument, or at least glimpsed a reality, it later resisted—that disadvantageous treatment of a woman because of her pregnancy and reproductive choice is a paradigm case of discrimination on the basis of sex?[101] What was the assumption underlying the differential treatment to which Captain Struck was exposed? The regulations that mandated her discharge were not even thinly disguised. They declared, effectively, that responsibility for children disabled female parents, but not male parents, for other work—not for biological reasons, but because society had ordered things that way.[102]

Captain Struck had asked the Court first to apply the highest level of scrutiny to her case, to hold that the sex-based classification she encountered was a "suspect" category for legislative or administrative action.[103] As a fallback, she suggested to the Court an intermediate standard of review, one under which prescriptions that worked to women's disadvantage would gain review of at least heightened, if not the very highest, intensity.[104] In the course of the 1970s, the Supreme Court explicitly acknowledged that it was indeed applying an elevated, labeled "intermediate," level of review to classifications it recognized as sex-based.[105]

Justice O'Connor carefully traced that development in last year's Madison Lecture,[106] and I will recall it only summarily. Until 1971, women did not prevail before the Supreme Court in any case charging unconstitutional sex discrimination.[107] In the years from 1971 to 1982, however, the Court held unconstitutional, as violative of due process or equal protection constraints, a series of state and federal laws that differentiated explicitly on the basis of sex.[108]

The Court ruled in 1973, for example, that married women in the military were entitled to the housing allowance and family medical care benefits that Congress had provided solely for married men in the military.[109] Two years later, the Court held it unconstitutional for a state to allow a parent to stop supporting a daughter once she reached the age of 18, while requiring parental support for a son until he turned 21.[110] In 1975, and again in 1979, the Court declared that state jury-selection systems could not exclude or exempt women as a class.[111] In decisions running from 1975 to 1980, the Court deleted the principal explicitly sex-based classifications in social insurance[112] and workers' compensation schemes.[113] In 1981, the Court said nevermore to a state law designating the husband "head and master" of the household.[114] And in 1982, in an opinion by Justice O'Connor, the Court held that a state could not limit admission to a state nursing college to women only.[115]

The backdrop for these rulings was a phenomenal expansion, in the years from 1961 to 1971, of women's employment outside the home,[116] the civil rights movement of the 1960s and the precedents set in that struggle,[117] and a revived feminist movement, fueled abroad and in the United States by Simone de Beauvoir's remarkable 1949 publication, *The Second Sex*.[118] In the main, the Court invalidated laws that had become obsolete, retained into the 1970s by only a few of the states.[119] In a core set of cases, however, those dealing with social insurance benefits for a worker's spouse or family,[120] the decisions did not utterly condemn the legislature's product. Instead, the Court, in effect, opened a dialogue with the political branches of government. In essence, the Court instructed Congress and state legislatures: rethink ancient positions on these questions. Should you determine that special treatment for women is warranted, i.e., compensatory legislation because of the sunken-in social and economic bias or disadvantage women encounter, we have left you a corridor in which to move.[121] But your classifications must be refined, adopted for remedial reasons, and not rooted in prejudice about "the way women (or men) are."[122] In the meantime, the Court's decrees removed no benefits; instead, they extended to a woman worker's husband, widower, or family benefits Congress had authorized only for members of a male worker's family.[123]

The ball, one might say, was tossed by the Justices back into the legislators' court, where the political forces of the day could operate. The Supreme Court wrote modestly, it put forward no grand philosophy;[124] but by requiring legislative reexamination of once-customary sex-based classifications, the Court helped to ensure that laws and regulations would "catch up with a changed world."[125]

Roe v. Wade,[126] in contrast, invited no dialogue with legislators. Instead, it seemed entirely to remove the ball from the legislators' court. In 1973, when *Roe* issued, abortion law was in a state of change across the nation. As the Supreme Court itself noted, there was a marked trend in state legislatures "toward liberalization of abortion statutes."[127] That movement for legislative change ran parallel to another law revision effort then under way—the change from fault to no-fault divorce regimes, a reform that swept through the state legislatures and captured all of them by the mid-1980s.[128]

No measured motion, the *Roe* decision left virtually no state with laws fully conforming to the Court's delineation of abortion regulation still permissible.[129] Around that extraordinary decision, a well-organized and vocal right-to-life movement rallied and succeeded, for a considerable time, in turning the legislative tide in the opposite direction.

Constitutional review by courts is an institution that has been for some two centuries our nation's hallmark and pride.[130] Two extreme modes of court intervention in social change processes, however, have placed stress on the institution. At one extreme, the Supreme Court steps boldly in front of the political process, as some believe it did in *Roe.*[131] At the opposite extreme, the Court in the early part of the twentieth century found—or thrust—itself into the rear guard opposing change, striking down, as unconstitutional, laws embodying a new philosophy of economic regulation at odds with the nineteenth century's laissez-faire approach.[132] Decisions at both of these poles yielded outcries against the judiciary in certain quarters. The Supreme Court, particularly, was labeled "activist" or "imperial," and its precarious position as final arbiter of constitutional questions was exposed.[133]

I do not suggest that the Court should never step ahead of the political branches in pursuit of a constitutional precept. *Brown v. Board of Education*,[134] the 1954 decision declaring racial segregation in public schools offensive to the equal protection principle, is the case that best fits the bill. Past the midpoint of the twentieth century, apartheid remained the law-enforced system in several states, shielded by a constitutional interpretation the Court itself advanced at the turn of the century—the "separate but equal" doctrine.[135]

In contrast to the legislative reform movement in the states, contemporaneous with *Roe*, widening access to abortion, prospects in 1954 for state legislation dismantling racially segregated schools were bleak. That was so, I believe, for a reason that distances race discrimination from discrimination based on sex. Most women are life partners of men; women bear and raise both sons and daughters. Once women's own consciousness was awakened to the unfairness of allocating opportunity and responsibility on the basis of sex, education of others—of fathers, husbands, sons as well as daughters—could begin, or be reinforced, at home.[136] When blacks were confined by law to a separate sector, there was no similar prospect for educating the white majority.[137]

It bears emphasis, however, that *Brown* was not an altogether bold decision. First, Thurgood Marshall and those who worked with him in the campaign against racial injustice, carefully set the stepping-stones leading up to the landmark ruling.[138] Pathmarkers of the same kind had not been installed prior to the Court's decision in *Roe.*[139]

Second, *Brown* launched no broadside attack on the Jim Crow system in all its institutional manifestations. Instead, the Court concentrated on segregated schools;[140] it left the follow-up for other days and future cases. A burgeoning civil rights movement—which *Brown* helped to propel—culminating in the Civil Rights Act of 1964,[141] set the stage for the Court's ultimate total rejection of Jim Crow legislation.

Significantly, in relation to the point I just made about women and men living together, the end of the Jim Crow era came in 1967, thirteen years after *Brown*: the case was *Loving v. Virginia*,[142] the law under attack, a state prohibition on interracial marriage. In holding that law unconstitutional, the Court effectively ruled that, with regard to racial classifications, the doctrine of "separate but equal" was dead—everywhere and anywhere within the governance of the United States.[143]

The framers of the Constitution allowed to rest in the Court's hands large authority to rule on the Constitution's meaning; but the framers, as I noted at the outset, armed the Court with no swords to carry out its pronouncements. President Andrew Jackson in 1832, according to an often-told legend, said of a Supreme Court decision he did not like: "The Chief Justice has made his decision, now let him enforce it."[144] With prestige to persuade, but not physical power to enforce, with a will for self-preservation and the knowledge that they are not "a bevy of Platonic Guardians,"[145] the Justices generally follow, they do not lead, changes taking place elsewhere in society.[146] But without taking giant strides and thereby risking a backlash too forceful to contain, the Court, through constitutional adjudication, can reinforce or signal a green light for a social change. In most of the post-1970 gender-classification cases, unlike *Roe*, the Court functioned in just that way. It approved the direction of change through a temperate brand of decisionmaking, one that was not extravagant or divisive. *Roe*, on the other hand, halted a political process that was moving in a reform direction and thereby, I believe, prolonged divisiveness and deferred stable settlement of the issue. The most recent *Planned Parenthood* decision[147] notably retreats from *Roe*[148] and further excludes from the High Court's protection women lacking the means or the sophistication to surmount burdensome legislation.[149] The latest decision may have had the sanguine effect, however, of contributing to the ongoing revitalization in the 1980s and 1990s of the political movement in progress in the early 1970s, a movement that addressed not simply or dominantly the courts but primarily the people's representatives and the people themselves. That renewed force, one may hope, will—within a relatively short span—yield an enduring resolution of this vital matter in a way that affirms the dignity and equality of women.[150]

Conclusion

To sum up what I have tried to convey in this lecture, I will recall the counsel my teacher and friend, Professor Gerald Gunther, offered when I was installed as a judge. Professor Gunther had in mind a great jurist, Judge Learned Hand, whose biography Professor Gunther is just now completing. The good judge, Professor Gunther said, is "openminded and detached . . . heedful of limitations stemming from the judge's own competence and, above all, from the presuppositions of our constitutional scheme; th[at] judge . . . recognizes that a felt need to act only interstitially does not mean relegation of judges to a trivial or mechanical role, but rather affords the most responsible room for creative, important judicial contributions."[151]

5

"A Decent Respect to the Opinions of [Human]kind"

The Value of a Comparative Perspective in Constitutional Adjudication*

I have titled this lecture "'A Decent Respect to the Opinions of [Human]kind': The Value of a Comparative Perspective in Constitutional Adjudication." The "Decent Respect" quotation, you likely noticed, comes from our Declaration of Independence. To explain why the thirteen colonies were severing their ties with the British Crown, Thomas Jefferson declared, at some length, the causes for "the Separation." He did so prompted by "a decent Respect to the Opinions of Mankind." The aim was to expose our reasons for becoming the "United States of America" to the scrutiny of "a candid World."

The founding generation recognized that becoming part of the world of nations meant that what we do would be watched in other lands; it also meant that we would become a participant in the formulation, recognition, and enforcement of international law. Thus, Article VI of the Constitution made treaties the supreme law of the

*Justice Ginsburg has delivered numerous versions of these remarks to various audiences over the years, including to students in the Tulane University Law School Summer Program in Paris in July 2013. We have edited the remarks for length and to ensure clarity outside the context in which they were originally delivered.

land, on a par with laws enacted by Congress. And among the powers of Congress enumerated in Article I, §8, the framers specified: "To define and punish . . . Offenses against the Law of Nations." John Jay, first Chief Justice of the United States, expressed the common understanding. He wrote, in 1793, that, "by taking a place among the nations of the earth," the United States had "become amenable to the law of nations." That term, "law of nations," is the core of what we today call international law.

Our fourth, longest-tenured, and supremely eminent Chief Justice, John Marshall, drew a distinction important to comprehend. He distinguished the "law of nations," which binds U.S. courts, and the law and judicial decisions of foreign countries, which do not. In an 1815 decision, Marshall explained that the law of nations is part of the law of our land because of our membership in a world of nations. But decisions of foreign tribunals about their own domestic law are not controlling authority for U.S. courts. Even so, Marshall added, decisions of the courts of other countries merit respectful attention for their potential persuasive value when they address problems similar to those we encounter.

For the most part, in the two centuries since John Marshall headed the U.S. judiciary, both federal and state courts have understood the difference: international law is part of our law; foreign law is not, but we can be informed by how jurists abroad have resolved problems resembling those we face. A comprehensive survey published in 2005 in the *William & Mary Law Review*, running some 166 example-filled pages, shows the considerable extent to which courts in the United States, from the start, have taken account of foreign law and decisions of foreign courts.

I will digress for some personal history. It will help you to understand why what I call "looking beyond our borders" seems to me altogether fitting and proper for lawyers and judges in the United States. Two years out of law school, in 1961, I was hired by the Columbia Law School Project on International Law to coauthor a book on the stirring topic: Civil Procedure in Sweden. The book was part of a series in which a U.S. author teamed with a lawyer from the country whose system was described. Sweden was chosen because, in the 1940s, it had revised its Code of Judicial Procedure, a typically civil law–style code, to infuse what Swedish jurists conceived to be the best of the Anglo-American system. The other two countries examined by the Columbia Project were France and Italy. (The German system had already been described in two comprehensive 1958 articles by Professors Kaplan and von Mehren published in the *Harvard Law Review*.)

I had no familial or other ties to Scandinavia so I wondered, why me? There was a commercial payoff in knowing something about the French and Italian systems, but Sweden had a rather small population, no larger than the population of my hometown, New York City, and the only clear benefit I grasped immediately would be understanding the language spoken in Ingmar Bergman films. I suspect Columbia looked down the list of women graduates (men were engaged to write about French and Italian procedure) and that is how the project came to me.

The work proved enormously enlightening. Not that there was anything in the Swedish system to be borrowed lock, stock, and barrel in the United States. But I came to see our way of doing things in comparative perspective, to understand that what was right for us was not necessarily right for others, but also to appreciate that we had something to learn from foreign systems in endeavors to reform our own modes of procedure. Other informing experiences, I served on the Board of Editors of the *American Journal of Comparative Law* from 1964 until 1972, and participated in meetings of the International Academy of Comparative Law in Hamburg, Uppsala, and, most memorably, Pescara in Abruzzi.

So, in the 1970s, when, as an advocate, I was urging U.S. courts to recognize the equal citizenship stature of men and women as constitutional principle, it seemed to me useful to cast a comparative sideglance. First case in point, *Reed v. Reed*. Decided in 1971, *Reed* was the Supreme Court's turning-point gender discrimination decision. [*For a detailed description of the* Reed *case, which challenged an Idaho law preferring men to women as administrators of the estates of relatives who died without leaving a will, see "Advocating the Elimination of Gender-Based Discrimination: The 1970s New Look at the Equality Principle," p. 154.*]

I referred in the *Reed* brief to two foreign decisions. Both were rulings of the then–West German Constitutional Court. One involved a provision of the German Civil Code stating: when the parents disagree about the education of the child, father decides. The West German Constitutional Court held that provision incompatible with the country's post–World War II constitution, which explicitly recognized the equal citizenship stature of men and women. The second case involved a restraint on succession to large farms. To avoid fragmenting the estate, the law provided that the eldest son would inherit the whole. Never mind that the eldest son had older sisters. That law, too, was held unconstitutional.

I cited the two decisions in the *Reed* brief, never expecting that the Supreme Court would refer to them in its opinion (it didn't), but in part for psychological effect. The message I tried to convey: if this is where the West German Constitutional Court is today in its understanding of equality, how far behind can the U.S. Supreme Court be? Our Court did not remain in the rear. It unanimously declared the Idaho male-preference statute unconstitutional.

Flash forward with me now to the hearings held in July 2010 on the nomination of Elena Kagan for a seat on the U.S. Supreme Court. Queries about international and foreign law were several times posed by members of the Senate Committee on the Judiciary. One senator expressed "dismay" that, during Kagan's tenure as dean of the Harvard Law School, "first year students [were required] to take a course in international law." Another ventured that "[n]owhere did the founders say anything about using foreign law." "[P]lease explain," that senator asked, "why it is OK sometimes to use foreign law to interpret our Constitution or statutes, our treaties." Yet another asked "whether [judges should] ever look to foreign laws for good ideas" or "get inspiration for their decisions from foreign law."

Nominee Kagan responded with her typical good humor: "I'm in favor of good ideas," she said, "wherever you can get them." "Having an awareness of what other nations are doing might be useful," she added. As an example, she referred to a brief she filed that year as solicitor general in a case concerning foreign officials' immunity from suit. Of course, she clarified, on a point of U.S. law, foreign decisions do not rank as precedent, but they could be informative in much the same way as one might gain insight from reading a law review article. "I'm troubled," said a senator dissatisfied with her answer, that she "believes we can turn to foreign law to get good ideas."

It is true that, for much of our history, U.S. courts were virtually alone in exercising judicial review for constitutionality. Most nations adhered to the principle of parliamentary supremacy, which left courts with no role to play in measuring ordinary laws and executive acts against the prescriptions contained in a fundamental instrument of government. But particularly in the years following World War II, many nations installed constitutional review by courts as one safeguard against oppressive government and stirred-up majorities. National, multinational, and international human rights charters and courts today play a prominent part in our twenty-first-century world.

On this development, former Chief Justice Rehnquist wrote in a 1999 foreword to a collection of essays on comparative constitutional law:

> For nearly a century and a half, courts in the United States exercising the power of judicial review [for constitutionality] had no precedents to look to save their own, because our courts alone exercised this sort of authority. When many new constitutional courts were created after the Second World War, these courts naturally looked to decisions of the Supreme Court of the United States, among other sources, for developing their own law. But now that constitutional law is solidly grounded in so many countries . . . it [is] time that the United States courts begin

> looking to the decisions of other constitutional courts to aid in their own deliberative process.

Justice O'Connor spoke to the same point a few years later: "While ultimately we must bear responsibility for interpreting our own laws," she said, "there is much to learn from . . . distinguished jurists [in other places] who have given thought to the same difficult issues that we face here." Exactly right, I believe, and the very point Justice Kagan made when she appeared before the Senate Judiciary Committee.

A related point I would stress. Recall that the founding generation showed concern for how adjudication in our courts would affect other countries' regard for the United States. John Marshall observed in 1816 that the U.S. judiciary would confront cases in which "foreign nations are deeply interested . . . [and] in which the principles of the law and comity of nations often form an essential inquiry." Today, even more than when the United States was a new nation, judgments rendered in the USA are subject to the scrutiny of "a candid World." A most recent example: the media in countries on every continent reported on three decisions announced the very last week of the Supreme Court's 2012–13 Term.

Yes, there have been discordant views on the attention we should pay to the "Opinions of Mankind." A mid-nineteenth-century Chief Justice wrote:

> No one, we presume, supposes that any change in public opinion or feeling . . . in the civilized nations of Europe or in this country, should induce the court to give the words of the Constitution a more liberal construction . . . than they were intended to bear when the instrument was framed and adopted.

Those words were penned in 1856. They appear in Chief Justice Roger Taney's opinion for a divided Court in *Dred Scott v. Sandford*, an opinion that invoked the majestic Due Process Clause to uphold one individual's right to hold another in bondage.

As shown by my quotations from senators' remarks at Justice Kagan's confirmation hearings, U.S. judges and political actors today divide sharply on the propriety of looking beyond our nation's borders, particularly on matters touching fundamental human rights. Expressing spirited opposition, my dear colleague, Justice Antonin Scalia, for example, counsels: The Court "should cease putting forth foreigners' views as part of the reasoned basis of its decisions. To invoke alien law when it agrees with one's own thinking, and ignore it otherwise, is not reasoned decisionmaking, but sophistry." In a 2005 published conversation with Justice Breyer, Justice Scalia said it was all right for Justice Breyer to inform himself on international legal developments, but he should keep the information out of his opinions.

A qualification. In March 2012, in a dissenting opinion, Justice Scalia took aim at a decision extending the right to effective assistance of counsel to plea bargaining. Justice Scalia observed: "In many—perhaps most—countries of the world, American-style plea bargaining is forbidden. . . . In Europe, many countries adhere to what they aptly call the 'legality principle' by requiring prosecutors to charge all prosecutable offenses. . . . Such a system reflects an admirable belief that the law is the law, and those who break it should pay the penalty provided." And on the last opinion hand-down day of the 2012–13 Term, Justice Scalia, dissenting in the Defense of Marriage Act case, cited, comparatively, a provision of Germany's Constitution, Article 93. Scalia observed that the United States Supreme Court cannot "say what the law is" except when necessary to do so to resolve a particular case or controversy. Germany's Constitutional Court, he observed, is not so confined. It can say what the German Basic Law means in contexts other than a lawsuit.

A trenchant critic of comparative sideglances, Seventh Circuit U.S. Court of Appeals Judge Richard Posner commented some years ago: "To cite foreign law as authority is to flirt with the discredited . . . idea of a universal natural law; or to suppose fantastically that the world's judges constitute a single, elite community of wisdom and conscience." Judge Posner's view rests, in part, on the concern that

U.S. judges do not comprehend the social, historical, political, and institutional background from which foreign opinions emerge. Nor do most of us even understand the language in which laws and judgments, outside the common law realm, are written.

Judge Posner is right, of course, to this extent: as Justice Kagan carefully stated in her responses to senators, foreign opinions set no binding precedent for the U.S. judge. But they can add to the store of knowledge relevant to the solution of trying questions. Yes, we should approach foreign legal materials with sensitivity to our differences and imperfect understanding, but imperfection, I believe, should not lead us to abandon the effort to learn what we can from the experience and wisdom foreign sources may convey.

What perplexes me most about the critics of looking beyond our borders is a point Justice Kagan made, in her typically engaging way, when the Senate Judiciary Committee was considering her nomination: Judges in the United States are, without doubt, free to consult all manner of commentary—restatements, treatises, what law professors or even law students write copiously in law reviews, and, in the Internet age, any number of legal blogs. If we can consult those sources, why not the analysis of a question similar to the one we confront contained, for example, in an opinion of the Supreme Court of Canada, the Constitutional Court of South Africa, the Supreme Court of Israel, the German Constitutional Court, or the European Court of Human Rights?

Henry Fielding wrote in one of his novels *(Joseph Andrews)* that examples work more forcibly on the mind than precepts. With that counsel in mind, I will note briefly some fairly recent Supreme Court decisions involving foreign or international legal sources as an aid to the resolution of constitutional questions. In a headline 2002 decision, *Atkins v. Virginia*, a six-member majority (all save the Chief Justice and Justices Scalia and Thomas) held unconstitutional the execution of a mentally retarded offender. The Court noted that "within the world community, the imposition of the death penalty for crimes committed by mentally retarded offenders is overwhelmingly disapproved."

The next year, the Court looked beyond our borders in a case titled *Lawrence v. Texas*. Overruling a 1986 decision, the judgment in *Lawrence* declared unconstitutional a Texas statute that prohibited two adult persons of the same sex from engaging, voluntarily, in intimate sexual conduct. On respect for "the Opinions of [Human]kind," the *Lawrence* Court emphasized: "The right the petitioners seek in this case has been accepted as an integral part of human freedom in many other countries." In support, the Court cited a leading 1981 European Court of Human Rights decision, *Dudgeon v. United Kingdom*, and subsequent European Human Rights Court rulings affirming the protected right of gay and lesbian adults to engage in intimate, consensual conduct. (*Lawrence v. Texas* was featured in the Court's recent decision holding unconstitutional a key provision of the federal Defense of Marriage Act.)

The current Supreme Court has several times shown "a decent respect for the opinions of humankind" in cases arising out of the war on terror. In June 2008, for example, the Court held, in *Boumediene v. Bush*, that Congress acted unconstitutionally when it eliminated federal court jurisdiction to hear petitions for habeas corpus filed by aliens detained at Guantanamo Bay.

The Court had established the groundwork for *Boumediene* in a 2004 decision, *Hamdi v. Rumsfeld*. There, the Court held that the president, acting without congressional authorization, could not order trial of Guantanamo Bay detainees by military commissions. Even in "our most challenging and uncertain moments" when "our Nation's commitment to due process is most severely tested," Justice O'Connor wrote for the four-Justice plurality in *Hamdi*, "we must preserve our commitment at home to the principles for which we fight abroad." "History and common sense," she reminded, "teach us that an unchecked system of detention carries the potential to become a means for oppression and abuse."

Two University of Chicago Law School professors (Eric A. Posner and Adrian Vermeule) promptly published their disagreement with Justice O'Connor's statement. People do not prefer liberty to death, they urged. A government that does not contract civil liberties in face of terrorist threats, they said, "is pathologically rigid, not enlightened." Yet what greater defeat could we suffer than to come to resemble the forces we oppose in their disrespect for human dignity?

I will conclude these illustrations with the Court's March 2005 decision in *Roper v. Simmons*. Holding unconstitutional the execution of persons under the age of eighteen who committed capital crimes, the Court acknowledged "the overwhelming weight of international opinion against the juvenile death penalty." Justice Kennedy wrote for the Court that the opinion of the world community provides "respected and significant confirmation of our own conclusions." "It does not lessen our fidelity to the [U.S.] Constitution," he explained, to recognize "the express affirmation of certain fundamental rights by other nations and peoples." (In a decision rendered last year, the Court held unconstitutional a mandatory sentence of life without the possibility of parole even for juveniles whose crime is murder.)

Recognizing that forecasts are risky, I nonetheless believe the U.S. Supreme Court will continue to accord "a decent Respect to the Opinions of [Human]kind" as a matter of comity and in a spirit of humility. Comity, because projects vital to our well-being—combating international terrorism is a prime example—require trust and cooperation of nations the world over. And humility because, in Justice O'Connor's words: "Other legal systems continue to innovate, to experiment, and to find . . . solutions to the new legal problems that arise each day, [solutions] from which we can learn and benefit."

In this regard, I was impressed by an observation made in September 2003 by Israel's then Chief Justice, Aharon Barak. September 11, he noted, confronts the United States with the dilemma of conducting a war on terrorism without sacrificing the nation's most cherished values, including our respect for human dignity. "We in Israel," Barak said, "have our September 11, and September 12 and so on." He spoke of his own Court's efforts to balance the government's no doubt compelling need to secure the safety of the state and of its citizens on the one hand, and a proper regard for "human dignity and freedom on the other hand." He referred, particularly, to a question presented to his Court: "Is it lawful to use violence [less euphemistically, torture] in interrogat[ing] [a] terrorist in a 'ticking bomb' situation." That is, the police think a person they have arrested knows where and when a bomb will explode. His Court's answer: No, "[n]ever use violence." He elaborated:

> [It] is the fate of a democracy [that] not all means are acceptable to it, . . . not all methods employed by its enemies are open to it. Sometimes, a democracy must fight with one hand tied behind its back. Nonetheless, it has the upper hand. Preserving the rule of law and recognition of individual liberties constitute an important component of [a democracy's] understanding of security. At the end of the day, [those values buoy up] its spirit and strength [and its capacity to] overcome [the] difficulties.

In that opinion, I concur without reservation.

6

Human Dignity and Equal Justice Under Law

Brown v. Board of Education in International Context
Centre for Human Rights*
University of Pretoria, South Africa
February 7, 2006

Although the *Brown* decision did not refer to international law or opinion, there is little doubt that the climate of the era explains, in significant part, why apartheid in America began to unravel in the late 1940s, in the aftermath of World War II. The United States and its Allies had fought, successfully, to destroy Hitler's Holocaust Kingdom and the rank racism that prevailed during the years of Nazi ascendancy in Europe. Yet our own troops, when we entered that war, were racially segregated. In the midst of the war, in 1942, Swedish economist Gunnar Myrdal published *The American Dilemma*, in which he observed: "America, for its international prestige, power and future security, needs to demonstrate to the world that American Negroes can be satisfactorily integrated into its democracy."

Illustrative of the growing awareness as the war progressed, a young rabbi, Roland B. Gittelsohn, then a service chaplain, delivered a eulogy over newly dug graves of U.S. Marines on the Pacific island of Iwo Jima. In words preserved at the Harry S. Truman

---

*Justice Ginsburg has delivered numerous versions of these remarks to various audiences over the years. We have edited the remarks for length and to ensure clarity outside the specific context in which they were originally delivered.

Presidential Library, Rabbi Gittelsohn spoke of the way it was, and the way it should be:

> Here lie men who loved America . . . , officers and men, Negroes and whites, rich men and poor, together. . . . Here no man prefers another because of his faith, or despises him because of his color. . . . Among these men there is no discrimination, no prejudice, no hatred. Theirs is the highest and purest democracy. . . . Whoever of us . . . thinks himself superior to those who happen to be in the minority, makes of this ceremony, and of the bloody sacrifice it commemorates, [a] . . . hollow mockery.
>
> To this, then, as our solemn, sacred duty do we, the living, now dedicate ourselves, to the right of Protestants, Catholics and Jews, of white men and Negroes alike, to enjoy the democracy for which all of them have here paid the price.

The author of the *Brown* decision, Chief Justice Earl Warren, reflected some eighteen years after the 1954 judgment:

> [The reversal of race relation policies in the United States] was fostered primarily by the presence of [World War II] itself. First, the primary enemy of the Allies, Nazi Germany, was perhaps the most conspicuously and brutally racist nation in the history of the world. . . . The segregation and extermination of non-Aryans in Hitler's Germany were shocking for Americans, but they also served as a troublesome analogy. While proclaiming themselves inexorably opposed to Hitler's practices, many Americans were tolerating the segregation and humiliation of nonwhites within their own borders. The contradiction between the egalitarian rhetoric employed against the Nazis and the presence of racial segregation in America was a painful one.

The Cold War between the United States and the Soviet Union was in full sway in 1954, the year *Brown v. Board* was decided. University of Virginia law professor Michael Klarman, author of a monumental 2004 publication, titled *From Jim Crow to Civil Rights*, wrote of the era: "U.S. democracy was on trial, and southern white supremacy was its greatest vulnerability, made all the more conspicuous by the postwar overthrow of colonial regimes throughout the world." President Truman's civil rights committee cautioned: "[T]he United States is not so strong, the final triumph of the democratic ideal is not so inevitable, that we can ignore what the rest of the world thinks of our record."

In an amicus brief for the United States filed in *Brown*, the attorney general urged:

> The existence of discrimination against minority groups in the United States has an adverse effect upon our relations with other countries. Racial discrimination . . . raises doubts even among friendly nations as to the intensity of our devotion to the democratic faith.

The brief included a letter from Secretary of State Dean Acheson on the negative impact of race discrimination upon the conduct of U.S. foreign relations. Acheson wrote:

> The United States is under constant attack in the foreign press, over the foreign radio, and in such international bodies as the United Nations because of various practices of discrimination against minority groups in this country. . . .
>
> [T]he continuance of racial discrimination in the United States remains a source of constant embarrassment to this Government in the day-to-day conduct of its foreign relations; and it jeopardizes the effective maintenance of our moral leadership of the free and democratic nations of the world.

Within an hour of the Chief Justice's announcement of the Court's unanimous conclusion that, "[i]n the field of public education, the doctrine of 'separate but equal' has no place," the Voice of America broadcast the news, in thirty-four languages, around the globe. The U.S. Information Agency promptly placed articles on *Brown* in almost every African journal. *Time* magazine commented: "In many countries, where U.S. prestige and leadership have been damaged by the fact of U.S. segregation, it will come as a timely reassertion of the basic American principle that 'all men are created equal.'" *Newsweek* magazine observed: "[S]egregation in the public schools has become a symbol of inequality. . . . Now that symbol lies shattered."

The press in Western Europe similarly applauded *Brown*. In Paris, *Le Monde* announced on its front page: "This long-awaited judgment marks a victory of justice over racial prejudice, a victory of democracy. . . ." The *Times* of London hailed the decision as "among the most important and far-reaching [the U.S. Supreme Court] has ever handed down." The *Manchester Guardian* expressed "immense relief" that the United States had "put behind it what has long been its worst reproach. . . ." South of the U.S. border, the Municipal Council in São Paulo, Brazil, cheered *Brown* as "establishing the just equality of the races, essential to universal harmony and peace."

In Africa, coverage was extensive. A dispatch from the American Consul in Dakar, Senegal, reported that the decision was "greeted with enthusiasm in French West Africa although the press [there] has expressed some slight skepticism over its implementation." The weekly *Afrique Nouvelle* reported on *Brown* under this headline: "At last! Whites and Blacks in the United States on the same school benches." Black members of Kenya's Legislative Council expressed the hope that their country would follow suit:

> Here in Kenya we are supposed to create one nation of all races. If we are not educated together, we will live in fear of one another. If we are to stay together forever, why should we have separate schools? Children will learn to know each other intimately in the same schools and fear will disappear.

Not all reactions to *Brown* were positive. A dispatch from the U.S. Embassy in South Africa reported: "Most South African Whites are segregationists. . . . [T]hough they may see some similarity in America's color problem, [they] regard their own racial situation as having no true parallel elsewhere. Their interest in the decision, then, would be very academic." But just four years later, British Prime Minister Harold Macmillan spoke out in South Africa's Parliament against apartheid. He referred to the "wind of change" blowing through the continent of Africa—change *Brown* helped to promote.

Massive resistance to *Brown* mounted in the South of the United States in the late 1950s, continuing into the 1960s. Foreign publications took note. Despite, or perhaps because of, the southern defiance, the world recognized that the U.S. Supreme Court had stepped ahead of the country's political branches (Congress and the president) and prevailing views in many states in pursuit of equal justice under law.

The pursuit of equal justice under law became a major part of the international human rights agenda. In 1965, the United Nations presented for ratification the International Convention on the Elimination of all Forms of Racial Discrimination. Signed by 180 states as of January 2006, and at last ratified by the United States in 1994, the Convention provides that the State Parties "particularly condemn racial segregation and apartheid and undertake to prevent, prohibit and eradicate all practices of this nature in territories under their jurisdiction."

Of the enduring legacy of *Brown*, Richard Goldstone, retired Justice of the South African Constitutional Court, and Brian Ray, Justice Goldstone's 2003 term foreign law clerk, wrote that *Brown* had demonstrated "the ability of courts to promote human rights and [of] lawyers to effect social change." Goldstone and Ray referred to decisions in Canada, South Africa, and Trinidad and Tobago citing *Brown* on the importance of education and equal access to it in a democratic society. Those authors also noted cases in New Zealand and South Africa citing *Brown* on the power of courts to "issu[e] orders that would impact budget decisions," orders that might require continuing court surveillance.

On a personal note, *Brown* and its forerunners, along with the movement for international human rights that ensued, powerfully influenced the women's rights litigation in the USA in which I was engaged in the 1970s. Thurgood Marshall and his coworkers sought to educate the U.S. Supreme Court, step by step, about the pernicious effects of race discrimination. Similarly, advocates for gender equality sought to inform the Court, through a series of cases, about the injustice of laws ordering or reinforcing separate spheres of human activity for men and women. The ACLU's Women's Rights Project, which I helped to launch and direct, was among the organizations inspired by the NAACP Legal Defense and Education Fund's example.

Advocates of equal citizenship stature for men and women laboring in the 1970s, of course, did not encounter the brand of opposition Thurgood Marshall and his aides experienced in his years at the helm of the NAACP's Legal Defense and Education Fund. Our lives were never in danger because of our advocacy, and we had no problem finding accommodations when we were litigating cases out of town. But of one thing there was no doubt. We gained courage and inspiration from the litigation campaign that led to and followed *Brown*. We copied the strategy of educating judicial audiences in measured movements, in ways digestible by, and palatable to, the decisionmakers.

Brown figured several years ago in a typically fine decision by Israel's Chief Justice, Aharon Barak. The Israel Land Administration had denied the asserted right of Arabs to build their homes on land in Israel open to the general public for home construction. The administration defended reservation of permission to build to non-Arab applicants on the promise that it would allocate land to establish an exclusively Arab communal settlement. Citing *Brown*, the Israeli Supreme Court ruled that such allegedly separate-but-equal treatment constituted unlawful discrimination on the basis of national origin.

To sum up, *Brown* both reflected and propelled the development of human rights protection internationally. It was decided with the horrors of the Holocaust in full view, and with the repressive regimes in the Soviet Union, Eastern Europe, and South Africa a then-current reality. It propelled an evolution yet unfinished toward respect, in law and in practice, for the human dignity of all the world's people.

Remarks on *Loving v. Virginia*
Federal Judicial Center High School Teachers Program*
United States Supreme Court, Washington, D.C.
June 22, 2009

I would like to speak, for just ten minutes or so, about one of the most important cases the U.S. Supreme Court has ever decided. Titled *Loving v. Virginia*, the case yielded a unanimous decision in 1967.

In May 2008, a *New York Times* obituary reported the death of Mildred Loving, co-plaintiff in the landmark case. Mildred was not a woman of means or sophistication. She held no academic degrees. But she was endowed with a caring heart and exemplary courage, and the case she pursued together with her husband, Richard Loving, changed America.

In 1958, my second year in law school, Mildred Jeter and Richard Loving drove from Caroline County, Virginia, to Washington, D.C., to get married. They could not marry in Virginia, where they had grown up, met, fell in love, and wanted to build their family. The reason: Richard was white, Mildred was of mixed African-American and Native American descent, and Virginia law (also the law in fifteen other states at that time) banned interracial marriage. The couple, Mildred later recounted, had no mind "to make a political statement or start a fight"; they "were [just] in love, and . . . wanted to be married."[1]

The Lovings returned to their home in Central Point, Virginia, after their marriage in D.C., and hung their marriage certificate on

---

*Justice Ginsburg has delivered numerous versions of these remarks to various audiences over the years. We have edited the remarks for length and to ensure clarity outside the specific context in which they were originally delivered.

a wall in their bedroom. Five weeks after their return, "the county sheriff and two deputies, acting on an anonymous tip, burst into their bedroom [at 2:00 a.m.,] [shined] flashlights in their eyes," and demanded of Richard: "Who is this woman you're sleeping with?"[2] When Richard pointed to the marriage certificate posted on the wall, the sheriff responded, "That's no good here,"[3] then carted the Lovings off to jail. Richard spent the rest of the night locked up. Mildred, the spouse of color, spent that night and the next five days and nights in jail.[4]

Frightened and uncounseled, the Lovings appeared before a judge and entered pleas to charges of violating Virginia's Racial Integrity Act. Their sentence, a year in jail, a term the judge would suspend provided that the Lovings "le[ft] the State and [did] not return to Virginia together for 25 years."[5] "Almighty God," the sentencing judge proclaimed, "created the races white, black, yellow, malay and red, and he placed them on separate continents. . . . The fact that he separated the races shows that he did not intend for [them] to mix."[6]

Banished from the community where their families had lived for generations, Mildred and Richard Loving managed as best they could as residents of D.C. Some years later, inspired by the civil rights movement, and particularly, the March on Washington, Mildred wrote to Attorney General Robert Kennedy. Kennedy replied, suggesting that Mildred contact the American Civil Liberties Union. She did, and with the aid of ACLU volunteer lawyers in Virginia (Bernard Cohen and Philip Hirschkop), the Lovings sued the state, seeking to vacate their convictions and gain Virginia's recognition of their marriage.

Their challenge, commenced in 1963, worked its way up to the Supreme Court, where, on June 12, 1967, Chief Justice Earl Warren announced the Court's unanimous holding: Virginia's miscegenation law was unconstitutional. "There can be no doubt," the Chief Justice wrote for the unified Court, "that restricting the freedom to marry solely because of racial classifications violates the central meaning of the Equal Protection Clause."[7] For good measure, the Court added, Virginia's ban on interracial marriage also "deprive[d] the Lovings of liberty without due process."[8] (The California Supreme Court had reached the same judgment nearly two decades earlier, in 1948, six years before *Brown v. Board of Education* was decided by the U.S. Supreme Court.)

How did the 1967 press greet the case that ended law-backed apartheid in America? Not with unreserved applause. A *New York Times* editorial commented: young people (that meant 1960s young people) would wise up, the editor hoped; they would no longer choose "racially mixed marriage as a gesture of defiance against law," pairings "rooted in rebellion more than . . . in affection."[9] "Naturally," the *Los Angeles Times* observed, "there was nothing in the opinion that could be taken as lending encouragement to the idea of interracial marriage."[10] The *Washington Post* described Mildred Loving, not as a woman of courage, but as "an attractive, slender 27-year-old Negro."[11]

Forty years after the muted zeal of first reactions to the landmark decision, Mildred Loving wrote: "I have lived long enough . . . to see big changes. The older generation's fears and prejudices have given way, and today's young people realize that if someone loves someone they have a right to marry."[12] The last state to rid its laws of a miscegenation ban was Alabama, in 2000. Today, 4.3 million interracial couples reside in the United States.[13]

Like Mildred Loving, I have lived long enough to see big changes. Who would believe, for example, in the 1950s when Justice O'Connor and I graduated from law school, that two women no law firm would hire simply because we were women, would one day be seated on the highest Court in the land? Or that the president of the United States would be an African-American, himself the child of an interracial marriage? Yes, we still have a way to go to ensure that all people in our land enjoy the equal protection of the laws, but considering how far we have come there is good cause for optimism about our country's future.

Remarks on the Value of Diversity: International Affirmative Action Institut d'Etudes Politiques* Paris, France July 17, 2009

Members of the faculty, graduating students and their families, and friends of Sciences Po, I am glad to speak at this celebration. I have read of Sciences Po's initiative to achieve excellence in diversity, made a priority by President Descoings. Through that initiative, talented students from all quarters of French society are drawn to this great school. The design is to deepen the complexion and life experiences of the student body and, eventually, the top ranks of government and business in France. Other institutions of higher education have copied the model set by Sciences Po, and that is a measure of the program's success.

I

In the United States, kindred efforts to embrace a wider society in schools and workplaces started in the late 1960s, and I have been told that affirmative action—or what Europeans call positive discrimination—would be an appropriate topic for this talk.

I will begin with a few comparative sideglances. Several post–World War II human rights charters recognize that a nondiscrimination principle alone will not ensure substantive equality. To combat centuries of inequality and to uplift people disadvantaged because they belong to long-subordinated populations, many modern constitutions allow, or even require, affirmative action. India's 1950 consti-

* Justice Ginsburg has delivered numerous versions of these remarks to various audiences over the years. We have edited the remarks for length and to ensure clarity outside the specific context in which they were originally delivered.

tution is a prime example. Among other affirmative action provisions, it broadly instructs the government to "promote with special care the educational and economic interests of the weaker sections of the people." For another example, South Africa's 1996 constitution provides that, to promote achievement of equality, "legislative and other measures [may be taken] to protect or advance persons, or categories of persons, disadvantaged by unfair discrimination." In nations forming the European Union, in contrast to India and South Africa, no similarly entrenched caste system existed and no suppression of the *majority* by the minority propelled positive discrimination. But European Union charters and directives, from the 1957 Rome Treaty to the 2000 Charter of Fundamental Rights, have advanced equal opportunity for women. The Charter confirms that "the principle of equal treatment" does not impede member states from adopting special measures to facilitate women's pursuit of vocational activities and professional careers.

On the world stage, two key United Nations covenants endorse affirmative action. First in time, the 1965 Convention on the Elimination of All Forms of Racial Discrimination declares: "Special measures taken for the [sole] purpose of securing adequate advancement of certain racial or ethnic groups . . . shall not be deemed racial discrimination." Next, the 1979 Convention on the Elimination of All Forms of Discrimination Against Women excludes from the definition of discrimination the "[a]doption . . . of temporary special measures aimed at accelerating *de facto* equality between men and women."

The constitutions of the United States and France contain no provisions resembling the two I have just read. The U.S. Constitution, as amended in 1868, simply prohibits denial of "the equal protection of the laws." The 1958 Constitution of France states in Article I a more precise principle: it declares the equality of citizens "without distinction of origin, race or religion." In keeping with that declaration and French tradition, I am told, no law or policy in France describes individuals or groups by race or ethnicity. Instead, educational priority zones, urban development strategies, and similar measures keyed to geographical location aim to advance the fortunes of people living in economically depressed areas.

Having barely sketched some prescriptions on equality nationally and internationally, I will devote the remainder of my remarks to some of the endeavors to make the equality ideal more than aspirational in the land in which I live and work, the United States.

II

Affirmative action efforts in the United States reflect distinctive aspects of our history. All people residing in France proper qualified for citizenship without regard to race or religion following the revolution. But in the United States slavery persisted in the South until outlawed by our Civil War and an 1865 constitutional amendment. So-called Jim Crow laws replaced slave codes in several states, laws that imposed a rigid and pervasive system of racial segregation that continued past the midpoint of the twentieth century. Although World War II made unmistakably clear to the world the evil of racism, one cannot erase the past in short order. "In the wake of a system of racial caste only recently ended," President Lyndon Johnson told the nation in 1965, "[f]reedom is not enough. You do not wipe away the scars of centuries by saying: 'Now you are free to go where you want . . . do as you desire, [elect your] leaders.' "

Affirmative action in the United States has had a seesaw, up-and-down history. The term was coined in 1961, but implementation of the concept did not shift into high gear until the administration of Republican President Richard Nixon. In 1969, Nixon's Labor Department published its pathmarking Philadelphia Plan, in large part to combat high rates of unemployment among African-American men, and to break down nepotism in the construction trades. The plan required construction enterprises that held contracts with the government to set goals and timetables for hiring minority workers. Enterprises that failed to comply risked termination of their contracts.

Within just a few years, the model was extended to cover the whole of the United States and all government contracts, including those held by universities. Coverage was also expanded to include women as well as racial and ethnic minorities. I was the beneficiary of the Nixon administration's affirmative action effort when, in 1972, I was engaged by the Columbia University law faculty as the first woman ever to hold a tenured position there.

During the period the administration was promoting affirmative action, the U.S. Supreme Court supplied important guidance on the scope of Title VII of the 1964 Civil Rights Act, the nation's principal law on antidiscrimination in employment. Title VII prohibits discrimination by employers, private and public, on the basis of race, color, religion, sex, or national origin. In *Griggs v. Duke Power Company*, a 1971 decision, the Supreme Court unanimously ruled that Title VII outlawed "not only overt discrimination but also practices . . . fair in form, but discriminatory in operation"—practices that had a "disparate impact" on minority group members or women. Merely stopping intentional discrimination, the Court acknowledged, would not accomplish Congress' objective. To open doors, employers had to examine their employment practices and eliminate requirements that screened out minorities and women, unless the policy or practice was manifestly related to job performance—necessary to the safe and efficient operation of the business.

The *Griggs* case itself involved a high school diploma requirement, even for low-level jobs that could be performed perfectly well by people who could not meet that measure. (In the state where Duke Power maintained its plant, North Carolina, most African-Americans, in the 1970s, were not high school graduates.) A host of exclusionary practices were dropped as a result of the *Griggs* disparate-impact ruling, for example, height or weight-lifting requirements for piloting planes or police officer jobs—requirements few women could meet.

The "disparate impact" or indirect discrimination concept reached selection criteria that operated as "built-in headwinds" for minorities or women. But the *Griggs* decision did not address the question whether express preferences could be given to minorities by employers or educational institutions.

The U.S. Supreme Court first ruled on the constitutionality of preferential systems in a university setting in 1978. The case, *Regents of the University of California v. Bakke*, involved a challenge by a disappointed white male applicant to a California medical school. The school's affirmative action plan reserved 16 out of 100 places in the entering class for members of minority groups. Dividing five to four, the Court held that the reservation violated the Constitution's equal protection principle. The controlling opinion in the *Bakke* case said that race could be considered as one factor among others in an admissions process that treated each individual discretely. But outright quotas or reservations of a set number of places for minority-group students, the majority held, are unconstitutional. Past societal discrimination, five Justices agreed, could not justify plans like the medical school's. While rejecting compensatory justifications for quotas or set asides, the dispositive opinion approved milder forms of affirmative action aimed at achieving a racially diverse student body. The educational experience for all students, the opinion reasoned, would be enhanced if members of different cultures live and learn together. That very understanding underlies the Sciences Po initiative.

The U.S. Supreme Court again addressed affirmative action in university admissions in 2003, in paired cases from the University of Michigan. One of the two cases, [*Gratz v. Bollinger*], involved the undergraduate school, which automatically awarded minority group members 20 points of the 100 needed to gain admission. The other case, [*Grutter v. Bollinger*], involved the law school, which assigned no additional points but treated race or ethnicity more flexibly as a plus factor. The Court disapproved of the undergraduate program because, the majority said, it put members of minority groups on a separate track. But it upheld the law school's program because that program advanced diversity without establishing a quota or separate track.

I would have upheld both University of Michigan programs and wrote in dissent in the undergraduate school case: "Actions designed to burden groups long denied full citizenship stature are not sensibly ranked with measures taken to hasten the day when entrenched discrimination and its after effects have been extirpated." "If honesty is the best policy," I added, the undergraduate school's transparent "affirmative action program is preferable to achieving similar numbers through winks, nods, and disguises."

Four years after the University of Michigan cases, the Court divided 5–4 again, this time on the constitutionality of lower school programs in Seattle, Washington, and Louisville, Kentucky—programs designed to keep kindergarten through twelfth-grade classes racially integrated despite the high degree of neighborhood separation along racial lines. To maintain integration, the cities' school boards took race into account in assigning children to particular schools. The Court [in *Parents Involved in Community Schools v. Seattle School District No. 1*] held the programs unconstitutional. Unlike the University of Michigan law school program, the Court said, race in the lower school plans was "decisive by itself." Moreover, the Court added, the Michigan case involved "considerations unique to higher education." The lead opinion ended with an attention-riveting line: "The way to stop discrimination on the basis of race is to stop discriminating on the basis of race."

The four dissenters—I was one of them—saw the Seattle and Louisville plans differently. There is a "legal and practical difference," we said, "between the use of race-conscious criteria . . . to keep the races apart, and the use of race-conscious criteria . . . to bring the races together."*

To complete the picture, I will note the Court's latest decision on disparate impact [*Ricci v. DeStefano*]. Making headlines, the Court held, on June 29, 2009, once again 5–4, that a city—New Haven, Connecticut, home to Yale University—could not set aside the results of promotional exams for firefighters, though certifying the results

---

* For an update on affirmative action, see pages 327–28.

would mean no African-Americans could be promoted for at least two years. In dissent, I pointed to multiple flaws in the test design, flaws that severely undermined the reliability of the exams and made it likely that black firefighters would not be promoted, despite their readiness to hold command positions. The Court's opinion in the firefighters case does not destroy the "disparate impact" concept, but it does significantly limit its application.

Comparing the unanimous 1971 *Griggs* decision with the U.S. Supreme Court's current decisions, a cynic might observe that the true symbol of the United States is not the bald eagle; it is the pendulum. Responding to a changed political climate, a few states have endeavored to reduce inequality in access to higher education by means that do not explicitly invoke a racial criterion. A decade ago, Texas enacted a "Top 10 Percent Law," under which any student who graduates in the top 10 percent of his or her high school class automatically qualifies for admission to any public undergraduate college in the state. A few other states have since adopted similarly designed, on the surface race-blind, policies. Because of residential segregation, these states have achieved a measure of diversity through their percentage plans.*

Ironically, schools in poor neighborhoods have gained greater popularity as a result of percentage plans. One can get into the top 10 percent more easily in lower-performing schools located in poor neighborhoods than in highly competitive schools located in more affluent neighborhoods.

III

In sum, affirmative action measures are controversial because they send both inspiring and disturbing messages. Affirmative action and the disparate-impact concept have potential to lessen substantive in-

---

* A separate aspect of the University of Texas admissions policy, which specifically designated race as one factor to be considered in the selection process, would twice end up in the Supreme Court. For Justice Ginsburg's role in *Fisher v. University of Texas*, see pp. 296–98 (Fisher I) and pp. 327–28 (Fisher II).

equality, foster diversity, and promote the economic and social well-being of people raised in unprivileged communities. But they also generate opposition, charges that they unfairly discriminate against individuals not personally responsible for society's transgressions. I do not downplay the opposition, but balancing the pros and cons, I subscribe to what Justice O'Connor wrote in the Michigan law school case: "[T]o cultivate . . . leaders with legitimacy in the eyes of the citizenry, . . . the path to leadership must be *visibly* open to the talented . . . individuals of every race and ethnicity." "Effective participation by members of [minority groups and women] in the civil life of our Nation is essential if the dream of one Nation, indivisible, is to be realized." We will all profit from a more diverse, inclusive society, understanding, accommodating, even celebrating our difference, while pulling together for the common good.

Congratulations on your graduation from a school known far and wide as one of the very best institutions of higher education. Cheers, too, to the parents and teachers who nurtured you and contributed to your will to aspire and achieve. And as you leave here and proceed along life's paths, try to leave tracks. Use the education you have received to help repair tears in your communities. Take part in efforts to move those communities, your nation, and our world closer to the conditions needed to ensure the health and well-being of your generation and generations following your own.

My applause on your achievement and every good wish.

7

The Role of Dissenting Opinions

In a lecture *titled "The Role of Dissenting Opinions," reprinted below, Justice Ginsburg reflects on the role of and proper occasion for dissents from the opinions of the Court's majority. And well she might. In recent years, with the advent of the Roberts Court, she and the Supreme Court's other three liberal Justices often found themselves in the minority when contentious legal issues divided the nine Justices along philosophical lines. Having become the liberal minority's most senior Justice after more than two decades on the Court, she, much more frequently than during the Rehnquist Court years, is a leading voice in such cases, penning some of its most important dissents.*

When the divide is especially deep and the case especially consequential, as Ginsburg explains in her lecture, dissenting Justices occasionally do more than simply write a dissent—they deliver an oral summary of the dissent from the bench, after the case has been announced by the author of the majority opinion. During her years on the Rehnquist Court (1993–2005) her bench dissents were few and far between—just six in twelve Terms. But beginning with the second Term of the Roberts Court, the pattern changed. That Term, 2006–07, she delivered not one but two bench dissents, a performance that made the front page of the New York Times. *Linda Greenhouse, the* Times' *veteran Supreme Court reporter, wrote two days after the second bench dissent, in* Ledbetter v. Goodyear Tire & Rubber Company, *that "oral dissent has not been, until now, Justice Ginsburg's style," and presciently predicted, "Whatever else may be said about the Supreme Court's current Term, which ends in about a month, it will be remembered as the time when Justice Ruth Bader Ginsburg found her voice, and used it."[1] By 2014, Justice Ginsburg had delivered twelve bench dissents, becoming the Roberts Court's most frequent bench dissenter. This included a record four such dissents in the 2012–13 Term alone—more than any other Justice in a single Term in almost three decades.*

Ever the law teacher, Justice Ginsburg brought handouts when she delivered her lecture on dissenting opinions to Tulane Law students in 2013. Specifically, she gave the students copies of two of the four dissents she had, just weeks before, summarized from the bench. She explained: The first one, Vance v. Ball, *involving interpretation of a federal law, "appeals to Congress to amend Title VII to say more explicitly what I believe Congress intended all along." The second,* Shelby County v. Holder, *involved constitutional interpretation, "and therefore appeals to the intelligence of a future day." She also read to the students a third of the four bench dissents,* Fisher v. University of Texas, *and discussed her earlier bench dissent in the* Ledbetter *case in 2007.*

Those four bench dissents appear below, following Justice Ginsburg's lecture. We have also included Justice Ginsburg's bench announcement in one of the most significant decisions of the Roberts Court, NFIB v. Sebelius *(2012), the case that threatened to dismantle President Obama's Affordable Care Act (ACA), and a second ACA case,* Burwell v. Hobby Lobby *(2014), a challenge to government regulations requiring employers to cover, in their employee health insurance policies, contraceptives for women employees. Over Justice Ginsburg's vigorous dissent, joined by Justices Breyer, Sotomayor, and Kagan, the majority extended the ACA's exemption for churches and religious organizations to cover closely held for-profit corporations like Hobby Lobby, a family-run corporation. Finally, we include Ginsburg's bench dissent in* Gonzales v. Carhart *(2007), protesting the majority's upholding of a state statute prohibiting a particular abortion method, even though the statute failed to make an exception to its rule when that method was necessary to protect a woman's health.*

The Role of Dissenting Opinions
Tulane University Law School Summer Program*
Paris, France
July 2013

My remarks concern the role of dissenting opinions in U.S. appellate courts generally, and the U.S. Supreme Court in particular. It is a subject I have been obliged to think about more than occasionally in recent Terms.

Although I sit on the top tier of the U.S. judiciary, I have often described trial judges as the real power holders in our justice system. Our trial judges sit alone and, in most instances, their rulings are not subject to review until the adjudication is completed and final judgment is entered. Even then, the vast majority of trial court rulings are never appealed, in large part because appeals may be taken only on matters of law. The fact determinations of trial courts may not be remade on appeal. In contrast, an appellate judge, typically sitting with two colleagues, is powerless unless at least one of her colleagues agrees she is right. And on the U.S. Supreme Court, where nine Justices sit together at all times, a Justice can write for the Court only if at least four of her colleagues endorse her opinion.

Chief Justice Roberts, in his 2005 confirmation hearings, expressed admiration for the nation's fourth Chief Justice, John Marshall—longest at the helm (from 1801 until his death in 1835) and frontrunner for the title greatest Chief Justice in U.S. history. Our current Chief admired, perhaps most of all, Chief Justice Marshall's unparalleled ability to achieve consensus among his colleagues. During John Marshall's thirty-four-year tenure, the Court spoke with one voice most of the time.

---

*Justice Ginsburg has delivered numerous versions of these remarks to various audiences over the years. We have edited the remarks for length and to ensure clarity outside the specific context in which they were originally delivered.

How did Marshall manage that feat? In his early years as Chief Justice, all members of the Court resided and dined together in the same boardinghouse whenever the Justices convened in the capital city. After dinner, so the legend goes, the Chief would serve Madeira from his own supply, talk about the argued cases, urge unanimity, then volunteer to write nearly all the opinions himself.

In Chief Justice Roberts' first year at the Court, notably also Justice O'Connor's last Term on our bench, it appeared that the new Chief's hope for greater unanimity might be realized. In the 2005–06 Term, 45 percent of the cases we took up for review were decided unanimously, with but one opinion for the Court, and 55 percent were unanimous in the bottom-line judgment. With Justice O'Connor no longer at our Conference table, that high level of unanimity has declined somewhat, but it is still impressive. This Term, 2012–13, for example, we agreed on the bottom line judgment in 38 (49 percent) of the 78 opinions issued during the Term. In 22 cases (28.2 percent), the Court issued only one opinion that all Justices joined in full. In contrast, the Court divided 5–4 in 23 (29 percent) of our post-argument dispositions.

Ordinarily, when Court decisions are announced from the bench, only the majority opinion is summarized. Separate opinions, concurring or dissenting, are noted, but not described. A dissent announced orally, therefore, garners immediate attention. It signals that, in the dissenters' view, the Court's opinion is not just wrong, but, to borrow Justice Stevens' words, "profoundly misguided." As an example, I will read my June 24 statement from the bench in the University of Texas affirmative action case. [*Justice Ginsburg then read her dissenting bench announcement in* Fisher v. University of Texas; *see p. 296.*]

Our practice of revealing dissents is hardly universal. In the civil law tradition that holds sway in Europe, and in countries once controlled by a continental European power, most multi-judge courts issue a collective judgment, cast in stylized, impersonal language. The judgment writer is neither named nor otherwise identifiable. Disagreement, if it exists, as inevitably it sometimes does, is not disclosed.

The British common law tradition lies at the opposite pole. [*For a description of that "opposite pole," in which each judge authors an individual opinion, see* Speaking in a Judicial Voice, *p. 228*.] Our system occupies a middle ground between the continental and the British traditions.

No doubt, as Chief Justice Roberts suggested in his confirmation hearings, the U.S. Supreme Court speaks with greater force, and provides clearer guidance, when it is not fractured. And I agree that a Justice, contemplating publication of a separate writing, should always ask herself: is this dissent or concurrence really necessary? Consider the extra weight carried by the Court's unanimous 1954 opinion in *Brown v. Board of Education*. All nine Justices signed one opinion making it clear that the Constitution does not tolerate legally enforced segregation in our nation's public schools.

Even for dissenters, I believe, one opinion speaks more impressively than four. In the rush to judgment in *Bush v. Gore* (2000), for example, there was no time to compose a single dissent, so the press and public had to read four separate, rather long, dissenting opinions to discern our views. Contrast the single opinion Justice Stevens composed expressing the view of all four in the minority in a case decided at the start of 2010, *Citizens United v. Federal Election Commission*. (The Court's 5–4 judgment in that case, you will recall, nullified a key constraint on corporate spending to elect or defeat candidates for public office.)

There was a repeat the next Term in *Arizona Free Enterprise Club v. Bennett*. A five-member majority invalidated Arizona's attempt to deter exorbitant campaign spending by gearing the amount a publicly financed candidate could receive to the amount his or her privately financed opponent spends. Justice Kagan wrote powerfully for the four dissenters. And this Term, I wrote for four, dissenting from the Court's decision to upset the preclearance procedure Congress prescribed in the Voting Rights Act. [*See Justice Ginsburg's dissenting bench announcement in* Shelby v. Holder, *p. 292*.]

On the utility of dissenting opinions, I will mention first their in-house impact. My experience confirms that there is nothing better than an impressive dissent to lead the author of the majority opinion to refine and clarify her initial circulation. An illustration: The *Virginia Military Institute* case, decided by the Court in 1996, held that VMI's denial of admission to women violated the Fourteenth Amendment's Equal Protection Clause. I was assigned to write the Court's opinion. [*See Justice Ginsburg's bench announcement of the majority opinion in* United States v. Virginia, *p. 150.*] The final draft, released to the public, was ever so much better than my first, second, and at least a dozen drafts more, thanks to Justice Scalia's attention-grabbing dissent, which he adjusted to meet each of my responsive circulations. In the Term's waning days, we agreed it was time to say Basta!

Sometimes a dissent is written, then buried by its author. An entire volume is devoted to the unpublished, quite extensive dissenting opinions written by Justice Louis Dembitz Brandeis during his 1916 to 1939 tenure on the Court. He would suppress his dissent if the majority made ameliorating alterations. (A few of my favorite separate writings remain unpublished for similar reasons.) And even when Brandeis gained no accommodations, he would retract his dissent if he thought the Court's opinion was of limited application and unlikely to cause real harm in future cases. He once explained: one must husband resources; dissenting too often will weaken the force of a dissent when it becomes important to write.

Constitutional law scholar Paul Freund, who clerked for Justice Brandeis in 1932, recalled his memory of the new Justice who came on board that year, Benjamin Nathan Cardozo. Freund "was surprised . . . how often Cardozo was in sole dissent in the vote at conference." Freund "was also struck by how preponderant [Cardozo's] course was of suppressing a dissent so that an opinion would come down unanimous. . . ." (We call dissenting votes so held back "graveyard dissents." They are buried.)

The most determined graveyard dissenter may have been Chief Justice Taft, who served on the Court from 1921 until 1930. His feeling about dissent resembled Thomas Jefferson's. Most dissents, Taft thought, are "a form of egotism," an expression of vanity. In many cases, he suppressed his dissent to, in his words, "stand by the Court and give its judgments weight." In his eight and a half years on the Court Taft stayed on the dissent side only 17 times, wrote only 3 dissents himself, and joined the majority in nearly 200 cases in which his initial vote was in the minority.

Although graveyard dissents are hardly as common as Chief Justice Taft thought they should be, on occasion, a dissent will be so persuasive that it attracts the votes necessary to become the opinion of the Court. That happens once or twice, no more than three times each Term. A former clerk to Justice Douglas tells this story. Douglas had circulated an opinion and was awaiting joins. Late on a Friday afternoon, Justice Harlan sent around his dissent. The clerk asked Justice Douglas if he wanted to make responsive changes. Douglas was about to depart for a hiking weekend. Without reading the Harlan dissent, Douglas told the clerk, "It won't make a difference," and left town. When Douglas returned to chambers Monday morning, he found to his chagrin that he had lost his majority. The Harlan dissent has become the opinion of the Court.

I had the heady experience once of writing a dissent for myself and just one other Justice; in time, it became the opinion of the Court from which only three of my colleagues dissented. Whenever I write in dissent, I aim for a repeat of that experience. Much more often than not, the conference vote holds, but hope springs eternal!

Are lasting rifts sparked by sharply worded dissents? Justice Scalia spoke to that question nicely. He said: "I doubt whether any two [J]ustices have dissented from one another's opinions any more regularly, or any more sharply, than did my former colleague Justice William Brennan and I. I always considered him, however, one of my best friends on the Court, and I think that feeling was reciprocated." (I might say something similar about my fondness for Justice Scalia.)

Describing the external impact of dissenting opinions, Chief Justice Hughes, in a book about the U.S. Supreme Court published in 1936, famously said: "A dissent in a court of last resort is an appeal . . .

to the intelligence of a future day, when a later decision may possibly correct the error into which the dissenting judge believes the court to have been betrayed." Dissents of this order occur in constitutional cases in which the only corrective is an overruling Court decision or a constitutional amendment. Congress cannot fix such errors.

A classic example of an opinion "appealing to the intelligence of a future day" is Justice Benjamin Curtis' dissent from the Court's notorious 1856 decision in *Dred Scott v. Sandford*. The Court held, 7–2, in *Dred Scott* that people of African descent whose ancestors were brought to the United States as slaves could never become citizens of the nation. Accordingly, an African-American could not invoke a federal court's diversity-of-citizenship jurisdiction to assert that, once brought to a free state, he was no longer his master's property. Justice Curtis disagreed, as did Justice McLean. Curtis wrote an opinion remarkable for its time. At the founding of our nation, he observed, African-Americans were "citizens of at least five States, and so in every sense part of the people of the United States," thus "among those for whom and whose posterity the Constitution was ordained and established."

Another example is the first Justice Harlan's dissent in the *Civil Rights Cases*. The Court, in that 1883 decision, invalidated a federal law entitling "citizens of every race and color" to the "full and equal enjoyment" of modes of transportation and places of public accommodation. If the Thirteenth and Fourteenth Amendments are to be enforced "according to the intent with which . . . they were adopted," Justice Harlan wrote, "there cannot be, in this republic, any class of human beings in practical subjection to another class."

Dissents of this order, Justice Scalia rightly commented, "augment rather than diminish the prestige of the Court." He explained: "When history demonstrates that one of the Court's decisions has been a truly horrendous mistake, it is comforting . . . to look back and realize that at least some of the [J]ustices saw the danger clearly and gave voice, often eloquent voice, to their concern."

Though Justice Scalia would not agree with me in these further examples, I would rank as dissents "appealing to the intelligence of a future day" Justice Stevens' dissent in *Citizens United* and Justice Kagan's in *Arizona Free Enterprise*, both disagreeing with a five-member majority's view that the First Amendment blocks controls on exorbitant spending in campaigns for public offices. I might also so rank my June 25, 2013 dissent in the Voting Rights Act case.

Another genre of dissent looks not to a distant future day, but seeks immediate action from the political branches of government—Congress and the president. Dissents of this order aim to engage or energize the public and propel prompt legislative overruling of the Court's decision. A fit example, perhaps, is the dissent I summarized from the bench in 2007 in *Ledbetter v. Goodyear Tire & Rubber Co.* [*See Justice Ginsburg's dissenting bench announcement, p. 287.*] The plaintiff, Lilly Ledbetter, worked as an area manager at a Goodyear tire plant in Alabama; in 1997, she was the only woman Goodyear employed in such a post. Her starting salary (in 1979) was in line with the salaries of men performing similar work. But over time, her pay slipped. By the end of 1997, there was a 15 to 40 percent disparity between Ledbetter's pay and the salaries of the fifteen men doing essentially the same work. A federal jury found it "more likely than not that [Goodyear] paid [Ledbetter] a[n] unequal salary because of her sex." The Supreme Court, dividing five to four, nullified the verdict. The majority held that Ledbetter had filed her claim too late.

It was incumbent on Ledbetter, the Court said, to file charges of discrimination each time Goodyear failed to increase her salary commensurate with the salaries of her male peers. Any annual pay decision not contested promptly (within 180 days), the Court ruled, became grandfathered, beyond the remedial reach of Title VII (our principal law prohibiting employment discrimination).

The Court's ruling, I observed, ignored real-world employment practices that Title VII was meant to govern: "Sue early on," the majority counseled, when it is uncertain whether discrimination accounts for the pay disparity you are beginning to experience, and when you may not know that men are receiving more for the same work. (Of course, you would likely lose such a premature, less than fully baked challenge.) But if you sue only when the pay disparity becomes steady and large, your now-winnable case will be blocked as untimely. Heads, the employer wins; tails, the employee loses. That situation, I urged, could not be what Congress intended when, in Title VII, it outlawed discrimination based on race, color, religion, sex, or national origin in our nation's workplaces. "The ball is in Congress' court," I wrote, "to correct [the Supreme] Court's parsimonious reading of Title VII."

Congress responded within days of the Court's decision. Bills were introduced in the House and Senate to amend Title VII to make it plain that each paycheck a woman in Ledbetter's situation received renewed the discrimination and restarted the time within which suit could be brought. Early in 2009, Congress passed the Lilly Ledbetter Fair Pay Act, and President Obama signed the corrective measure as one of his first actions after taking office.

I had a sense of déjà vu last Term in the *Wal-Mart* case [*Wal-Mart v. Dukes* (2011)]. The issue on which the Court divided 5–4 concerned the plaintiffs' satisfaction of the threshold "commonality" requirement for class action certification. The women's complaint, their chances of being hired for, or promoted to, management-level posts were distinctly lower than the chances of male applicants for supervisory posts. No "common" question of law or fact united the class, the Court ruled, because the plaintiffs were complaining about millions of discrete employment decisions.

I observed, in dissent, that managers had wide discretion in deciding on pay and promotions. The commonality requirement was satisfied, I tried to explain, by this phenomenon: managers were overwhelmingly male and they tended, perhaps unconsciously, to favor people who looked like themselves. As a graphic example, I noted that women did not appear in numbers in symphony orchestras until a curtain was dropped, so that the auditioners could not tell whether the person auditioning was male or female. (To make certain there would be no cues, auditioners were required to take off their shoes.)

To sum up, although I appreciate the value of unanimous opinions, I will continue to speak in dissent when important matters are at stake. I stress *important* matters because I try to follow Justice Brandeis' counsel. He cautioned that in most matters of statutory interpretation, "it is more important that [the applicable] rule of law be settled than that it be settled right." One might put in that category ambiguous provisions of complex legislation—for example, the Internal Revenue Code or the Employee Retirement Income Security Act.

I recall, too, that Oliver Wendell Holmes, who graced the Court from 1902 until 1932, was called "the Great Dissenter." In fact, he dissented less often than most of his colleagues. As Holmes put it, "I sometimes endorse an opinion with which I do not agree, I acquiesce, I'll shut up." But when he elected to dissent, he did so to great effect.

On when to acquiesce in the majority's view, and when to take an independent stand, Arizona lawyer and legal scholar, John Frank, wrote in 1958 of the model Brandeis set:

> Brandeis was a great institutional man. He realized that . . . random dissents . . . weaken the institutional impact of the Court and handicap it in the doing of its fundamental job. Dissents . . . need to be saved for major matters if the Court is not to appear indecisive and quarrelsome. . . . To have discarded some of [his separate] opinions is a supreme example of [Brandeis'] sacrifice to [the] strength and consistency of the Court. And he had his reward: his shots [were] all the harder because he chose his ground.

In the years I am privileged to serve on the Court, I pray that I will be granted similar wisdom in choosing my ground.

Bench Announcement

Ledbetter v. Goodyear Tire & Rubber Co.

Tuesday, May 29, 2007

Lilly Ledbetter worked for Goodyear for nearly two decades. At the outset, her pay was the same as others doing the same work, but as the years passed, a pay gap between Ledbetter and her male colleagues emerged and grew. In 1998, shortly after retiring, Ledbetter sued Goodyear for sex discrimination in violation of Title VII of the Civil Rights Act of 1964. When the case reached the Supreme Court, Justice Samuel Alito, writing on behalf of a five-Justice majority, ruled that Ledbetter had filed her lawsuit too late. In her dissent, which she summarized from the bench, Justice Ginsburg argued that the Court's interpretation of Title VII was too narrow and encouraged Congress to take corrective action. It ultimately did so, passing the Lilly Ledbetter Fair Pay Act in 2009.

Four members of this Court, Justices Stevens, Souter, Breyer, and I, dissent from today's decision. In our view, the Court does not comprehend, or is indifferent to, the insidious way in which women can be victims of pay discrimination. Today's decision counsels: sue early on, when it is uncertain whether discrimination accounts for the pay disparity you are beginning to experience. Indeed, initially you may not know that men are receiving more for substantially similar work. (Of course, you are likely to lose such a less than fully baked case.) If you sue only when the pay disparity becomes steady and large enough to enable you to mount a winnable case, you will be cut off at the court's threshold for suing too late. That situation cannot be what Congress intended when, in Title VII, it outlawed discrimination based on race, color, religion, sex, or national origin in our nation's workplaces.

Lilly Ledbetter, the plaintiff in this case, was engaged as an area manager at a Goodyear Tire and Rubber plant in Alabama in 1979.

Her starting salary was in line with the salaries of men performing similar work. But over time, her pay slipped in comparison to the pay of male employees with equal or less seniority. By the end of 1997, Ledbetter was the only woman left working as an area manager and the pay discrepancy between Ledbetter and her fifteen male counterparts was stark: Ledbetter's pay was *15 to 40 percent less* than every other area manager.

Ledbetter complained to the Equal Employment Opportunity Commission in March 1998. She charged that, in violation of Title VII, Goodyear paid her a discriminatorily low salary because of her sex. The charge was eventually brought to court and tried to a jury. The jury found it "more likely than not that [Goodyear] paid [Ledbetter] a[n] unequal salary because of her sex." The Court today nullifies that verdict, holding that Ledbetter's claim is time barred.

Title VII provides that a charge of discrimination "shall be filed within [180] days after the alleged unlawful employment practice occurred." Ledbetter charged, and proved at trial, that the paychecks she received within the 180-day filing period were substantially lower than the paychecks received by men doing the same work. Further, she introduced substantial evidence showing that discrimination accounted for the pay differential, indeed, that discrimination against women as supervisors was pervasive at Goodyear's plant. That evidence was unavailing, the Court holds, because it was incumbent on Ledbetter to file charges of discrimination year-by-year, each time Goodyear failed to increase her salary commensurate with the salaries of her male peers. Any annual pay decision not contested promptly (within 180 days), the Court affirms, becomes grandfathered, beyond the province of Title VII ever to repair.

Title VII was meant to govern real-world employment practices, and that world is what the Court today ignores. Pay disparities often occur, as they did in Ledbetter's case, in small increments; only over time is there strong cause to suspect that discrimination is at work. Comparative pay information is not routinely communicated to employees. Instead, it is often hidden from the employee's view. Small initial discrepancies, even if the employee knows they exist, may not be seen as grounds for a federal case. An employee like Ledbetter, trying to succeed in a male-dominated workplace, in a job filled only by men before she was hired, understandably may be anxious to avoid making waves.

Pay discrimination that recurs and swells in impact is significantly different from discrete adverse actions promptly communicated and "easy to identify" as discriminatory. Events in that category include firing, denial of a promotion, or refusal to hire. In contrast to those unambiguous actions, until a pay disparity becomes apparent and sizable, an employee is unlikely to comprehend her plight and, therefore, to complain about it. Ledbetter's initial readiness to give her employer the benefit of the doubt should not preclude her from later seeking redress for the continuing payment to her of a salary depressed because of her sex.

Yet, as the Court reads Title VII, each and every pay decision Ledbetter did not promptly challenge wiped the slate clean. Never mind the cumulative effect of a series of decisions that, together, set her pay well below that of every male area manager. Knowingly carrying past pay discrimination forward must be treated as lawful. Ledbetter may not be compensated under Title VII for the lower pay she was in fact receiving when she complained to the EEOC. Notably, the same denial of relief would occur had Ledbetter encountered pay discrimination based on race, religion, age, national origin, or disability.

This is not the first time the Court has ordered a cramped interpretation of Title VII, incompatible with the statute's broad remedial purpose. In 1991, Congress passed a Civil Rights Act that effectively overruled several of this Court's similarly restrictive decisions, including one, *Lorance*, upon which the Court relies today. Today, the ball again lies in Congress' court. As in 1991, the Legislature has cause to note and correct this Court's parsimonious reading of Title VII.

Bench Announcement
Vance v. Ball State University
Monday, June 24, 2013

On June 24, Justice Ginsburg summarized the dissents on behalf of herself and the three liberal Justices in two cases, thematically related, in which the Court split five to four. Both, like* Ledbetter, *involved a "parsimonious reading of Title VII" by the majority, which Justice Ginsburg and her fellow dissenters viewed as oblivious to "real world employment practices" and congressional intent. The portion of the announcement discussing the first of those two cases,* Vance v. Ball State University, *follows.*

In two of the decisions announced today, the Court has corralled Title VII, an Act designed to stop discrimination on the basis of race, color, religion, sex, or national origin in our nation's workplaces. Both decisions dilute the strength of Title VII in ways Congress could not have intended. For that reason, Justices Breyer, Sotomayor, Kagan, and I dissent.

The decision Justice Alito just announced, *Vance v. Ball State University*, answers the question: Who is a supervisor for Title VII purposes? The answer is important, because this Court has held that an employer is vicariously liable for a supervisor's harassing conduct. If the harasser is a coworker, and not a supervisor, however, we have held that the employer is not responsible unless the victim of the harassment proves negligence on the part of the employer. To do so, the employee must show that the employer knew or should have known of the harassing conduct and failed to stop it. That is a burden not easily carried. An employee may have a reputation as a harasser among those in his vicinity, but if no complaint makes its way up to management, the employer will escape liability.

---

* University of Texas Southwestern Medical Center v. Nassar, 133 S. Ct. 2517 (2013); Vance v. Ball State University, 133 S. Ct. 2434 (2013).

The supervisor/coworker distinction makes sense. An employee can walk away from a harassing coworker, or tell him to "buzz off." The harassment of a supervisor, however, is harder to avoid given the control rein held by an in-charge superior.

So who qualifies as a supervisor? All agree that an employee with authority to take tangible employment actions, that is, to hire, fire, promote, or demote qualifies. In addition, the Equal Employment Opportunity Commission (EEOC), the agency charged with interpretation and administration of Title VII, defines as a supervisor one authorized "to direct [other] employee[s'] daily work activities." The EEOC's definition was accepted by both plaintiff and defendant in this case. Remarkably, the Court rejects it and confines the supervisory category to those authorized to take tangible employment actions.

Who does that leave out? A typical, and not at all hypothetical, example: A female highway maintenance worker is given assignments by employees called "lead workers." Sex-based invectives are hurled at the female worker and a pornographic image is taped to her locker. The lead worker forces her to wash her truck in subzero weather, assigns her to undesirable yard work instead of road-crew work, and directs other employees to give her no aid in fixing a malfunctioning heating system in her truck. Harassing conduct? Concededly yes. Was the lead worker in charge of the harassed employee's daily work activities? Certainly. But the lead worker lacked authority to hire, fire, or take other tangible employment actions. So, under today's decision, the lead worker would be ranked merely a coworker, not a supervisor.

As anyone with employment experience can easily grasp, in-charge employees authorized to assign and control subordinate employees' daily work are aided in accomplishing their harassment by the superintending position in which their employer places them, and for that reason, the employer is properly held responsible for the misconduct. The Court's disregard for the realities of the workplace means that many victims of workplace harassment will have no effective remedy.

The result, Title VII's capacity to prevent and redress discriminatory conduct is notably diminished.

Six years ago, in *Ledbetter v. Goodyear Tire and Rubber Company*, the Court read Title VII in a similarly restrictive way. In 2009, Congress corrected that error.

Today, the ball again lies in Congress' court to correct this Court's wayward interpretations of Title VII.

Bench Announcement
Shelby County v. Holder
Tuesday, June 25, 2013

The Voting Rights Act bans any "standard, practice, or procedure" that "results in a denial or abridgment of the rights of any citizen . . . to vote on account of race or color." Under one provision of the Act, states and political subdivisions with a history of curtailing the voting rights of African-Americans were required to submit all proposed changes in voting procedures to the Justice Department for approval before putting them into effect, a procedure called "preclearance." Shelby County, Alabama, one such jurisdiction, challenged the constitutionality of the preclearance requirement and the formula for selecting the jurisdictions subjected to that requirement.

Five members of the Court, in an opinion by Chief Justice Roberts, declared the formula antiquated and unconstitutional in light of significantly improved "current conditions." Writing for the four dissenting Justices, Justice Ginsburg wrote a thirty-seven-page dissent whose core argument was summed up in this single, memorable sentence: "Throwing out preclearance when it has worked and is continuing to work is like throwing away your umbrella in a rainstorm because you are not getting wet." The formula, she said, "accurately identifies the jurisdictions with the worst conditions of voting discrimination." Her dissent in Shelby County, *as Justice Ginsburg told her students in her lecture on the role of dissenting opinions, involves constitutional interpretation, "and therefore appeals to the intelligence of a future day."*

In the following bench announcement summarizing her dissent, Justice Ginsburg's meticulous attention to telling details and her deep commitment to racial equality are both on display.

The majority and the dissenters agree on two points. First, race-based voting discrimination still exists; no one doubts that. Second, the Voting Rights Act addresses an extraordinary problem—a near century of disregard for the dictates of the Fifteenth Amendment—and Congress has taken extraordinary measures to meet the problem. Beyond those two points, the Court divides sharply.

Congress' failure to redo the coverage formula, the Court holds, renders inoperative the preclearance remedy of §5, the provision far more effective than any other in securing minority voting rights and stopping backsliding. Justices Breyer, Sotomayor, Kagan, and I are of the view that Congress' decision to renew the Act and keep the coverage formula was an altogether rational means to serve the end of achieving what was once the subject of a dream: the equal citizenship stature of all in our polity, a voice to every voter in our democracy undiluted by race.

Most fundamentally, we see the issue as a "who decides" question. In this regard, we note that the very First Amendment to our Constitution exhibits a certain suspicion of Congress. It instructs: Congress shall make no law abridging the freedom of speech or of the press. The Civil War Amendments are of a distinctly different thrust. Thus the Fifteenth Amendment instructs that the right to vote shall not be denied or abridged on account of race, and it vests in Congress, as do the Thirteenth and Fourteenth Amendments, power to enforce the guaranteed right by appropriate legislation. As the standard-setting decision, *South Carolina v. Katzenbach*, put it: "As against the reserved powers of the States, Congress may use any rational means to effectuate the constitutional prohibition of race discrimination in voting."

Congress sought to do just that in 1965, when it initially passed the Voting Rights Act, and in each reauthorization, including the most recent one. Indeed, the 2006 reauthorization was the product of the most earnest consideration. Over a span of more than 20 months, the House and Senate Judiciary Committees held 21 hearings, heard from scores of witnesses, received numerous investigative reports and other documentation showing that "serious and widespread intentional discrimination persists in covered jurisdictions."

In all, the legislative record filled more than 15,000 pages. Representative Sensenbrenner, then chair of the House Judiciary Committee, described the record supporting reauthorization as "one of the most extensive considerations of any piece of legislation that the United States Congress has dealt with in the 27½ years" he had served in the House. The reauthorization passed the House by a vote of 390 to 33. The vote in the Senate was 98 to 0. President Bush signed the reauthorization a week after he received it, noting the need for "further work . . . in the fight against injustice" and calling the extension "an example of our continued commitment to a united America where every person is treated with dignity and respect."

Why was Congress intent on renewing §5 particularly? As the Chief Justice explained, §5 requires covered jurisdictions to obtain preclearance before making changes in voting laws that might introduce new methods of voting discrimination. Congress found, first of all, that §5 had been enormously successful in increasing minority registration and access to the ballot. But it also learned how essential §5 was to prevent a return to old ways. In 1995, for example, the state of Mississippi was stopped by §5 from bringing back its Jim Crow–era dual voter registration system, and in 2006, Texas was stopped from curtailing early voting in a predominantly Latino district, in defiance of this Court's order to reinstate the district after Texas tried to eliminate it. Congress confronted similar examples of discrimination in covered jurisdictions by the score.

Of signal importance, Congress found that as registration and voting by minority citizens impressively increased, other barriers sprang up to replace the tests and devices that once impeded access to the ballot. These second generation barriers included racial gerrymandering, switches from district-by-district voting to at-large voting, discriminatory annexations—methods more subtle than the visible methods used in 1965, but serving effectively to diminish a minority community's ability to exercise clout in the electoral process.

Congress retained §5 to put down the second-generation barriers before they got off the ground.

But the coverage formula is no good, the Court insists, for it is based on "decades-old data and eradicated practices," so Congress must start from scratch. Suppose the record shows, however, as engaging with it would reveal, that the formula continues to identify the jurisdictions of greatest concern, jurisdictions with the worst current records of voting discrimination. If Congress could determine from the reams of evidence it gathered that these jurisdictions still belonged under the preclearance regime, why did it need to alter the formula?

Bear in mind that Shelby County has mounted a facial challenge to the reauthorization. By what right does the Court address the County's claim? On other days, this Court has explained that facial challenges are the most difficult to mount successfully. The challenger will not be heard to complain on the ground that the statute in question might be applied unconstitutionally to others in situations not before the Court. Congress continued preclearance over Alabama, including Shelby County, only after considering barriers there to minority voting clout. There were many, they were shocking, and they were recent. They are spelled out in the dissenting opinion. What has become of the Court's usual restraint, its readiness to turn away facial attacks unless there is "no set of circumstances . . . under which [an] Act would be valid"?

The Court points to the success of §5 in eliminating the tests and devices extant in 1965 and in increasing minority citizens' registration and ballot access. Does that provide cause to believe §5's potent remedy is no longer needed? The notion that it does is hardly new. The same assumption, that the problem can be solved when particular methods of voting discrimination are identified and eliminated, was indulged and proved wrong repeatedly prior to enactment of the Voting Rights Act. That is why the 2006 renewal targeted no particular practices, but instead aimed to reach, in all their variety and persistence, measures that effectively impaired minority voting rights. And it is why Congress found in the second-generation barriers demonstrative evidence that a remedy as strong as preclearance remains vital and should not be removed from the federal arsenal.

It was the judgment of Congress that "40 years has not been a sufficient amount of time to eliminate the vestiges of discrimination following nearly 100 years of disregard for the dictates of the 15th Amendment." That judgment of the body empowered to enforce the Civil War Amendments "by appropriate legislation" should garner this Court's unstinting approbation. The great man who led the march from Selma to Montgomery and there called for the passage of the Voting Rights Act foresaw progress, even in Alabama. "The arc of the moral universe is long," he said, but "it bends toward justice," if there is a steadfast commitment to see the task through to completion. That commitment has been disserved by today's decision.

Bench Announcement
Abigail Fisher v. University of Texas at Austin
Monday, June 24, 2013

The Top Ten Percent Law, guaranteeing Texas high school seniors in the top 10 percent of their class automatic admission to a Texas university, fills three-quarters of the University of Texas freshman class. To select the remaining members of its entering class, UT evaluates applicants on factors including their talents, leadership qualities, family circumstances, and race. Abigail Fisher, a rejected white applicant who ranked below the top 10 percent of her class, sued the university for race discrimination, claiming that the use of race as a factor in the selection process discriminated against her in violation of the Equal Protection Clause.

The District Court and the Fifth Circuit Court of Appeals ruled in favor of the University, citing Grutter v. Bollinger, *a 2003 Supreme Court case holding that the University of Michigan Law School's holistic assessment of student applicants, in which race was just one "plus factor," was sufficiently targeted ("narrowly tailored") to achieve its compelling interest in ensuring a diverse student body. (By contrast, in* Grutter's *companion case,* Gratz v. Bollinger, *the Court found that the University of Michigan's undergraduate admissions process, which assigned numerical points for minority race or ethnicity, failed to pass the "narrowly tailored" requirement and was therefore unconstitutional.)*

In Abigail Fisher's case against the University of Texas, the Supreme Court majority, concluding that the Fifth Circuit had been insufficiently strict in its application of the Grutter/Gratz *precedent, vacated the Circuit decision and sent the case back to the Fifth Circuit to correct its legal error. Justice Ginsburg, the sole dissenter, not only viewed the lower federal court as faithful to the* Grutter *precedent and would have upheld its ruling, but felt strongly enough to announce her dissent from the bench. In the process, she also challenged the majority's characterization of the Top Ten Percent law as racially "neutral." Both of the University's admissions methods were adopted with an eye toward increasing racial diversity, she argued, and both were constitutionally legitimate.*

Justice Ginsburg's bench announcement of her dissent appears below. However, the Fisher *story does not end here. As the Court's majority ordered, the case went back to the Fifth Circuit, which concluded, for the second time, that the University's use of race as one factor in its admissions process was constitutional. The Supreme Court once again reviewed the Fifth Circuit's decision, as described in more detail in Highlights of the U.S. Supreme Court's 2015–16 Term at pp. 318–21 and 327–28.*

In my view, the courts below adhered to this Court's pathmarking decisions and there is no need for a second look.

My dissenting opinion questions the starting premise on which this case has proceeded. Texas' Top Ten Percent Law requires public universities to admit any graduate of a Texas high school ranked in the top 10 percent of her class. Petitioner calls the law race-neutral, and the Court accepts that characterization. The diversity achieved by the Top Ten Percent Law, petitioner urges, is accomplished without resort to a racial criterion, so the University has no constitutionally permissible basis for treating race as a relevant factor in reviewing individual admissions applications.

In truth, is the Top Ten Percent Law racially neutral in comparison to the University's explicit regard of race as one among many factors relevant to its educational mission? Is it not blindness to race, but race consciousness instead, that drives percentage plans such as the one Texas has adopted? But for *de facto* racial segregation in Texas' neighborhoods and schools, there would be no Top Ten Percent Law. The Texas Legislature deliberately used the State's demographics primarily to achieve a measure of racial diversity in the State's public universities.

The notion that the Top Ten Percent Law is race-neutral calls to mind Professor Thomas Reed Powell's famous statement: "If you think that you can think about a thing inextricably attached to something else without thinking about the thing which it is attached to, then you have a legal mind." Only that kind of legal mind could conclude that an admissions plan specifically designed to produce racial diversity is not race-conscious.

I have several times explained why government actors, including state universities, need not blind themselves to the still-lingering, everyday evident, effects of centuries of law-sanctioned inequality. Among constitutionally permissible options, I remain convinced, those that candidly disclose their consideration of race are preferable to those that conceal or obscure what drives them.

Like so many educational institutions across the nation, the University of Texas modeled its admissions plan after the law-school policy approved in *Grutter v. Bollinger* and the Harvard plan referenced as exemplary in Justice Powell's opinion in *Regents of the University of California v. Bakke*.

The Court rightly declines to cast off the equal protection framework settled ten years ago in *Grutter*. Yet it stops short of reaching the conclusion that framework warrants. Instead, the Court vacates the Court of Appeals' judgment and remands for the Court of Appeals to "assess whether the University has offered sufficient evidence [to] prove that its admissions program is narrowly tailored to obtain the educational benefits of diversity." As I see it, the Court of Appeals has already completed that inquiry, and its judgment, trained on this Court's *Bakke* and *Grutter* pathmarkers, merits our approbation.

Bench Announcement
National Federation of Independent Business v. Sebelius
June 28, 2012

On June 28, 2012, the last day of the Supreme Court's 2011–12 Term, the courtroom was packed. A thousand people gathered outside and many thousands more turned on their televisions and radios to learn the outcome in the most-watched case since Bush v. Gore. *The question in the* NFIB v. Sebelius *case: would the Patient Protection and Affordable Care Act of 2010 (the "ACA") survive the constitutional challenges marshalled against it?*

That complex and controversial act, designed to ensure virtually everyone in the United States access to health care, adopted two basic mechanisms to achieve that goal. First, it required individuals who were not covered by employer-provided insurance or by Medicaid to purchase insurance. The ACA provided for "insurance exchanges" where such individual insurance could be purchased, and created a penalty, collectible by the IRS, for those who failed to obtain insurance by the 2014 deadline.

Second, the ACA expanded Medicaid. That federal-state program, which had been adopted by all the states, provides medical services for low-income persons who are disabled, blind, or elderly and for needy families with dependent children. The ACA added all non-elderly adults with incomes below 133 percent of the federal poverty level.

The two provisions under constitutional attack were, first, the Act's "individual mandate" to purchase insurance, and, second, a mechanism to induce states to adopt the Medicaid expansion: possible revocation of resisting states' federal funding for its previously existing Medicaid program.

As Chief Justice Roberts began to announce the majority opinion, supporters of the Act had reason to hold their breath. After all, he was one of the five Justices labeled conservative; if he was speaking for them, the ACA might be doomed. Those fears seemed confirmed as he explained that the Constitution's "commerce clause," which bestowed upon Congress power "to regulate commerce . . . among the several states," did not authorize a provision such as the individual insurance mandate. (At least one television network, alerted by one of its reporters within the courtroom, announced that the Supreme Court had held that the ACA was unconstitutional.)

But the Chief Justice wasn't done with his bench announcement: although the Commerce Clause did not authorize Congress to enact the individual mandate, he continued, another constitutionally granted congressional power—the power to "lay and collect taxes"—did provide the necessary authorization, a conclusion in which he was joined by Justices Ginsburg, Breyer, Sotomayor, and Kagan. The individual mandate, the linchpin of the ACA's insurance scheme, had survived by a vote of five to four.

Not so the ACA's inducement to get states to adopt the ACA's Medicaid expansion. Unconstitutional, the Chief Justice declared. When Congress, in addition to extending the carrot of generous funding for the expansion, threatened states with the stick of terminating federal support for their preexisting Medicaid programs, "pressure turn[ed] into compulsion" and the legislation "runs contrary to our system of federalism." From this conclusion only Justice Ginsburg, joined by Justice Sotomayor, dissented.

Justice Ginsburg's twenty-minute dissenting bench announcement, the most lengthy she has delivered, addressed both of the Court's holdings.

In the 1930s, Congress responded to the need of senior citizens for old age and survivors insurance. It did so by making Social Security a tax-based, entirely federal program. In 2010, Congress addressed the public need for affordable health care when sickness or injury occurs. Congress did so by taking a path unlike the one it took for Social Security. Instead of an entirely federal program, the Affordable Care Act gives states and private insurers important roles in ensuring medical care for those who need it. The question the Court must answer is whether the Constitution stops Congress from taking the course it did. I would answer, emphatically No.

I agree with the Chief Justice that Congress' power to tax and spend supports the so-called individual mandate or minimum coverage provision. But I would make that an auxiliary holding. As I see it, Congress' vast authority to regulate interstate commerce solidly undergirds the Affordable Care legislation. I would uphold the legislation, first and foremost, on that ground.

Since 1937, the Court has deferred, as it should, to Congress' policymaking in the economic and social realm. Today, a majority of the Court rules that the commerce power is not adequate to the task. That ruling harks back to the era, ended seventy-five years ago, when the Court routinely thwarted legislative efforts to regulate the economy in the interest of those who labor to sustain it. It is a stunning step back that should not have staying power.

The Court's majority would compare health insurance to broccoli. If the government can compel people to buy insurance, then there is no commodity the government can't force people to purchase, so the argument goes. But health care is not like vegetables or other items one is at liberty to buy or not to buy. All of us will need health care, some sooner, some later, but we can't tell when, where, or how dire our need will be. A healthy twenty-one-year-old, for example, may tomorrow be the victim of an accident that leaves him or her an invalid, in need of constant and costly medical care. Further, to get broccoli, one must pay at the counter. Not so of health care. The accident victim who cannot pay the steep price of medical services will nevertheless receive emergency and follow-up care, because the law and professional ethics so require, and because ours is a humane society. But people who do purchase insurance end up footing the bill. By requiring the healthy uninsured either to obtain insurance or pay a toll, Congress sought to end this free ride.

It is shortsighted, moreover, to see the mandate as a decree that hale and hardy young people subsidize care rendered to older, less healthy people. In the fullness of time, today's young and healthy will become society's old and infirm. Viewed over a life span, the costs and benefits even out. And as I just noted, the youth who does not want insurance today may find that tomorrow, she desperately needs the services insurance is designed to secure.

What the mandate does, essentially, is to require people to prepay for medical care through insurance, instead of waiting, expecting to pay out of pocket at the point of service, when, in reality, many will lack the money to cover the cost. (Establishing payment terms for goods or services in or affecting interstate commerce is the kind of economic regulation that lies well within Congress' domain.)

The Chief Justice reasons that Congress can use its commerce power to regulate something already in existence, but cannot create that something in order to regulate it. But the interstate health insurance and health care markets are not Congress' creations; both existed well before the enactment of the Affordable Care Act.

I have already emphasized the unique attributes of the health care market: the fact that all of us will be in it sooner or later and cannot predict exactly when; the huge free-rider problem caused by people who refrain from purchasing insurance, then become sick or injured and get care cost-free to them, but costly for those of us who have paid in advance. Because there is no comparable market, the slippery slope envisioned by the Court's majority (if health insurance today, then broccoli tomorrow) is far more imaginary than real. As a learned jurist once commented: "Judges and lawyers live on the slippery slope of analogies; they are not supposed to ski it to the bottom."

Yes, the insurance purchase mandate is novel, but novelty is no reason to reject it. As our economy grows and changes, Congress must be competent to devise legislation meeting current-day social and economic realities. For that very reason, the Necessary and Proper Clause was included in the Constitution, to ensure that the federal government would have the capacity to provide for conditions and developments the framers knew they could scarcely foresee.

In enacting the Affordable Care Act, Congress' aim was to reduce the large number of U.S. residents, some 50 million in 2009, who lack health insurance. Congress was aware that the vast majority of those who lack insurance are not uninsured by choice. One group of particular concern to Congress were individuals with preexisting medical conditions. Before the ACA's enactment, the insurance industry charged these individuals steep prices or flatly denied them coverage. Congress understood, however, that a simple ban on those practices would not work. Without the mandate to acquire insurance, covering those with preexisting conditions would trigger a death spiral in the health insurance market: many people would not buy insurance until they suffered sickness or injury, premiums would skyrocket, more people would be added to the ranks of the uninsured because they could not pay the steep premiums, and, eventually, insurance companies, left with a pool of high-risk policyholders, would exit the market. With the mandate, the job could be done: access to insurance would be available and affordable; and uncompensated care would be hugely reduced.

In no way was Congress' action improper. The mandate acts directly on individuals; it does not commandeer the states as intermediaries. And along with other provisions of the Act, it addresses the sort of countrywide problem that made the Commerce Clause essential. The crisis created by the many millions of U.S. residents who lack health insurance is hardly contained within state boundaries. Far from encroaching on state prerogatives, the Affordable Health Care Act supplies a federal response to a need the states, acting separately, are incapable of meeting.

This Court has long recognized that the power to regulate interstate commerce "is an affirmative power commensurate with the national needs." While the Court upholds the mandate, as it surely should, it also, regrettably, hems in Congress' commerce power. In doing so, the Court invites assaults on national legislation irreconcilable with the framers' anticipation. Their understanding and expectation was that the Commerce Clause would empower Congress to act "in all Cases for the general Interests of the Union, and also in those instances in which the States are separately incompetent."

My dissent from the Court's retrogressive reading of the Commerce Clause is joined by Justices Breyer, Sotomayor, and Kagan.

There is a further issue: Congress' expansion of Medicaid to include a larger portion of the nation's poor. Medicaid is the prototypical example of federal-state cooperation. Rather than authorizing a federal agency to administer a uniform national health care system for the poor, as Congress did in establishing Medicare for seniors, Congress offered states the opportunity to tailor Medicaid grants to their particular needs, so long as they remain within bounds set by federal law. Congress reserved the "right to alter, amend, or repeal" any provision of the Medicaid Act; and participating states, for their part, agreed to amend their Medicaid plans consistent with alterations in the federal law. From 1965 until 2010, states regularly conformed to amendments expanding Medicaid, sometimes quite sizably.

The 2010 expansion is different in kind, the Court concludes, 7 to 2. Justice Sotomayor and I disagree. According to the Chief Justice, the expansion was misnamed. It did not expand Medicaid as it existed in 2010, he maintains. Instead, Congress established a wholly new program alongside "old Medicaid," and coerced the states to accept "new Medicaid" by threatening them with loss of funds from the old program if they hold out. On this reasoning, the Court, for the first time ever, finds an exercise of Congress' spending power unconstitutionally coercive.

In truth, however, Medicaid is a single program with but one constant aim—to enable poor persons to receive basic health care when they need it. What the expansion does is simply this: it adds more people, all of them poor, to the Medicaid-eligible population. Congress did not otherwise change the operation of the program.

The Chief Justice justifies his characterization of the expansion as a new program on three grounds. First, he says, by covering those earning up to 133 percent of the federal poverty line, the expansion, unlike Medicaid as originally enacted, does not "care for the neediest among us." The expansion covers adults earning less than $15,000 annually. Those low earners, on any fair assessment, rank among the nation's poor.

Second, the Chief observes that newly eligible people receive a level of coverage less comprehensive than the traditional Medicaid package. But the ACA did not introduce the less comprehensive package. Since 2006, states have been free to use it for many of their Medicaid beneficiaries.

Third, the reimbursement rate for participating states is different. True, but that rate is markedly more generous than the usual federal contribution, hardly something the states can complain about. The federal government picks up 100 percent of the tab initially, gradually reducing to 90 percent.

Suppose Congress had from the start made Medicaid-eligible all those originally covered, plus those added by the expansion. That would be unobjectionable under the Chief Justice's reasoning. But we have never held that a grant program becomes two rather than one when Congress lays a foundation and later builds on it. Congress can, and often does, expand programs, adding new conditions that grant recipients must meet in order to continue receiving funds.

Our decisions, I acknowledge, have hypothesized that a financial inducement might "pass the point where pressure becomes coercion," and therefore exceed Congress' spending power. But until today, that prospect has remained theoretical. The Court had found no case fitting the bill.

Recall that Congress reserved to itself, when it adopted Medicaid in 1965, the right to alter, amend, even repeal any provision. This Court long ago explained what those words mean. They mean Congress retains "full and complete power to make such alterations and amendments . . . as come within the just scope of the legislative power."

States have not missed that meaning. Each time a state notified the federal government of a change it made in its own Medicaid plan, it certified both that it knew the federally set terms of participation could change, and that it would abide by the changes as a condition of continued participation.

Today's decision holds that Congress can alter a spending program "somewhat, but not too much." We can anticipate bolder challenges than in the past urging that a congressional amendment goes too far, turning "pressure . . . into compulsion." When those challenges arrive, my colleagues may comprehend the wisdom of the observation that conceptions of "impermissible coercion" premised on a state's perceived inability to decline federal funds "are just too amorphous to be judicially administerable."

At bottom, my colleagues' position is that the states' reliance on federal funds limits Congress' authority to alter its spending programs. This gets things backwards. Congress, not the states, is tasked by the Constitution with spending federal money in service of the general welfare. And each successive Congress is empowered to appropriate funds as it sees fit. When the 111th Congress reached a conclusion about the portion of the nation's poor that should qualify for Medicaid, a portion larger than a predecessor Congress covered, the later Congress abridged no state's right to "existing" or "preexisting" funds. For, in truth, there are no such funds. There is only money states *anticipate* receiving, but can scarcely insist on receiving, from future Congresses.

Seven members of the Court, however, buy the argument that prospective withholding of anticipated funds exceeds Congress' spending power. Given that holding, I entirely agree with the Chief Justice as to the appropriate remedy: it is to bar the withholding found impermissible, not to scrap the expansion altogether. This Court has many times explained that when it confronts a statute marred by a constitutional infirmity, its endeavor must be to salvage, not demolish, the legislation. The Court does that by declaring the statute invalid "to the extent that it reaches too far, but otherwise [leaving the statute] intact." Because the Court finds the withholding—not the granting—of federal funds incompatible with the Spending Clause, Congress' extension of Medicaid remains available to any state affirming its willingness to accept the uncommonly generous federal grant.

So, in the end, the Affordable Care Act survives largely unscathed. But the Court's Commerce and Spending Clause jurisprudence has been set awry. My expectation is that the setbacks will be temporary blips, not permanent obstructions.

Bench Announcement

Burwell v. Hobby Lobby Stores, Inc.

Conestoga Wood Specialties Corp. v. Burwell

June 30, 2014

Hobby Lobby and Conestoga Wood Specialties each sued Sylvia Burwell, the secretary of the Department of Health and Human Services (HHS), the federal agency that administers the Affordable Care Act (ACA), also known as "Obamacare." The ACA requires employer health plans to furnish preventive care and screenings for women. HHS, in regulations implementing this provision, specifies that employer plans must provide women with coverage for the twenty contraceptive methods approved by the Food and Drug Administration, but exempts religious employers, such as churches and religious nonprofit organizations, from the requirement. Hobby Lobby and Conestoga are both for-profit corporations and therefore not exempt under the HHS regulation. The main stockholders of these corporations objected on religious grounds to providing insurance for approved contraceptives that operate post-conception. They asserted that their corporations are protected under the provisions of the Religious Freedom Restoration Act (RFRA) of 1993. RFRA prohibits the federal government from "substantially burden[ing] a person's exercise of religion" unless it "demonstrates that application of the burden to the person—(1) is in furtherance of a compelling governmental interest; and (2) is the least restrictive means of furthering that compelling governmental interest." Hobby Lobby prevailed in the Tenth Circuit, Conestoga lost in the Third Circuit, and the Supreme Court granted review to resolve the conflict between the circuits.

The Supreme Court split five to four, with Justice Alito delivering the opinion of the Court. Agreeing with the Tenth Circuit, the Court held that corporations (at least if they are "closely held" corporations, meaning most of their shares are held by a family or a small group of investors) are "persons" under RFRA, that HHS's contraceptive mandate substantially burdened their exercise of religion, and that, even assuming the government's interest in guaranteeing employees cost-free access to the four objectionable contraceptives is a compelling one, it had failed to show that the contraceptive mandate was the least restrictive means of furthering that interest. Justice Ginsburg delivered the following dissent announcement from the bench.

Under the Affordable Care Act, employers with health plans must provide women with access to contraceptives at no cost to the insured employee. The Court holds today that commercial enterprises, employing workers of diverse faiths, can opt out of contraceptive coverage if contraceptive use is incompatible with the employers' religious beliefs. When an employer's religious practice detrimentally affects others, however, the First Amendment's Free Exercise Clause does not require accommodation to that practice. Because precedent to that effect is well established, the Court rests its decision not on the Free Exercise Clause of the Constitution, but solely on the Religious Freedom Restoration Act (RFRA).

Justices Breyer, Sotomayor, Kagan, and I find in that act no design to permit the opt-outs in question. RFRA targeted this Court's decision in a particular case, one holding that Native Americans could be denied unemployment benefits because they had ingested peyote at, and as an essential part of, a religious ceremony. Congress sought to override that decision and to restore by statute the respect for religious exercise as it existed before the sacramental peyote decision was rendered. Nothing more.

Reading the Act expansively, as the Court does, raises a host of "Me, too" questions. Can an employer in business for profit opt out of coverage for blood transfusions, vaccinations, antidepressants, or medications derived from pigs, based on the employer's sincerely held religious beliefs opposing those medical practices? What of the employer whose religious faith teaches that it is sinful to employ a single woman without her father's consent, or a married woman, without her husband's consent? Can those employers opt out of Title VII's ban on gender discrimination in employment? These examples, by the way, are not hypothetical.

A wise legal scholar famously said of the First Amendment's free speech guarantee: "Your right to swing your arms ends just where the other [person's] nose begins." The dissenters believe the same is true of the Free Exercise Clause, and that Congress meant RFRA to be interpreted in line with that principle.

The genesis of the contraceptive coverage regulations should have enlightened the Court's decision. "The ability of women to participate equally in the economic and social life of the Nation," the Court appreciated over two decades ago, "has been facilitated by their ability to control their reproductive lives." Congress acted on that understanding when it called for coverage of preventive care responsive to women's needs as part of the Affordable Care Act, a nationwide insurance program intended to be comprehensive.

Carrying out Congress' direction, the Department of Health and Human Services (HHS) promulgated regulations requiring group health plans to cover, without cost-sharing, all contraceptives approved by the Food and Drug Administration (FDA). The scientific studies informing the HHS regulations demonstrate compellingly the benefits to public health and to women's well-being attending improved contraceptive access.

Notably, the Court assumes that contraceptive coverage under the Affordable Care Act furthers compelling interests. The Court's reasoning, however, subordinates those interests. Nor is the subordination limited to the four contraceptives Hobby Lobby and Conestoga object to. At oral argument, counsel for Hobby Lobby forthrightly acknowledged that his argument "would apply just as well" if an employer's religion ruled out use of every one of the twenty contraceptives the FDA has approved.

A threshold issue the parties dispute: does RFRA, which speaks of "a person's" exercise of religion, even apply to for-profit corporations, for they are not flesh-and-blood "person[s]," they are artificial entities created by law. True enough, the First Amendment's free exercise protections, and RFRA's safeguards, shelter not only natural persons, they shield as well churches and other nonprofit religion-based organizations. Yes, the Court's decisions have accorded "special solicitude" to religious institutions. But until today, no similar solicitude has been extended to for-profit commercial entities.

The reason why is not obscure. Religious organizations exist to foster the interests of persons subscribing to the same religious faith. Not so of for-profit corporations. Workers who sustain the operations of for-profit corporations commonly are not drawn from one religious community. Indeed, by law, no religion-based criterion can restrict the workforce of for-profit corporations. The difference between a community of believers in the same religion and a business embracing persons of diverse beliefs is slighted in today's decision.

Justice Sotomayor and I would hold that for-profit corporations should not be equated to nonprofits existing to serve a religious community, and would place them outside RFRA's domain. Justices Breyer and Kagan would not decide the threshold question whether for-profit corporations or their owners can bring RFRA claims, and therefore do not join this part of the dissenting opinion. All four of us, however, agree in unison that RFRA gives Hobby Lobby and Conestoga no right to opt out of contraceptive coverage.

The Court rejects the contraceptive coverage requirement on the ground that it fails to meet RFRA's least restrictive means test. But the government has shown that there is no less restrictive, equally effective means that would both satisfy the challengers' religious objections and ensure that women employees receive, at no cost to them, the preventive care needed to safeguard their health and well-being.

Well, let the government pay for the contraceptives (rather than the employees who do not share their employer's faith), the Court suggests. The Care Act, however, requires coverage of preventive services through the existing employer-based system of health insurance, not through substitution of the government (in effect, the general public) as payor.

And where is the stopping point to the "let the government pay" solution? Suppose it offends an employer's religious belief to pay the minimum wage, or to accord women equal pay for substantially similar work. Such claims, in fact, have been made and accepted as sincere. Does it rank as a less restrictive alternative to require the government to provide the pay to which the employer has a religion-based objection?

Perhaps because these questions are not so easy to answer, the Court rests on a different solution: extend to commercial enterprises the accommodation already afforded to nonprofit religion-based organizations. This extension solution was barely addressed in the parties' briefs. Asked about it at oral argument, Hobby Lobby's counsel responded: "We haven't been offered that accommodation, so we haven't had to decide what kind of objection, if any, we would make to that."

Ultimately, the Court hedges. It declines to decide whether the extension solution "complies with RFRA for purposes of all religious claims." The fatal flaw, in any event, bears reiteration. The extension cure would equate two dissimilar categories: on the one hand, commercial businesses like Hobby Lobby and Conestoga, whose workforces, by law, are open to persons of all faiths, and on the other, nonprofit organizations designed to further the mission of a particular community of believers.

A pathmarking 1982 decision RFRA preserved is highly instructive in this regard: *United States v. Lee*. *Lee* rejected the exemption claim of an Amish entrepreneur whose religious tenets were offended by the payment of Social Security taxes. Tax cases are in a discrete category, today's Court responds. But *Lee* made two key points that cannot be confined to tax cases. First, "[w]hen followers of a particular sect enter into commercial activity as a matter of choice," the *Lee* Court observed, "the limits they accept on their own conduct as a matter of conscience and faith are not to be superimposed on statutory schemes . . . binding on others in that activity." Second, the *Lee* Court said, allowing a religion-based exemption to a commercial employer would "operat[e] to impose the employer's religious faith on the employees." Working for Hobby Lobby or Conestoga, in other words, should not deprive employees holding different beliefs of the employer-insured preventive care available to workers at the shop next door.

Hobby Lobby and Conestoga, as shown by the real cases I described, hardly stand alone as commercial enterprises seeking religion-based exemptions from generally applicable laws, among them, laws prohibiting discrimination in the workplace. How is the Court to divine when a religious belief is feigned "to escape legal sanction," or which genuine beliefs are worthy of accommodation and which are not? Those questions are all the more perplexing given the majority opinion's repeated insistence that "courts may not presume to determine . . . the plausibility of a religious claim."

In sum, today's potentially sweeping decision minimizes the government's compelling interest in uniform compliance with laws governing workplaces, in particular, the Affordable Care Act. And it discounts the disadvantages religion-based opt-outs impose on others, in particular, employees who do not share their employer's religious beliefs.

Our cosmopolitan nation is made up of people of almost every conceivable religious preference. In passing RFRA, Congress did not alter a tradition in which one person's right to free exercise of her religion must be kept in harmony with the rights of her fellow citizens, and with the common good.

For the reasons I summarized, all of them and others developed in the dissenting opinion, I would reverse the judgment of the Tenth Circuit and affirm the judgment of the Third Circuit.

Bench Announcement
Gonzales v. Carhart
Gonzales v. Planned Parenthood
Wednesday, April 18, 2007

Gonzales v. Carhart *upheld the Partial Birth Abortion Act of 2003, a federal law that criminalizes a procedure referred to as "intact dilation and evacuation," or "D&E," one of several abortion methods used by doctors after the twelfth week of pregnancy. In this first abortion case decided after Sandra Day O'Connor retired from the Court, the Justices upheld the Act, splitting five to four. Justice Kennedy wrote the majority opinion, joined by Chief Justice Roberts, then in his second Term as Chief Justice, Justice Scalia, Justice Thomas, and Justice Alito, the Court's newest member and O'Connor's replacement.*

The majority opinion claimed to be faithful to the Court's precedents on the right to abortion, despite an earlier case in which the Court declared a state ban on D&E unconstitutional. That earlier case, Stenberg v. Carhart *(2000), had also been decided 5–4, but Justice Breyer, joined by Justices Stevens, O'Connor, Souter, and Ginsburg, had ruled the statute unconstitutional on its face. The reason: it did not contain an exception allowing a doctor to perform the D&E procedure if it was "necessary, in appropriate medical judgment, for the preservation of the . . . health" of the pregnant woman. The Partial Birth Abortion Act also lacked the woman's health exception, but Justice Kennedy's opinion in* Gonzales, *by contrast to Justice Breyer's in* Stenberg, *emphasized not the absence of an exception to protect the woman's health, but the government's "legitimate and substantial interest in preserving and promoting fetal life," which, it said, existed throughout a woman's pregnancy. Justices Thomas and Scalia issued a concurring opinion reiterating their view that* Roe v. Wade *and its progeny should be explicitly overruled.*

The majority's claim of adherence to precedent was disputed by the four dissenters, in an opinion by Justice Ginsburg. Underscoring their mutual concern, Justice Ginsburg in her bench announcement "strongly" dissented from the majority opinion.

Four members of this Court, Justices Stevens, Souter, Breyer, and I, strongly dissent from today's decision.

Fifteen years ago, in *Planned Parenthood of Southeastern Pennsylvania v. Casey*, the Court declared that "[l]iberty finds no refuge in a jurisprudence of doubt." There was, the Court said, an "imperative" need to dispel doubt as to "the meaning and reach" of the Court's 7-to-2 judgment, rendered nearly two decades earlier, in *Roe v. Wade*. One of the clarifications *Casey* provided concerned the state's unconditional obligation to safeguard a woman's health. At all stages of pregnancy, the Court reconfirmed, state regulation of abortion procedures must protect "the health of the woman."

In reaffirming *Roe*, the *Casey* Court described the centrality of "the decision whether to bear . . . a child" to a woman's "dignity and autonomy," her "destiny," her "conception of . . . her place in society." Challenges to undue restrictions on abortion procedures, the Court comprehended in *Casey*, do not seek to vindicate some vague or generalized notion of privacy. Rather, they home in on a woman's autonomy to decide for herself her life's course, and thus to enjoy equal citizenship stature.

In keeping with this understanding of the right to reproductive choice, we have consistently required that laws regulating abortion, at any stage of pregnancy and in all cases, safeguard not only a woman's existence—her life—but her health as well. Faithful to precedent unbroken from 1973 until today, the Court held seven years ago in *Stenberg v. Carhart* that a state statute banning the very procedure at issue today—intact D&E—was unconstitutional in part because it lacked a health exception. If substantial medical authority maintains that banning a particular abortion procedure could endanger women's health, we held, a health exception cannot be omitted by the legislators.

Despite our unambiguous ruling, Congress passed the Partial-Birth Abortion Ban Act—without an exception for women's health—a ban that would operate nationwide. After lengthy trials and thorough review of volumes of medical evidence, each of the district courts to consider the statute found that it was unconstitutional for the same reason: significant medical authority identified intact D&E as the safest procedure for some women.

In an alarming decision, the Court today reverses the judgments other federal courts have uniformly made. Today's decision refuses to take *Casey* and *Stenberg* seriously. The Court's opinion tolerates, indeed applauds, federal intervention to ban nationwide a procedure found necessary and proper in certain cases by the American College of Obstetricians and Gynecologists. For the first time since *Roe*, the Court blesses a prohibition with no exception protecting a woman's health.

The Court asserts that its ruling furthers the government's interest in "promoting fetal life." But the Act scarcely furthers that interest, for it targets only a *method* of abortion. The woman may abort the fetus, so long as her doctor uses another method, one her doctor judges less safe for her. The Court further pretends that its decision protects women. Women might come to regret their physician-counseled choice of an intact D&E and suffer from "[s]evere depression and loss of esteem," the Court worries. Notably, the solution the Court approves is *not* to require doctors to inform women adequately of the different procedures they might choose, and the risks each entails. Instead, the Court shields women by denying them any choice in the matter. This way of protecting women recalls ancient notions about women's place in society and under the Constitution—ideas that have long since been discredited.

If there is anything at all redemptive about today's opinion, it is that the Court is not willing to foreclose entirely a challenge to the constitutionality of the Act. But the "as-applied challenge[s] in discrete case[s]" the Court would allow put women's health in danger and place doctors in an untenable position. Even if courts were able slowly to carve out health exceptions for "discrete and well-defined instances" through hard fought, protracted piecemeal litigation, women whose circumstances have not been anticipated by prior litigation could well remain unprotected. In treating those women, physicians would risk criminal prosecution, conviction, and imprisonment if they exercise their best judgment as to the safest medical procedure for their patients. The Court is thus gravely mistaken to conclude that narrow, as-applied challenges are "the proper manner to protect the health of the woman."

As the Court wrote in *Casey*, "overruling *Roe*'s central holding would not only reach an unjustifiable result under principles of *stare decisis*, it would seriously weaken the Court's capacity to exercise the judicial power and to function as the Supreme Court of a Nation dedicated to the rule of law." Although today's opinion does not go so far as to discard *Roe* or *Casey*, the Court—differently composed than it was when we last considered a restrictive abortion regulation—is hardly faithful to *Casey*'s invocations of "the rule of law" and the "principles of *stare decisis*."

In candor, the Partial-Birth Abortion Ban Act, and the Court's defense of it, cannot be understood as anything other than an effort to chip away at a right declared again and again by this Court—and with increasing comprehension of its centrality to women's lives. A decision of the character the Court makes today should not have staying power.

8

Highlights of the U.S. Supreme Court's 2015–16 Term

The federal judicial map of the United States is divided into thirteen "circuits," most of which are subdivided into "districts." Each circuit is the home of a "circuit court of appeals." (Justice Ginsburg, for example, served on the U.S. Court of Appeals for the District of Columbia Circuit from 1980 until 1993.) The circuit courts take appeals from the federal trial courts—called "district courts"—within their circuit. Above the circuit courts sits the United States Supreme Court.

In the early days of the republic, each of the Supreme Court Justices, assigned to a particular circuit, would "ride circuit," sitting as a judge with the circuit's judges to hear cases. Today the Justices are still assigned a circuit or two, but they almost never hear cases. Their main responsibility is to deal with applications from their assigned circuits for emergency stays (most notably, stays of execution in death penalty cases) and injunctions.

Justice Ginsburg's assigned circuit is the Second Circuit, which includes Connecticut, New York, and Vermont. Each year she attends the annual Judicial Conference of the Second Circuit and delivers her "Highlights" reports to the attendees, in which she comments on the "most watched" cases decided by the Supreme Court for the Term, as well as notable actions in cases that came to the Court from the Second Circuit, and she leavens the report with a taste of the lighter side of life at the Court. Since these "Highlights" are usually delivered before the end of the Term, Justice Ginsburg updates them once all the decisions are "in," usually by the end of June.

The Court's 2015–16 Term was, as Justice Ginsburg's Highlights below reveal, affected by the mid-Term death of Justice Scalia. One consequence was that some cases which likely would have been decided by a 5–4 vote ended up with a 4–4 tie, leaving resolution of the issues they raised for a later case and future Term. Another may have been a somewhat heavier workload for the Court's remaining Justices. Fortunately, most of the Court's cases are not decided by narrow majorities, and, as Justice Ginsburg's review of the Court's Term output and "closely watched" cases makes evident, much of the Court's work proceeded as usual. But, she says, without the exuberant presence of Justice Scalia, the Court is "a paler place."

The two cases at the top of Justice Ginsburg's most-watched list for 2015–16, both from Texas, were Fisher v. University of Texas, *an equal protection challenge to the university's affirmative action admissions policy, and* Whole Woman's Health v. Hellerstedt, *a due process challenge to a law imposing standards on abortion clinics and their doctors that reduced women's access to abortions. In both of these cases, it was Justice Kennedy who called the shots. Tweaking his prior positions on affirmative action and abortion, he joined the Court's liberal members to preserve the Court's challenged precedents on abortion and affirmative action.*

Although Justice Ginsburg did write for the majority in some of the other high-profile cases discussed in her Highlights, she wrote neither a majority nor dissenting opinion in Fisher *or* Whole Woman's Health. *Nonetheless, she left her mark on both. Before turning to her "rapid review" of the Court's 2015–16 Term, a few extra paragraphs on her role in those two most-watched cases are in order.*

Fisher

Three years and one day after its first ruling in Fisher v. University of Texas *had sent the case back to the Court of Appeals for a second look* *(see p. 296), the Court, on June 23, 2016, issued its second decision in* Fisher. *As in* Fisher I, *Elena Kagan, the Court's junior Justice, recused herself because, during her previous job as solicitor general, her office of the Justice Department submitted an amicus brief in the case. In the absence of Justice Kagan, and with the death of Justice Scalia earlier in the Term, the Court, reduced* to seven Justices, was likely to split 4–3. Justice Kennedy had written the majority opinion that sent Fisher I back to the Fifth Circuit for reassessment; now the question was, which three Justices would he join to make a majority in Fisher II?

Justice Ginsburg had been the sole dissenter to Justice Kennedy's Fisher I decision. She had written:

> The University of Texas . . . seeks to achieve student-body diversity through an admissions policy patterned after the Harvard plan referenced as exemplary in Justice Powell's opinion in Regents of the University of California v. Bakke (1978). And, like so many educational institutions across the Nation, the University has taken care to follow the model approved by the Court in Grutter v. Bollinger (2003) [citations omitted].

"Accordingly, I would not return this case for a second look," she declared:

> As the thorough opinions below show, the University's admissions policy flexibly considers race only as a "factor of a factor of a factor of a factor" in the calculus; followed a yearlong review through which the University reached the reasonable, good-faith judgment that supposedly race-neutral initiatives were insufficient to achieve, in appropriate measure, the educational benefits of student-body diversity; and is subject to periodic review to ensure that the consideration of race remains necessary and proper to achieve the University's educational objectives.
>
> The Court rightly declines to cast off the equal protection framework settled in Grutter. Yet it stops short of reaching the conclusion that [the Grutter] framework warrants. Instead, . . . it remands for the Court of Appeals to "assess whether the University has offered sufficient evidence [to] prove that its admissions program is narrowly tailored to obtain the educational benefits of diversity." As I see it, the Court of Appeals has already completed that inquiry, and its judgment, trained on this Court's Bakke and Grutter pathmarkers, merits our approbation. [Footnotes and citations omitted.]

Although Justice Kennedy was never the adamant opponent of affirmative action that his colleagues Justices Scalia and Thomas were, in no prior case had he actually approved a race-conscious admissions program. Now, in Fisher II, *he changed course, joining Justices Ginsburg, Breyer, and Sotomayor to make a 4–3 majority declaring the University of Texas's race-conscious admissions program lawful under the Equal Protection Clause of the Constitution, and, as the senior Justice in that majority, he chose to keep the opinion-drafting task for himself.*

The university, Kennedy wrote, had, after careful and thorough study, "articulated concrete and precise goals"—among them, destruction of stereotypes, promotion of cross-racial understanding, preparation of a student body for an increasingly diverse workforce and society, and the "cultivation of a set of leaders with legitimacy in the eyes of the citizenry"—all objectives that "mirror the 'compelling interest' this Court has approved in its prior cases." And this time around, he was persuaded that the university had carried its burden of proving that its race-conscious program was necessary and narrowly tailored to its interest in a diverse student body.

None of the suggested alternatives to the university's approach, he concluded, "had been shown to be 'available' and 'workable' means through which the university could have met its educational goals." In particular, Kennedy rejected petitioner Fisher's suggestion that the university already had at hand a race-neutral device to meet its goals: namely, an uncapped version of the university's Top Ten Percent Plan under which it could admit all or nearly all of its students. Explaining why such a percentage scheme did not constitute a more narrowly tailored way of achieving the university's interest in diversity, Kennedy invoked Justice Ginsburg's dissenting words in Fisher I, *writing:*

> *As an initial matter, petitioner [Fisher] overlooks the fact that the Top Ten Percent Plan, though facially neutral, cannot be understood apart from its basic purpose, which is to boost minority enrollment. Percentage plans are "adopted with racially segregated neighborhoods and schools front and center stage."* Fisher I, *570 US at ___ (Ginsburg, J., dissenting) (slip op., at p. 2). "It is race consciousness, not blindness to race that drives such plans."* Ibid. *Consequently, petitioner*

cannot assert simply that increasing the University's reliance on a percentage plan would make its admissions policy race neutral.

The university, he concluded, had "met its burden of showing that the admissions policy it used at the time it rejected petitioner's application was narrowly tailored." In Fisher II, *Justice Kennedy had ended up where Justice Ginsburg already stood in her dissent in* Fisher I.

Whole Woman's Health

In one of the most significant abortion cases in several decades, the Court was asked to pass on the constitutionality of a Texas law that, purportedly in the name of women's health, had reduced women's access to pre-viability abortions in that state. The Court's three women Justices, Ruth Bader Ginsburg, Sonia Sotomayor, and Elena Kagan, joined by Justice Stephen Breyer, made news with their vigorous, informed, and pointed questions from the bench at oral argument in early March.

Justice Ginsburg asked the first question of the lawyer for Whole Woman's Health, Stephanie Toti. When, mid-argument, the questioning bogged down, she tried to move her fellow questioners along, but, even after a clarifying intervention by Justice Kagan, couldn't manage to guide Justices Kennedy and Alito past threshold procedural issues before Toti reached the end of her allotted time. At that point, Justice Ginsburg intervened again, asking the Chief Justice if Toti could "have some time to address the merits"—whether the state's legal requirements imposed an undue burden on women's right to choose abortion. The Chief granted an extra five minutes, at the end of which Justice Sotomayor took up the questioning and didn't let go for at least another five minutes. But it was when the lawyer for Texas, Scott Keller, stood up to defend the legislation that Justices Ginsburg, Sotomayor, and Kagan dominated the bench. Justice Ginsburg again asked the first question—and also, the argument again in overtime, the last. The Washington Post *noted that Justices Ginsburg and Sotomayor had questioned the lawyers for so long that the one hour allotted for the arguments in the case went almost a half-hour overtime. Dahlia Lithwick, in a long blog for* Slate *titled "How Three Fierce Female Justices Took Control of the Supreme Court," crowed: "It felt as if, for the first time in history, the gender playing field at the high court was finally leveled." The* Post *quoted Justice Ginsburg's cut-to-the-chase comment as Scott's argument drew to a close: "What it's about," she had reminded Scott, "is that a woman has a fundamental right to make this [abortion] choice for herself."*

During oral argument, Justice Kennedy had seemed of two minds, on the one hand exploring at length whether there was some way to postpone or avoid a decision on the constitutional question, and on the other inquiring about the medical wisdom of one of the Texas law's consequences, fueling considerable speculation among Court watchers about where he would come out. When the time came to decide, he cast his vote with the liberals, joining Justices Ginsburg, Kagan, Sotomayor, and Breyer to form a majority of five to invalidate the Texas law. Being the senior Justice in the majority, he got to assign the authorship of the Court's opinion, and he chose Justice Breyer to do the job.

Reaching back to Planned Parenthood v. Casey, *a case decided the year before Justice Ginsburg joined the Supreme Court, Justice Breyer clarified the "undue burden" standard for evaluating the constitutionality of abortion regulations. "We recognize," he wrote, quoting* Roe v. Wade, *that the "State has a legitimate interest in seeing to it that abortion, like any other medical procedure, is performed under circumstances that insure maximum safety for the patient." But, he noted, citing* Casey, *"unnecessary health regulations that have the purpose or effect of presenting a substantial obstacle to a woman seeking an abortion impose an undue burden on that right." The* Casey *rule, he stated, "requires that courts consider the burdens a law imposes on abortion access together with the benefits those laws confer." Applying that balancing test, Justice Breyer engaged in an intensive examination of the evidence and findings relating to the Texas law's health benefits (negligible) and burdens on women's access to abortion (considerable), and concluded that the Texas law failed the constitutional test.*

Justice Ginsburg joined Breyer's forty-page opinion, but, as she mentions in her Highlights, she also wrote a concurring opinion. This short concurrence, consisting of one long paragraph, amplified the Breyer opinion's most telling facts: The Texas law "inevitably will reduce the number of clinics and doctors allowed to provide abortion services," making abortions more difficult to obtain. Complications from abortions "are both rare and rarely dangerous"; abortion is "one of the safest medical procedures performed in the

United States" and "is at least as safe as other medical procedures performed in outpatient settings"; and "medical procedures, including childbirth, are far more dangerous to patients."

"Given those realities," she wrote, "it is beyond rational belief that [the Texas law] could genuinely protect the health of women, and certain that the law 'would simply make it more difficult for them to obtain abortions.'" (Later, speaking with a reporter, she was blunt about the law's purpose: "It seemed to me it was a sham to pretend this was about a woman's health" rather than about making it harder to obtain an abortion.)

Then she made a point, nowhere addressed in the Breyer opinion, but embedded in the memories of women old enough to remember the days when abortion was illegal: "When a State severely limits access to safe and legal procedures, women in desperate circumstances may resort to unlicensed rogue practitioners, faute de mieux, at great risk to their health and safety." Her conclusion: "So long as this Court adheres to* Roe *v.* Wade *(1973) and* Planned Parenthood of Southeastern Pa. *v.* Casey *(1992), [laws like Texas's] that 'do little or nothing for health, but rather strew impediments to abortion' . . . cannot survive judicial inspection." Just days after the decision was announced, Justice Ginsburg told an Associated Press reporter, "I fully subscribed to everything Breyer said, but it was long, and I wanted something pithy. I wrote to say, 'Don't try this anymore.'"*[1]

Highlights of the U.S. Supreme Court's 2015–16 Term

July 1, 2016†

It is fitting to open these remarks with a remembrance of my dear colleague, Antonin Scalia. His death was the most momentous occurrence of the Court's 2015–16 Term, and his absence will be felt

---

*Translation: "for lack of a better alternative."

† A version of these remarks was delivered at the U.S. Court of Appeals for the Second Circuit Judicial Conference in Saratoga Springs, New York, on May 25, 2016. They have been updated and edited.

in many Terms to follow. [*Justice Ginsburg's tribute in these remarks included memories she recounted in "Remembering Justice Scalia," p. 38. We do not repeat those remembrances here.*]

Justice Scalia was a man of many talents, a jurist of captivating brilliance, high spirits, and quick wit, possessed of a rare talent for making even the most somber judge smile. The press wrote of his "energetic fervor," "astringent intellect," "peppery prose," "acumen," and "affability."

It was my great good fortune to have known him as working colleague and dear friend. The Court is a paler place without him.

My rapid review of the Term just ended starts with a numerical snapshot. From June 2015 to May 2016, the Court received about 6,375 petitions for review, down from 6,500 in the previous Term. From the thousands of requests, we selected only 67 for full briefing and argument, not counting the one petition we dismissed as improvidently granted. To the 67, the same number we selected last Term, add 12 per curiam decisions—opinions rendered without full briefing or oral argument. That brings total opinions produced to 79.

Records set during the Term: According to a law professor who keeps tabs on these things, then blogs about them, Justice Breyer asked the longest question at oral argument. In *United States v. Texas*,[2] a challenge to the president's deferred-action immigration policy, Breyer's inquiry ran 52 transcript lines. In total questions asked, however, Justice Breyer ranked only fourth, asking 381 questions. He stood behind Justice Alito, whose questions numbered 401, and the Chief Justice, who questioned counsel 417 times. Far out in front with 477 questions, Justice Sotomayor replaced Justice Scalia as the Justice who asked the most questions at oral argument.

Justice Thomas, after a ten-year silence, astonished all in attendance by asking nine questions, all in the same case, *Voisine v. United States*.[3] The issue that sparked his interest: whether misdemeanor assault convictions for reckless conduct trigger the statutory ban on possessing firearms contained in 18 U.S.C. §922(g).

With all returns in, the Court completed the Term's work on

June 27. We divided 5–3 or 4–3 in 8 of the 67 argued cases[4] and were unanimous, at least as to the bottom-line judgment, in 25 cases.[5] And in 4, we affirmed judgments of the courts of appeals by an equally divided Court. When the Court is evenly divided, no opinions are released and the automatic affirmance of the court below has no precedential value; an even division, therefore, is essentially the same as a denial of review. Three of the 4–4 automatic affirmances were among the Term's most closely watched cases. I will essay a capsule description of each.

First of the 4–4 splits announced, *Friedrichs v. California Teachers Association:*[6] The petitioners in *Friedrichs* asked the Court to overrule *Abood v. Detroit Board of Education*[7] and hold that requiring public-sector employees to pay anything to a union violates the First Amendment's free speech guarantee. *Abood*, which held that all workers could be required to contribute to the cost of collective bargaining and union-operated grievance procedures, thus survives, at least until the Court numbers nine.

On June 23, four days before we finished, the Court reported equal divisions in *Dollar General v. Mississippi Band of Choctaw Indians*[8] and *United States v. Texas*.[9] The issue in *Dollar General:* whether tribal courts may adjudicate civil claims filed by members of a tribe against nonmembers who engage in wrongful conduct on Indian reservations.

In *United States v. Texas*, several states joined in a challenge to the legality of President Obama's policy of deferring deportation of some four million unlawfully present aliens whose children are U.S. citizens or lawful permanent residents. Under long-standing government policy, aliens granted deferred action are eligible to receive certain benefits, prime among them permission to work legally in the United States. A divided Fifth Circuit panel affirmed a district court decision preliminarily enjoining implementation of that policy.

The case will now return to the trial court for a likely full airing on Texas's request for a permanent injunction. Chances are the controversy will be back in our Court after round two in the lower courts.

We resolved another headline case on May 16, without an opinion on the merits. *Zubik v. Burwell*[10] and the cases consolidated with it involved objections by religious nonprofits to providing contraceptive services coverage in their employees' health plans, as required by the Affordable Care Act. The litigation was based primarily, not on the First Amendment's free exercise of religion guarantee, but on a law passed by Congress, the Religious Freedom Restoration Act. Attempting to accommodate the nonprofits' objections, the government had called upon third parties, mainly insurers, to provide contraceptive coverage in the religious employers' stead. Even that accommodation, the nonprofits asserted, burdened the exercise of their religious beliefs because it made use of health plans offered by employers.

After hearing argument, the Court requested supplemental briefing to determine whether the parties might compose their differences. The additional briefs in hand, the Court issued a per curiam order remanding the cases so that the courts of appeals could consider what the new briefs conveyed. Justice Sotomayor filed a concurring opinion, which I joined, emphasizing that the Court's order in no way tipped the scales in the nonprofits' direction.

I turn now to some of the Term's headline cases that yielded dispositive rulings. *Evenwel v. Abbott*[11] concerned who counts under the one-person, one-vote principle derived from the Fourteenth Amendment's Equal Protection Clause. In drawing state and local legislative districts, should the state count only eligible voters, as the plaintiffs, Texas voters, urged, or does everyone—the district's total population—count? We held that jurisdictions may draw legislative districts to equalize total population.

The Framers of the Fourteenth Amendment, we emphasized, selected total population as the basis for congressional apportionment. They wrote: "Representatives shall be apportioned among the several States according to their respective numbers, counting the whole number of persons in each State." "It cannot be," I wrote for the Court, "that the Fourteenth Amendment calls for the apportionment of congressional districts based on total population, but simultaneously prohibits States from apportioning their own legislative districts on that same basis."[12]

High on the list of the Term's leading decisions, *Fisher v. University of Texas at Austin*[13] returned to the Court for a second look. The question: does the university's affirmative action admissions policy meet the Court's equal protection measurement? When the Fifth Circuit invalidated the university's initial plan, the Texas Legislature adopted a Top Ten Percent Law, under which all Texas students who graduate in the top 10 percent of their high school classes gain admission. That plan accounts for up to 75 percent of the entering class. To complete the class, the university considers a number of factors, including a student's race.

Last time around, in 2012, the Court sent the case back to the Fifth Circuit, determining that the Court of Appeals, which had upheld the university's policy, had applied with insufficient rigor the close review the Court's decisions required for all race-based classifications.[14] I dissented on the ground that the university had followed assiduously the holistic, race-conscious model the Court had approved in *Grutter v. Bollinger*,[15] the University of Michigan Law School affirmative action case. Like Michigan's law school, the University of Texas used race as only one factor among many. The Top Ten Percent Law, which the majority regarded as race neutral, I suggested, could not fairly bear that description, for it was adopted with the state's racially segregated neighborhoods and schools in full view.

On remand, the Fifth Circuit again upheld the university's admissions policy. This time, in a 4–3 decision written by Justice Kennedy and announced June 23, the Court affirmed the judgment of the Court of Appeals. Justice Kennedy wrote for the majority: "Though a college must continually reassess its need for race-conscious review, here that assessment appears to have been done with care, and a reasonable determination was made that the University had not yet attained its goals."[16] "[P]ublic universities, like the States themselves," the Court's opinion stated, "can serve as laboratories for experimentation. The University of Texas at Austin has a special opportunity to learn and to teach."[17]

Rivalling *Fisher* at the top of the most-watched slate was *Whole Woman's Health v. Hellerstedt*.[18] In that controversy, Texas abortion providers challenged the constitutionality of two severely restrictive abortion access regulations imposed by the state's legislature: first, a requirement that abortion clinic physicians obtain admitting privileges at local hospitals; second, a mandate that clinics meet minimum standards required of ambulatory surgical centers. If the law had become fully operative, the District Court found, only 7 or 8 contraception and abortion clinics out of some 40 would remain.

The Fifth Circuit upheld the Texas restrictions in principal part. On the Term's last opinion announcement day, June 27, we reversed the Court of Appeals judgment, 5–3, in an opinion by Justice Breyer. The Texas requirements did not genuinely protect women's health, the Court observed. Instead, they burdened a woman's access to an abortion for no tenable reason. In a concurring opinion, I emphasized that Texas trained its restrictions on abortion providers alone, and placed no similar restraints on medical procedures considerably more dangerous to patients, including tonsillectomies, colonoscopies, and childbirth.

The 2015–16 Term cases closely watched abroad included *RJR Nabisco, Inc. v. European Community*[19] and *Bank Markazi v. Peterson*.[20] In *RJR Nabisco*, the European Union invoked our Racketeer Influenced and Corrupt Organizations Act, commonly known as RICO, to sue a corporation, organized and headquartered in the United States, for allegedly orchestrating a complex, global money-laundering scheme. The EU asserted losses sustained by European financial institutions and member states' lost opportunities to collect duties. The Court ordered dismissal of the EU's suit. It held that, absent a domestic injury, private civil actions could not be maintained under RICO. No such limitation, the Court also held, applies to RICO civil action instituted by the United States. I agreed that the U.S. could sue, but dissented as to the Court's exclusion of suits by private parties injured abroad. Joined by Justices Breyer and Kagan, I wrote that the domestic-injury requirement invoked by the Court to stop the EU's suit was nowhere prescribed by RICO, but rather was the Court's own invention.

Bank Markazi involved the constitutionality of a provision of the 2012 Iran Threat Reduction and Syria Human Rights Act. The provision identified a set of assets held at a New York bank for Bank Markazi, the Central Bank of Iran; it made those assets available to satisfy some sixteen district court judgments against Iran for its part in terrorist attacks abroad that took the lives of many U.S. citizens. The cases were consolidated for post-judgment execution in a proceeding the statute named by docket number. The question presented: Did the provision violate the separation of powers by directing a particular result in a pending case?

In an opinion I wrote, the Court upheld the statute, and thus freed the assets for distribution among the judgment creditors. Congress, we reaffirmed, can't tell a court how a case should be decided under existing law, but ordinarily it can amend the law applicable to a pending case, even when the amendment will determine the outcome in that case. The decision drew a strong dissent from the Chief Justice, joined only by Justice Sotomayor, and an irate response from Iran, including a suit against the United States filed by Iran in the International Court of Justice.

Finally, I cannot resist reporting the Term's most memorable slip by an attorney. On April 27, the last day for oral argument, an advocate responded to my question thus: "There are lots of other statutes that would prohibit precisely what you are suggesting, Justice O'Connor. . . ."[21] I gently reminded counsel: "That hasn't happened in quite some time."[22] The first woman on the Supreme Court retired a decade ago, yet confusion of the two of us lingers. Eight, as the Term's 4–4 splits show, is not a good number for a multimember Court. When the 2016–17 Term ends, I anticipate reporting on decisions rendered by a full bench.

Conclusion

AT EIGHTY-THREE, *Justice Ruth Bader Ginsburg is still going strong. She works out twice a week in the Supreme Court gym. She watches the evening news on TV while on the elliptical glider. Under the guidance of her longtime trainer, she lifts weights and does 20 push-ups—with a short stretch in the middle to catch her breath. This is down from the 30 push-ups she did a few years ago—but more than most of us do at half her age, if ever. She has twice conquered cancer, in 1999 and 2009, and never missed a day on the bench. On Sunday, June 27, 2010, she lost her life partner of fifty-six years—and carried on. The day after Martin Ginsburg's death, the last day of the Supreme Court's Term, she appeared with her fellow Justices and announced one of the Court's decisions from the bench. Marty, she said, would have wanted it that way.*

Since the retirement of Justice Stevens in June 2010, she has become the senior Justice among the Court's four liberal members, significant because when the Court splits 5–4 on philosophically divisive issues of great public importance, she now decides who will write the dissenting opinion. Her own voice, in dissent, has never been stronger or more important to the reasoned dialogue in which the Court's majority and dissenters engage as they shape the law of the land.

In recent years, to Justice Ginsburg's bemusement, she has become something of a cultural rock star. There's the opera, Scalia/Ginsburg *(see Part One) and a play about a Supreme Court case (the actor who played Ginsburg, wearing a robe and lace collar, portrayed her to a tee). She has had a blog dedicated to following her life and career, her image has appeared on numerous and varied T-shirts, and she has been the subject of a bestselling book, admiringly titled* The Notorious RBG. *(The authors nicknamed her after her fellow Brooklynite, the rapper Notorious B.I.G.) Her daughter-in-law, Patrice Michaels, an opera singer and teacher, has composed a song cycle in her honor. There are RBG mugs, RBG portraits, RBG birthday cards, RBG tattoos, and most recently, not one but two RBG coloring books. The three- and four-year-olds of the Bee Hive Class at Temple Emanu-El in Dallas, Texas, named their class fish "Ruth Beta Ginsburg," after the Justice. Researchers Sydney Brannoch and Gavin Svenson at the Cleveland Museum of Natural History went a step further, naming an entire species of praying mantis,* Ilomantis ginsburgae, *in honor of the Justice. Natalie Portman will portray her in an upcoming movie about a case she litigated, in partnership with her husband, in 1971.*

On a more academic note, another book, Sisters in Law, *a "dual biography," recounts, to quote its subtitle, "How Sandra Day O'Connor and Ruth Bader Ginsburg Went to the Supreme Court and Changed the World." A third book,* The Legacy of Ruth Bader Ginsburg, *features chapters by legal scholars and commentators assessing her contributions as lawyer, law professor, judge, and Justice. She has more than thirty honorary degrees, and counting. She has won numerous awards and honors, most recently including the American Bar Association Medal, which honors "a leader of the Bench or Bar" who has "truly 'rendered conspicuous service to the cause of American Jurisprudence,'" and she has been counted among* Time*'s 100 Most Influential People,* Forbes*' 100 Most Powerful Women, and* Elle*'s 2015 Women in Washington Power. The New York City Bar sponsors an annual Justice Ruth Bader Ginsburg Distinguished Lecture on Women and the Law, and the Association of American Law Schools' Section on Women in Legal Education bestows a Ruth Bader Ginsburg Lifetime Achievement Award (of which Justice Ginsburg herself was the inaugural recipient).*

To Ruth Ginsburg's deep satisfaction, the two newest Justices on the Court are women, Sonia Sotomayor and Elena Kagan. When, more than two decades ago, President Bill Clinton announced his choice of Ginsburg for the Supreme Court, she responded that for her, the significance of her nomination was that "it contributes to the end of the days when women, at least half the talent pool in our society, appear in high places only as one-at-a-time performers." (See Part Four.) When Justice Sandra Day O'Connor, until Ginsburg's confirmation a "one-at-a-time performer," retired in 2006,

Ruth Ginsburg was left as the only woman on the Court. "Neither of us ever thought this would happen again," she said. "The word I would use to describe my position on the bench," she told a reporter a year after O'Connor's departure, "is lonely."[1] *She is lonely no more: "Now Kagan is on my left, and Sotomayor is on my right. So we look like we're really part of the Court and we're here to stay."*[2] *In recent years, when people ask her when she thinks there will be enough women on the Court, she answers, with a twinkle in her eye, "My answer is, when there are nine."*[3]

Does Justice Ginsburg plan to retire? A few years ago, she said she wanted to match the record of Justice Louis Brandeis, who retired after twenty-three years on the bench. By April 2016, she had matched the Brandeis record. On another occasion, she said she would not leave the Court until the Smithsonian Museum of American Art returned the Josef Albers painting it had borrowed from her to take on tour. That painting has been restored to its place facing the desk in her chambers. When Justice Stevens retired at ninety after thirty-five years on the Court in 2010, making Ruth Ginsburg the Court's oldest member and senior liberal, she said he was her new "model." The test, she has said, "has to be, 'am I equipped to do the job?'" She will stay, she says, "as long as I can do the job full steam."[4]

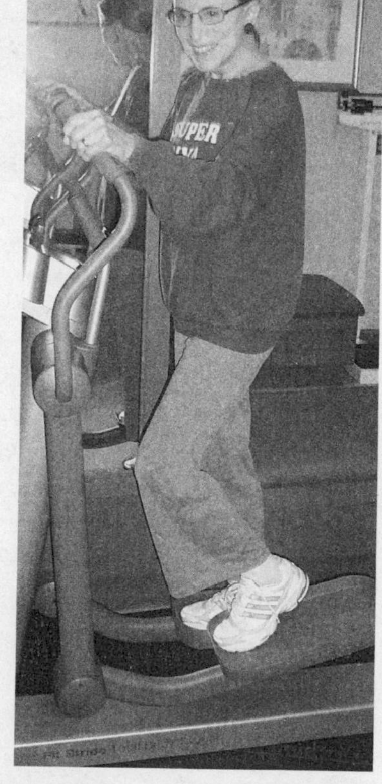

Justice Ginsburg works out on elliptical during a training session at the Supreme Court, sporting her "Super Diva" sweatshirt. August 30, 2007.

Justice Ginsburg in her Chambers with her October Term 2015 law clerks, Chambers staff and Natalie Portman, February 29, 2016.

To judge by the measures that matter most—the quality of her reasoning (her opinions are as skillfully wrought and compelling as ever), her mental acuity (apparent in her questioning at oral argument and in her public appearances), her stamina (she remains probably the most efficient and timely producer of opinions for the Court; when need be, she still stays up all night to get the job done), and her public engagement (she still indefatigably travels the country and the world, teaching and learning)—there is no question that Justice Ruth Bader Ginsburg continues to "do the job full steam."

Acknowledgments

FIRST AND FOREMOST WE would like to thank the bright, incredible, and unflappable Kim McKenzie, who manages Justice Ginsburg's chambers, and the Justice's talented assistants Lauren Brewer and Andrew Schlegel, for their cheerful, able, and tireless assistance every step along the way to publication of *My Own Words*. Huge appreciation goes also to Daniel Hartnett Norland, who has helped captain and corral the manuscript and has lived, breathed, and edited this book with us to completion. A big shout-out to Justice Ginsburg's Term 2015–16 law clerks, Payvand Ahdout, Joshua Bone, Samuel Harbourt, and Amy Marshak, and to Sam Rothschild (on loan from retired Justice David Souter), whose thoughtful review and suggestions were extremely helpful in our effort to "get it right and keep it tight." We would also like to thank profusely two terrific Georgetown Law student research assistants, Lindsey Stearns and Eric Kay, now newly minted lawyers, who supported our efforts with enthusiasm, skill, and elbow grease.

We are most grateful for the indispensable assistance from the U.S. Supreme Court's gifted and agile photographer Steve Petteway, who is willing to share the fruits of his labor, and for the proficient assistance of the Supreme Court's Public Information Office. Immense thanks also to Georgetown University Law Center Dean William Treanor and Vice Dean Jane Aiken for providing a warm and generous academic home, as well as intellectual and administrative support without which this book would not have been possible. We are deeply appreciative of key Georgetown Law staff members including Mary Ann DeRosa, who has patiently, professionally, and accurately transcribed thousands of pages of interviews and speeches; Chris Critchfield, an audio-genius who expertly records interviews with even the most soft-spoken of Justices, and Steve Eckhoff for able and repeated AV office support; the entire Faculty Support team, especially Monica Stearns and Anna Selden; and Associate Dean for Library Services Michelle Wu, Associate Law Librarian Marylin Raisch, and Special Collections Librarian Hannah Miller-Kim.

We are tremendously fortunate to be represented by Agent Extraordinaire Esther Newberg with ICM and extremely grateful for her vigorous advocacy on our behalf, and we also wish to thank her team, especially John DeLaney and Zoe Sandler. At Simon & Schuster, our hearty thanks to an incomparable editor, the legendary Alice Mayhew, for her wisdom and guidance, and to assistant editor Stuart Roberts for his steady, talented, and professional hand in every phase of production. Thanks also to Simon & Schuster's Lisa Healy, Tom Pitoniak, Julia Prosser, Richard Rhorer, Ellen Sasahara, Jackie Seow, and Dana Trocker for their very able assistance.

Saving the very best for the very last, we wish to thank, from the bottom of our hearts, our incredibly supportive families, especially our spouses: Martin D. Ginsburg *in memoriam*, Richard Diamond, and Richard Norland; our children and their spouses: Jane Ginsburg and George Spera, James Ginsburg and Patrice Michaels, Luke Diamond and Penelope Crocker, Ethan Diamond and Kristen Danforth, Daniel Hartnett Norland and Jennifer Barkley, and Kathleen Norland List and Phil List; and all of our grandchildren.

With deep gratitude,

Ruth Bader Ginsburg, Wendy W. Williams & Mary Hartnett

An important postscript

To all those institutions and individuals who have provided support to biographers Mary Hartnett and Wendy W. Williams for our forthcoming biography of Justice Ginsburg, including at Georgetown Law, the Library of

Congress, the Wilson Center and numerous other institutions; a generation of research assistants at Georgetown Law and elsewhere; the hundreds of individuals whom we have interviewed, including Justice Ginsburg's friends, family, colleagues, clerks, and others; and the many who have provided varied and sundry support (like David Norland for providing us use of his New York apartment for over a decade): ***We have not forgotten you—thank you, thank you, thank you, and—please stay tuned for the next book!***—MEH, WWW.

Notes

A Note on Sources

My Own Words includes a variety of materials, including speeches that have no citations, and legal briefs and law review articles that are rife with citations. Our publisher recommended that instead of including the full citations in the print edition of the book, it would benefit the environment and most of our readers to instead house the majority of the legal citations from briefs and articles on the book's website MyOwnWordsBook.com. We have retained notes from the introductory text and the *Scalia/Ginsburg* opera excerpt in the print edition.

Part One: Early Years and Lighter Side

1. Interview by Mary Hartnett and Wendy Williams with Ruth Bader Ginsburg (Aug. 12, 2010) (on file with authors).
2. Interview by Mary Hartnett and Wendy Williams with Ruth Bader Ginsburg (Aug. 27, 2009) (on file with authors).
3. "Justice Ginsburg Grade School Tour," C-SPAN, June 3, 1994, http://www.c-spanvideo.org/program/57503-1 (quote begins at 1:22:42 mark of video clip).
4. Interview by Maeva Marcus with Ruth Bader Ginsburg (Aug. 10, 1995) (on file with authors).
5. Ibid.
6. Interview by Mary Hartnett with Beth Amster Hess (Apr. 11, 2005) (on file with authors).
7. Letter from Ruth Bader Ginsburg to Mary Hartnett and Wendy Williams (Aug. 16, 2004) (on file with authors).
8. Interview by Larry Josephson with Ruth Bader Ginsburg, "Only in America—Celebrating 350 Years of the Jewish Experience," NPR, Sept. 2, 2004, http://www.onlyinamerica.info/ginsburg.shtml.
9. Interview by Mary Hartnett and Wendy Williams with Ruth Bader Ginsburg (Aug. 27, 2009) (on file with authors).
10. Interview by Ron Grele with Ruth Bader Ginsburg (Aug. 17, 2004) (on file with authors).
11. Interview by Larry Josephson with Ruth Bader Ginsburg, "Only in America—Celebrating 350 Years of the Jewish Experience," NPR, Sept. 2, 2004, http://www.onlyinamerica.info/ginsburg.shtml.

12. Interview by Ron Grele with Ruth Bader Ginsburg (Aug. 17, 2004) (on file with authors).
13. Interview by Mary Hartnett and Wendy Williams with Ruth Bader Ginsburg (Sept. 5, 2008) (on file with authors).
14. Interview by Mary Hartnett and Wendy Williams with Ruth Bader Ginsburg (Aug. 27, 2009) (on file with authors).
15. Ibid.
16. Ibid.
17. Ibid.
18. Ibid.
19. Ibid.

2. One People

1. Interview by Mary Hartnett and Wendy Williams with Ruth Bader Ginsburg (Aug. 27, 2009) (on file with authors).
2. Interview by Larry Josephson with Ruth Bader Ginsburg, "Only in America—Celebrating 350 Years of the Jewish Experience," NPR, Sept. 2, 2004, http://www.onlyinamerica.info/ginsburg.shtml.
3. Interview by Mary Hartnett and Wendy Williams with Ruth Bader Ginsburg (Aug. 5, 2005) (on file with authors).
4. Interview by Sarah Wilson with Ruth Bader Ginsburg (Sept. 25, 1995) (on file with authors).
5. Interview by Larry Josephson with Ruth Bader Ginsburg, "Only in America—Celebrating 350 Years of the Jewish Experience," NPR, Sept. 2, 2004, http://www.onlyinamerica.info/ginsburg.shtml.
6. Ruth Bader Ginsburg, "Tribute to Rabbi Stephen S. Wise," *East Midwood Jewish Center Bulletin*, June 21, 1946, p. 2 (on file with authors).
7. Interview by Research Assistant Leila Abolfazli with Seymour "Si" Bessen (Mar. 17, 2007) (on file with authors).
8. Interview by Mary Hartnett with Anita Fial (May 12, 2006) (on file with authors).
9. Interview by Mary Hartnett with Ann Burkhardt Kittner (May 22, 2006) (on file with authors).

3. Wiretapping: Cure Worse than Disease?

1. Interview by Maeva Marcus with Ruth Bader Ginsburg (Aug. 10, 1995) (on file with authors).
2. Interview by Mary Hartnett and Wendy Williams with Ruth Bader Ginsburg (Aug. 5, 2004) (on file with authors).
3. Ibid.
4. Conversation between Mary Hartnett and Ruth Bader Ginsburg (Feb. 3, 2010).

4. Marty Ginsburg's Favorite Subject

1. Interview by Mary Hartnett and Wendy Williams with Martin Ginsburg (Aug. 2, 2004) (on file with authors).
2. Interview by Maeva Marcus with Ruth Bader Ginsburg (Aug. 10, 1995) (on file with authors).
3. Ibid.
4. Ibid.
5. Interview by Mary Hartnett and Wendy Williams with Martin Ginsburg (Aug. 2, 2004) (on file with authors).
6. Interview by Maeva Marcus with Ruth Bader Ginsburg (Aug. 10, 1995) (on file with authors).

5. Law and Lawyers in Opera

1. Interview by Mary Hartnett and Wendy Williams with Ruth Bader Ginsburg (Aug. 12, 2010) (on file with authors).

6. Remembering Justice Scalia

1. Interview by Mary Hartnett with Antonin Scalia (Aug. 1, 2007) (on file with authors).
2. Ibid.

7. The Scalia/Ginsburg Opera

1. *Cf.* St. Mary's Honor Ctr. v. Hicks, 509 U.S. 502, 512 (1993) ("Only one unfamiliar with our case law will be upset by the dissent's alarum that we are today setting aside 'settled precedent,' . . . ."); Melendez-Diaz v. Massachusetts, 557 U.S. 305, 312 (2009) ("[W]e must assure the reader of the falsity of the dissent's opening alarum . . . .").
2. *See* Antonin Scalia, A Matter of Interpretation: Federal Courts and the Law 40 (Amy Gutmann ed., 1997) ("It certainly cannot be said that a constitution naturally suggests *changeability*; to the contrary, its whole purpose is to prevent change—to embed certain rights in such a manner that future generations cannot readily take them away." (emphasis added)); *see also* Lee v. Weisman, 505 U.S. 577, 632 (1992) (Scalia, J., dissenting) ("Today's opinion shows more forcefully than volumes of argumentation why our Nation's protection, that fortress which is our Constitution, cannot possibly rest upon the *changeable* philosophical predilections of the Justices of this Court, but must have deep foundations in the historic practices of our people." (emphasis added)). Changeability is the subject

of one particularly well-known operatic aria. *See* GIUSEPPE VERDI & FRANCESCO MARIA PIAVE, *La donna è mobile* [*Woman is changeable*], *in* RIGOLETTO act 1, sc. 11 (1851), *available at* http://perma.cc/3KX-ZCBG.

3. *Cf.* GEORGES BIZET, HENRI MEILHAC & LUDOVIC HALÉVY, *Habañera (L'amour est un oiseau rebelle)* [*Habañera (Love is a rebellious bird)*], *in* CARMEN act 1, sc. 5 (1875), *available at* http://perma.cc/6LTM-YJAH ("L'amour est enfant de Bohême, / il n'a jamais, jamais connu de loi" ["Love is a gypsy's child, / It has never, ever known the law"]).
4. *See, e.g.*, GEORGE FRIDERIC HÄNDEL & NICOLA FRANCESCO HAYM, *Empio, dirò, più sei* [*I say, you are a villain*], *in* GIULIO CESARE IN EGITTO [JULIUS CAESAR IN EGYPT] act 1, sc. 3 (1724) (HWV 17), *available at* http://perma.cc/CWU7-4GGU.
5. *See* Planned Parenthood of Se. Penn. v. Casey, 505 U.S. 833, 980 (1992) (Scalia, J., concurring) (stating that "the Constitution says absolutely nothing about" whether the power of a woman to abort her unborn child is a liberty protected by the Constitution).
6. *See* United States v. Virginia, 518 U.S. 515, 567 (1996) (Scalia, J., dissenting) ("Today [this Court] *enshrines* the notion that no substantial educational value is to be served by an all-men's military academy . . . ." (emphasis added)); *id.* at 597 ("The enemies of single-sex education have won; by persuading only seven Justices (five would have been enough) that their view of the world is *enshrined* in the Constitution, they have effectively imposed that view on all 50 States." (emphasis added)). *Contra* McCreary County v. Am. Civil Liberties Union of Ky., 545 U.S. 844, 896-97 (2005) (Scalia, J., dissenting) ("The Establishment Clause, upon which Justice Stevens would rely, *was* enshrined in the Constitution's text, and these official actions show *what it meant*. . . . What is more probative of the meaning of the Establishment Clause than the actions of the very Congress that proposed it, and of the first President charged with observing it?" (emphasis in original)); Dist. of Columbia v. Heller, 554 U.S. 570, 584-85 (2008) ("Nine state constitutional provisions written in the 18th century or the first two decades of the 19th . . . *enshrined* a right of citizens to 'bear arms in defense of themselves and the state' or 'bear arms in defense of himself and the state.'" (emphasis added) (citations omitted)); *id.* at 634-36 ("Constitutional rights are *enshrined* with the scope they were understood to have when the people adopted them, whether or not future legislatures or (yes) even future judges think that scope too broad. . . . [T]he *enshrinement* of constitutional rights necessarily takes certain policy choices off the table." (emphasis added)).
7. *See, e.g.*, Ushma Patel, *Scalia Favors "Enduring," Not Living, Constitution*, PRINCETON UNIV. (Dec. 11, 2012, 1:00 PM), http://perma.cc/M7R2-3G9H ("'I have classes of little kids who come to the court, and they recite very proudly what they've been taught, 'The Constitution is a living document.' It isn't a living document! It's dead. Dead, dead, dead!' Scalia said, drawing laughs from the crowd. 'No, I don't say that. . . . I call it the enduring Constitution. That's what I tell them.'").
8. *Cf. The First Nowell*, *in* CHRISTMAS CAROLS NEW & OLD (Henry Ramsden Bramley & John Stainer eds., ca. 1878) ("The First Nowell the Angel did say, / Was to certain poor shepherds in fields as they lay . . .").

9. *See* McDonald v. City of Chicago, 561 U.S. 742, 805 (2010) (Scalia, J., concurring) ("Justice Stevens abhors a system in which 'majorities or powerful interest groups always get their way' . . . but replaces it with a system in which unelected and life-tenured judges always get their way." (citation omitted)); Webster v. Reproductive Health Servs., 492 U.S. 490, 535 (1989) (Scalia, J., concurring) ("We can now look forward to at least another Term with carts full of mail from the public, and streets full of demonstrators, urging us—their unelected and life-tenured judges who have been awarded those extraordinary, undemocratic characteristics precisely in order that we might follow the law despite the popular will—to follow the popular will.").
10. *Cf.* HÄNDEL & HAYM, *Svegliatevi nel core* [*Awaken in my heart*], *in* GIULIO CESARE IN EGITTO, *supra* note 4, at act 1, sc. 5 ("L'ombra del genitore / accorre a mia difesa / e dice: a te rigor, / Figlio, si aspetta." ["The specter of [my] father / Rushes to my defense / And says: from you, severity, / [My] son, is expected."]).
11. *Cf.* FRANCIS SCOTT KEY & JOHN STAFFORD SMITH, *The Star-Spangled Banner* (1814) ("O! say can you see by the dawn's early light, / What so proudly we hailed at the twilight's last gleaming").
12. *Cf.* GEORGE FRIDERIC HÄNDEL, *Ombra mai fu*, *in* SERSE [XERXES] act 1, sc. 1 (1738) (HWV 40), *available at* http://perma.cc/6XRJ-AUK5 (Händel's "Largo") ("Ombra mai fu / Di vegetabile, / Cara ed amabile / Soave più." ["Never was a shade / Of any plant / Dearer and lovelier, / [Or] sweeter."]).
13. *Cf. The First Nowell*, *supra* note 8 ("Nowell, Nowell, Nowell, Nowell, / Born is the King of Israel.").
14. *See 60 Minutes: Justice Scalia on the Record, Both Online and Off* (CBS television broadcast Apr. 27, 2008) (transcript available at http://perma.cc/A64C-QNBB) ("'When I first came on the court I thought I would for sure get off as soon as I could which would have been when I turned 65. Because you know, justices retire at full salary. So there's no reason not to leave and go off and do something else. So you know, essentially I've been working for free, which probably means I'm too stupid to be on the Supreme Court,' Scalia says, laughing. 'You should get somebody with more sense. But I cannot—what happened is, simply I cannot think of what I would do for an encore. I can't think of any other job that I would find as interesting and as satisfying.'").
15. *See id.* ("'I mean after a while, you know, I'm saying the same things in today's dissent that I said in a dissent 20 years ago,' Scalia explains.").
16. *Cf.* WOLFGANG AMADEUS MOZART & EMANUEL SCHIKANEDER, DIE ZAUBERFLÖTE [THE MAGIC FLUTE] act 2, sc. 8 (1791) (K. 620), *available at* http://perma.cc/444R-UDUT ("Die Königin der Nacht kommt unter Donner aus der mittlern Versenkung und so, dass sie gerade vor Pamina zu stehen kommt." ["The Queen of the Night emerges amid thunder from the central trapdoor so that she stands just in front of Pamina."]); RICHARD WAGNER, DAS RHEINGOLD [THE RHINE GOLD] sc. 4 (1869), *available at* http://perma.cc/U6VV-PLAL ("[W]ird plötzlich Erda sichtbar, die . . . aus der Tiefe aufsteigt; sie ist von edler Gestalt . . ." ["Erda is suddenly visible, rising . . . from the depths; she is of noble figure . . ."]).

17. *See* Nat'l Fed'n of Indep. Bus. v. Sebelius, 132 S. Ct. 2566, 2623-24 (2012) (Ginsburg, J., concurring) ("Underlying the Chief Justice's view that the Commerce Clause must be confined to the regulation of active participants in a commercial market is a fear that the commerce power would otherwise know no limits. . . . As an example of the type of regulation he fears, The Chief Justice cites a Government mandate to purchase green vegetables. . . . One could call this concern 'the broccoli horrible.'").
18. *See* United States v. Windsor, 133 S. Ct. 2675, 2704 (2013) (Scalia, J., dissenting) ("Unimaginable evil this is not.").
19. *Cf.* McCulloch v. Maryland, 17 U.S. (4 Wheaton) 316, 407 (1819) ("[W]e must never forget, that it is *a constitution* we are expounding."); Antonin Scalia, Remarks at the Woodrow Wilson International Center for Scholars (Mar. 14, 2005) (transcript available for download at http://perma.cc/WAB5-EGV3) ("Although it is a minority view now, the reality is that, not very long ago, originalism was orthodoxy. . . . [C]onsider the opinions of John Marshall in the Federal Bank case, where he says . . . we must always remember it is a constitution we are expounding. And since it's a constitution, he says, you have to give its provisions expansive meaning so that they will accommodate events that you do not know of which will happen in the future. Well, if it is a constitution that changes, you wouldn't have to give it an expansive meaning. You can give it whatever meaning you want and, when future necessity arises, you simply change the meaning. But anyway, that is no longer the orthodoxy.").
20. *See* United States v. Virginia, 518 U.S. 515, 567 (1996) (Scalia, J., dissenting) ("The virtue of a democratic system with a First Amendment is that it readily enables the people, over time, to be persuaded that what they took for granted is not so, and to change their laws accordingly. That system is destroyed if the smug assurances of each age are removed from the democratic process and written into the Constitution. So to counterbalance the Court's criticism of our ancestors, let me say a word in their praise: They left us free to change. The same cannot be said of this most illiberal Court, which has embarked on a course of inscribing one after another of the current preferences of the society (and in some cases only the countermajoritarian preferences of the society's law-trained elite) into our Basic Law."). *See generally* David F. Forte, *The Illiberal Court*, 48 NAT'L REV., July 29, 1996, at 40; *cf. also* [Jennifer Senior, *In Conversation: Antonin Scalia*, N.Y. MAG., Oct. 6, 2013, *available at* http://perma.cc/Q9ZW-ZFYN] ("[W]e get newspapers in the morning. . . . We used to get the Washington *Post*, but it just . . . went too far for me. I couldn't handle it anymore. . . . It was the treatment of almost any conservative issue. It was slanted and often nasty. . . . I think they lost subscriptions partly because they became so shrilly, *shrilly* liberal.").
21. *Cf.* GIUSEPPE VERDI & FRANCESCO MARIA PIAVE, *Sempre libera* [*Always free*], *in* LA TRAVIATA [THE FALLEN WOMAN] act 1, sc. 5 (1853), *available at* http://perma.cc/6EZF-AUKY ("Follie! follie . . . !" ["What folly! what folly . . . !"]).
22. *Cf.* Antonin Scalia, *God's Justice and Ours*, FIRST THINGS (May 2002), http://perma.cc/FY87-852V ("This dilemma, of course, need not be confronted by a proponent

of the 'living Constitution,' who believes that it means what it ought to mean. If the death penalty is (in his view) immoral, then it is (hey, presto!) automatically unconstitutional. . . . (You can see why the 'living Constitution' has such attraction for us judges.")).

23. The words sung by the character of Scalia correspond approximately to the poetic structure of the Verdi aria "Sempre libera" ["Always free"]. *See* VERDI & PIAVE, *Sempre libera [Always free]*, *in* LA TRAVIATA, *supra* note [21], at act 1, sc. 5 ("Sempre libera degg'io / folleggiare di gioia in gioia" ["Always free, I must frolic from delight to delight"]).
24. The words sung by the character of Ginsburg correspond approximately to the rhythms of a Mozart duet. *See* MOZART & DA PONTE, *Aprite, presto, aprite [Open it, quickly, open it]*, *in* [LE NOZZE DI FIGARO [THE MARRIAGE OF FIGARO] act 2, sc. 4 (1786) (K. 492), *available at* http://perma.cc/32JK-Q3PR] ("Fermate, Cherubino!" ["Stop, Cherubino!"]).
25. Justice Scalia joined the majority opinion in *Shelby County v. Holder*. *See* 133 S. Ct. 2612, 2648 (2013) (Ginsburg, J., dissenting) ("[T]he Court's opinion can hardly be described as an exemplar of restrained and moderate decisionmaking. Quite the opposite.").
26. *See* Adam Liptak, *How Activist Is the Supreme Court?*, N.Y. TIMES, Oct. 12, 2013, at SR4 ("Justices Antonin Scalia and Ruth Bader Ginsburg are ideological antagonists on the Supreme Court, but they agree on one thing. Their court is guilty of judicial activism.").
27. *See id.* ("'If it's measured in terms of readiness to overturn legislation, this is one of the most activist courts in history,' Justice Ginsburg said in August [2013] in an interview with The New York Times. 'This court has overturned more legislation, I think, than any other.'"); *Justice Ruth Bader Ginsburg Talks About Judicial Activism*, NAT'L CONST. CTR. (Sept. 9, 2013), http://perma.cc/7R6V-ZKAX ("[An activist court] is a court that is not at all hesitant to overturn legislation passed by the Congress. . . . The worst case was [*Shelby County v. Holder*,] the Voting Rights Act case.").
28. Shelby Cnty. v. Holder, 133 S. Ct. 2612 (2013) (Ginsburg, J., dissenting).
29. *See id.* at 2636 (2013) (Ginsburg, J., dissenting) ("Congress' power to act [was] at its height.").
30. *See Justice Ruth Bader Ginsburg Talks About Judicial Activism*, *supra* note [27] ("Despite the overwhelming majority in Congress that passed the Voting Rights Act, the Court said, 'that won't do.'").
31. *See* Nat'l Fed'n of Indep. Bus. v. Sebelius, 132 S. Ct. 2566, 2676 (2012) (Scalia, Kennedy, Thomas and Alito, JJ., dissenting) ("The Court regards its strained statutory interpretation as judicial modesty. It is not. It amounts instead to a vast judicial overreaching. . . . The values that should have determined our course today are caution, minimalism, and the understanding that the Federal Government is one of limited powers. But the Court's ruling undermines those values at every turn. In the name of restraint, it overreaches.").
32. *Cf., e.g.*, Atkins v. Virginia, 536 U.S. 304, 338 (2002) (Scalia, J., dissenting) ("Sel-

dom has an opinion of this Court rested so obviously upon nothing but the personal views of its Members.").

33. *Cf.* United States v. Virginia, 518 U.S. 515, 601 (1996) (Scalia, J., dissenting) ("It is one of the unhappy incidents of the federal system that a self-righteous Supreme Court, acting on its Members' personal view of what would make a 'more perfect union' (a criterion only slightly more restrictive than a 'more perfect world') can impose its own favored social and economic dispositions nationwide.").
34. *Cf. Shelby Cnty.*, 133 S. Ct. 2612, 2632 (2013) (Ginsburg, J., dissenting) ("Recognizing that large progress has been made, Congress determined, based on a voluminous record, that the scourge of discrimination was not yet extirpated."); Fisher v. Univ. of Tex., 133 S. Ct. 2411, 2434 n.4 (2013) (Ginsburg, J., dissenting) ("'Actions designed to burden groups long denied full citizenship stature are not sensibly ranked with measures taken to hasten the day when entrenched discrimination and its aftereffects have been extirpated.'" (quoting Gratz v. Bollinger, 539 U.S. 244, 301 (2003) (Ginsburg, J., dissenting))).
35. *Cf., e.g.*, City of Richmond v. J.A. Croson Co., 488 U.S. 469, 520 (1989) (Scalia, J., concurring) ("I do not agree, however, with Justice O'Connor's dictum suggesting that, despite the Fourteenth Amendment, state and local governments may in some circumstances discriminate on the basis of race in order (in a broad sense) 'to ameliorate the effects of past discrimination.'").
36. *Cf.* Mozart & Da Ponte, *Voi che sapete* [*You who know*], *in* The Marriage of Figaro, *supra* note [24], at act 2, sc. 2.
37. *Cf.* Antonin Scalia, *The Disease as Cure: "In Order to Get Beyond Racism, We Must First Take Account of Race,"* 1979 Wash. U. L.Q. 147 (1979) (discussing Regents of Univ. of Cal. v. Bakke, 438 U.S. 265 (1978)).
38. *Cf.* Mozart & Schikaneder, *Der Hölle Rache kocht in meinem Herzen* [*Hell's vengeance boils in my heart*], *in* The Magic Flute, *supra* note [16], at act 2, sc. 7 ("Verstoßen sei auf ewig, / verlassen sei auf ewig" ["Be disowned forever, / be forsaken forever"]).
39. *See Fisher*, 133 S. Ct. at 2433 (Ginsburg, J., dissenting) ("As for holistic review, if universities cannot explicitly include race as a factor, many may 'resort to camouflage' to 'maintain their minority enrollment.'" (quoting *Gratz*, 539 U.S. at 304 (Ginsburg, J., dissenting))); *Fisher*, 133 S. Ct. at 2434 ("As the thorough opinions below show . . . the University's admissions policy flexibly considers race only as a 'factor of a factor of a factor of a factor' in the calculus. . . ." (citation omitted)).
40. *See Shelby Cnty.*, 133 S. Ct. at 2633 (Ginsburg, J., dissenting) ("A century after the Fourteenth and Fifteenth Amendments guaranteed citizens the right to vote free of discrimination on the basis of race, the 'blight of racial discrimination in voting' continued to 'infec[t] the electoral process in parts of our country.' Early attempts to cope with this vile infection resembled battling the Hydra." (quoting South Carolina v. Katzenbach, 383 U.S. 301, 308 (1966))).
41. *See Gratz*, 539 U.S. at 288-89 (Ginsburg, J., dissenting) ("This insistence on [judicial consistency] would be fitting were our Nation free of the vestiges of

rank discrimination long reinforced by law. But . . . . [i]n the wake 'of a system of racial caste only recently ended,' large disparities endure." (citations omitted) (quoting Adarand Constructors, Inc. v. Pena, 515 U.S. 200, 273-76 & n.8 (1995) (Ginsburg, J., dissenting))). *Cf. generally* GIUSEPPE VERDI & TEMISTOCLE SOLERA, *Va, pensiero* [*Fly, thought, on wings of gold*], *in* NABUCCO [NEBUCHADNEZZAR] act 3, sc. 2 (1842) ("Chorus of the Hebrew Slaves").

42. See *Fisher*, 133 S. Ct. at 2433-34 (Ginsburg, J., dissenting) ("I have said before and reiterate here that only an ostrich could regard the supposedly neutral alternatives as race unconscious. . . . [T]he University reached the reasonable, good-faith judgment that supposedly race-neutral initiatives were insufficient to achieve, in appropriate measure, the educational benefits of student-body diversity." (citations omitted)).

43. *See Adarand*, 515 U.S. at 239 (Scalia, J., concurring) ("In my view . . . . [i]ndividuals who have been wronged by unlawful racial discrimination should be made whole but under our Constitution there can be no such thing as a either a creditor or debtor race. . . . In the eyes of government, we are just one race here. It is American."); City of Richmond v. J.A. Croson Co., 488 U.S. 469, 527-28 (1989) (Scalia, J., concurring) ("[T]hose who believe that racial preferences can help to 'even the score' display, and reinforce, a manner of thinking by race that was the source of the injustice and that will, if it endures within our society, be the source of more injustice still.").

44. *See Shelby Cnty.*, 133 S. Ct. at 2648 (Ginsburg, J., dissenting) ("Hubris is a fit word for today's demolition of the [Voting Rights Act].").

45. *Cf.* BIZET, MEILHAC & HALEVY, *Seguidilla (Près des remparts de Séville)* [*Seguidilla (Near the ramparts of Seville)*], *in* CARMEN, supra note 3, at act 1, sc. 9 ("Près des remparts de Séville, / Chez mon ami, Lillas Pastia, / J'irai danser le séguedille / Et boire du Manzanilla. / J'irai chez mon ami Lillas Pastia." ["Near the ramparts of Seville, / At the place of my friend, Lillas Pastia, / I will go to dance the Seguidilla / And drink Manzanilla. / I will go to the place of my friend Lillas Pastia."]); *see also* ABA Journal—Law News Now, *Justice Ruth Bader Ginsburg Talks Opera, the Law and Tells of a Plácido Domingo Serenade*, YOUTUBE (Aug. 5, 2012), http://perma.cc/4ZCV-W48R?type=source [hereinafter ABA Journal, *Justice Ginsburg Talks Opera*] ("[T]he most famous plea bargain in opera is Carmen's bargain with Don José: if he will allow her to escape, then she promises him that she will meet him at her friend's café.").

46. *See, e.g.*, VERDI & PIAVE, *Libiamo ne' lieti calici* [*Let us drink from joyful chalices*], *in* LA TRAVIATA, *supra* note [21], at act 1, sc. 2.

47. *See Lawyers Enjoy a Morning at the Opera with Justice Ginsburg and Solicitor General Verrilli*, ABANOW (Aug. 4, 2012), http://perma.cc/L3NW-A5X3 ("The founders of our country were great men with a vision. They were held back from realizing their ideas by the times in which they lived. But I think their notion was that society would evolve and the meaning of some of the grand clauses in the Constitution, like due process of law, would grow with society so that the Constitution would always be attuned with the society that law is meant to serve.");

see also Adarand, 515 U.S. at 276 (Ginsburg, J., dissenting) ("I see today's decision as one that allows our precedent to evolve, still to be informed by and responsive to changing conditions.").

48. This section of the aria prioritizes the lower register of the soprano voice. *Cf.* ABA Journal, *Justice Ginsburg Talks Opera*, *supra* note [45] ("[If I were an opera singer,] my first reaction would be, well, [my voice] would be a great soprano: I would be Renata Tebaldi or perhaps Beverly Sills. But then I think of Risë Stevens and say, well, perhaps I'd be a mezzo, like Marilyn Horne.").
49. *See, e.g.*, United States v. Virginia, 518 U.S. 515, 531 (1996) ("Through a century plus three decades and more of [our Nation's] history, women did not count among voters composing 'We the People.'").
50. *See id.* at 557 ("A prime part of the history of our Constitution . . . is the story of the extension of constitutional rights and protections to people once ignored or excluded.").
51. *See id.* at 532 ("[T]he Court has repeatedly recognized that neither federal nor state government acts compatibly with the equal protection principle when a law or official policy denies to women, simply because they are women, full citizenship stature—equal opportunity to aspire, achieve, participate in and contribute to society based on their individual talents and capacities.").
52. *See* Ledbetter v. Goodyear Tire & Rubber Co., Inc., 550 U.S. 618, 645 (Ginsburg, J., dissenting) (challenging "the unlawful [employment] practice [that] is the *current payment* of salaries infected by gender-based (or race-based) discrimination—a practice that occurs whenever a paycheck delivers less to a woman than to a similarly situated man"). Congress later adopted Justice Ginsburg's position by passing the Lilly Ledbetter Fair Pay Act of 2009. Pub. L. No. 111-2, 123 Stat. 5 (2009).
53. *Cf.* Ruth Bader Ginsburg, *Closing Remarks for Symposium on Justice Brennan and the Living Constitution*, 95 Cal. L. Rev. 2217, 2219 (2007) ("Justice Brennan was also instrumental in the 1970s, I should not fail to note, in moving the Court in a new direction regarding women's rights. The very first case I argued before the Court, *Frontiero v. Richardson*, yielded, in 1973, the first in a line of Brennan opinions holding that *our living Constitution* obligates government to respect women and men as persons of equal stature and dignity." (emphasis added)).
54. *See* Adarand Constructors, Inc. v. Pena, 515 U.S. 200, 274 (1995) (Ginsburg, J., dissenting) ("Bias both conscious and unconscious, reflecting traditional and unexamined habits of thought, keeps up barriers that must come down if equal opportunity and nondiscrimination are ever genuinely to become this country's law and practice.").
55. *Cf.* Ruth Bader Ginsburg, The 20th Annual Leo and Berry Eizenstat Memorial Lecture: The Role of Dissenting Opinions (Oct. 21, 2007) (transcript available at http://perma.cc/Z6E8-6NUM) ("Our Chief Justice . . . expressed admiration for the nation's fourth Chief Justice, John Marshall, in my view, shared by many, the greatest Chief Justice in U.S. history. Our current Chief admired, particularly, Chief Justice Marshall's unparalleled ability to achieve consensus among his colleagues. During his tenure, the Court spoke with one voice most of the time.").

56. As Justice Ginsburg notes, "There are a number of cases . . . they're not picked up by the press too often, where Justice Scalia and I are in total agreement, and if you think of this last Term, of Fourth Amendment cases, the one where Nino was . . . in dissent. [The] question was whether the police, when they arrest someone suspected of a felony, . . . can take a DNA sample." *Justice Ginsburg on Supreme Court Rulings and Political Activism* (C-SPAN television broadcast Sept. 6, 2013), *available at* http://perma.cc/S5LZ-68GA; *see* Maryland v. King, 133 S. Ct. 1958, 1980 (2013) (Scalia, J., dissenting) ("Justice Scalia, with whom Justice Ginsburg, Justice Sotomayor, and Justice Kagan join, dissenting.").
57. *Cf.* Zuni Pub. Sch. Dist. v. Dep't of Educ., 550 U.S. 81, 113 (2007) (Scalia, J., dissenting) ("The sheer applesauce of this statutory interpretation should be obvious.").
58. *Cf., e.g.*, *Piers Morgan Tonight: Interview with Antonin Scalia* [(CNN television broadcast July 18, 2012) (transcript available at http://perma.cc/6ZPA-HGB5)] ("My best buddy on the Court is Ruth Bader Ginsburg, has always been.").
59. *See, e.g.*, Emmarie Huetteman, *Breyer and Scalia Testify at Senate Judiciary Hearing*, N.Y. Times, Oct. 6, 2011, at A21 ("Justice Scalia expounded on what sets the United States apart from other countries: not the Bill of Rights, which 'every banana republic has,' but the separation of powers. Americans 'should learn to love the gridlock,' he said. 'It's there for a reason, so that the legislation that gets out will be good legislation.'")
60. The original composition of the Court was six justices. Judiciary Act of 1789, ch. 20, § 1, 1 Stat. 23. In 1869, the number of justices was increased to nine. Judiciary Act of 1869, ch. 22, § 1, 16 Stat. 44 ("[T]he Supreme Court of the United States shall hereafter consist of the Chief Justice of the United States and eight associate justices . . . .").
61. *Cf.* Scalia, A Matter of Interpretation, *supra* note 2, at 13-14 ("By far the greatest part of what I and all federal judges do is to interpret the meaning of federal statutes and federal agency regulations.").
62. *See, e.g.*, Rob Seal, *Scalia: Judges Should Consider Tradition in Church and State Cases*, U. Va. L. Sch. (Apr. 11, 2008), http://perma.cc/3PYB-R8E4 ("What Shakespeare is to the high school English student, the society's accepted constitutional traditions are to the prudent jurist. He doesn't judge them, but is judged by them. . . . [Rules] ought to be rooted in—ought to be derived from—the text of the Constitution, and where that text is in itself unclear, the settled practices that the text represents.").
63. *See, e.g.*, *Morning Edition: Ruth Bader Ginsburg and Malvina Harlan: Justice Revives Memoir of Former Supreme Court Wife* [(NPR radio broadcast May 2–3, 2002), *available at* http://www.npr.org/templates/story/story.php?storyId=1142685] ("Dissents speak to a future age. It's not simply to say, 'My colleagues are wrong and I would do it this way.' But the greatest dissents do become court opinions and gradually over time their views become the dominant view. So that's the dissenter[s'] hope: that they are writing not for today but for tomorrow.").
64. *Compare* Daniel J. Hemel, *Scalia Describes "Dangerous" Trend*, Harvard Crimson (Sept. 29, 2004), http://perma.cc/B8JU-U5BF ("The Supreme Court's recent

decisions . . . represent a 'dangerous' trend, Justice Antonin Scalia told a Harvard audience last night."), *with At the Supreme Court: A Conversation with Justice Ruth Bader Ginsburg and Stanford Law School Dean M. Elizabeth Magill*, STANFORD LAWYER (Oct. 4, 2013), http://perma.cc/ZNS2-VMZU ("If you reflect on the history of the Court, there have been periods in which the Court is stemming the tide of progress in the nation at large. I think this may be one such time, but, eventually, this time will pass.").

65. *See* SCALIA, A MATTER OF INTERPRETATION, *supra* note 2, at 7, 12 ("[A]n absolute prerequisite to common-law lawmaking is the doctrine of *stare decisis*—that is, the principle that a decision made in one case will be followed in the next. Quite obviously, without such a principle common-law courts would not be making any 'law'; they would just be resolving the particular dispute before them. It is the requirement that future courts adhere to the principle underlying a judicial decision which causes that decision to be a legal rule. (There is no such requirement in the civil-law system, where it is the text of the law rather than any prior judicial interpretation of that text which is authoritative. Prior judicial opinions are consulted for their persuasive effect, much as academic commentary would be; but they are not binding.) . . . I am content to leave the common law, and the process of developing the common law, where it is. It has proven to be a good method of developing the law in many fields—and perhaps the very best method.").
66. *See Justice Ginsburg on Supreme Court Rulings and Political Activism*, *supra* note [56] ("I should say that one of the hallmarks of the Court is collegiality, and we could not do the job the Constitution gives to us if we didn't—to use one of [Justice Antonin] Scalia's favorite expressions—'get over it.' We know that—even though we have sharp disagreements on what the Constitution means, we have a trust, we revere the Constitution and the Court, and we want to make sure that, when we leave it, it will be in as good shape as it was when we joined the Court.").
67. *See id.*

Part Two: Tributes to Waypavers and Pathmarkers

1. Justice Ginsburg, who often uses the terms "pathmarking" and "waypaving," not only in these tributes but also in her legal writings and judicial opinions, came across the term when she read former UN Secretary General Dag Hammarskjöld's book *Vägmärken* (1965). *See* Interview by Mary Hartnett and Wendy Williams with Ruth Bader Ginsburg (Aug. 5, 2004) (on file with authors).

Part Three: On Gender Equality: Women and the Law

1. Interview by Mary Hartnett and Wendy Williams with Ruth Bader Ginsburg (Aug. 25, 2005) (on file with authors).

2. *See* Ruth Bader Ginsburg, *Treatment of Women by the Law: Awakening Consciousness in the Law Schools*, 5 Val. U. L. Rev. 480, 481 (1971).
3. Ruth Bader Ginsburg, Remarks for Rutgers (Apr. 11, 1995), *cited in* Herma Hill Kay, *Claiming a Space in the Law School Curriculum: A Casebook on Sex-Based Discrimination*, 25 Colum. J. Gender & L. 54, 55 (2013).

3. The *Frontiero* Reply Brief

1. Gerald Gunther, *The Supreme Court, 1971 Term—Forward: In Search of Evolving Doctrine on a Changing Court: A Model for a Newer Equal Protection*, 86 Harv. L. Rev. 1, 8 (1972).

4. The Need for the Equal Rights Amendment

1. *See, e.g.*, Nikki Schwab, *Ginsburg: Make ERA Part of the Constitution*, U.S. News & World Report, Apr. 18, 2014, *available at* http://www.usnews.com/news/blogs/washington-whispers/2014/04/18/justice-ginsburg-make-equal-rights-amendment-part-of-the-constitution (quoting Justice Ginsburg).

Part Four: A Judge Becomes a Justice

1. Interview by Mary Hartnett with Ron Klain (Nov. 30, 2007) (on file with authors).
2. Interview by Maeva Marcus with Ruth Bader Ginsburg (Sept. 6, 2000) (on file with authors).
3. Interview by Mary Hartnett and Wendy Williams with Martin Ginsburg (Aug. 3, 2004) (on file with authors).
4. Interview by Mary Hartnett with Ron Klain (Nov. 30, 2007) (on file with authors).
5. Interview by Mary Hartnett with President William Jefferson Clinton (June 26, 2014) (on file with authors).
6. Interview by Mary Hartnett with Bernie Nussbaum (Nov. 15, 2007) (on file with authors).
7. Interview by Mary Hartnett and Wendy Williams with Ruth Bader Ginsburg (Aug. 25, 2005) (on file with authors).
8. Ibid.
9. Ibid.
10. Interview by Mary Hartnett with President William Jefferson Clinton (June 26, 2014) (on file with authors).
11. Interview by Mary Hartnett with Bernie Nussbaum (Nov. 15, 2007) (on file with authors).

12. Background Briefing by Senior Administration Officials (June 14, 1993), available at the American Presidency Project, http://www.presidency.ucsb.edu/ws/?pid=59985.
13. Ibid.
14. Interview by Maeva Marcus with Ruth Bader Ginsburg (Sept. 6, 2000) (on file with authors).

1. Rose Garden Acceptance Speech

1. Transcript of president's announcement and Judge Ginsburg's remarks, *New York Times*, June 15, 1993.
2. Ibid.
3. Ibid.
4. Interview by Mary Hartnett and Wendy Williams with Ruth Bader Ginsburg (Aug. 25, 2005) (on file with authors).
5. Background Briefing by Senior Administration Officials (June 14, 1993), available at the American Presidency Project, http://www.presidency.ucsb.edu/ws/?pid=59985.
6. Ruth Bader Ginsburg Supreme Court Nomination Announcement, White House Rose Garden, Washington, D.C. (June 14, 1993) (recording available on C-SPAN at http://www.c-span.org/video/?42908-1/ginsburg-supreme-court-nomination).
7. Interview by Mary Hartnett with President William Jefferson Clinton (June 26, 2014) (on file with authors).
8. Ibid.
9. Ibid.

2. Senate Confirmation Hearing Opening Statement

1. Nomination of Ruth Bader Ginsburg, to Be Associate Justice of the Supreme Court of the United States: Hearings Before the Committee on the Judiciary, 103rd Congress, July 20–23, 1993, S. Hrg. 103-482 [hereinafter Nomination Hearings], at 1 (statement of Chairman Biden).
2. Ibid., p. 32 (statement of Senator Heflin).
3. Ibid., p. 46 (statement of Judge Ginsburg).
4. Ibid.
5. Ibid., p. 166 (statement of Judge Ginsburg).
6. Linda P. Campbell, "Soft-spoken Ginsburg Gets Points Across," *Chicago Tribune*, July 25, 1993, p. 1.
7. Nomination Hearings, *supra* note 1, p. 404 (statement of Senator Feinstein).
8. Ibid., p. 503 (statement of Rosa Cumare).
9. Ibid., p. 517 (statement of Susan Hirschmann).
10. Ibid., p. 565 (statement of Chairman Biden).

11. Interview by Mary Hartnett with Joel Klein (Sept. 16, 2014) (on file with authors).
12. Nomination of Ruth Bader Ginsburg to Be an Associate Justice of the United States Supreme Court: Executive Report, 103rd Congress, Aug. 5, 1993, Exec. Rept. 103-6, at 2 (submitted by Chairman Biden).

Part Five: The Justice on Judging and Justice

1. Interview by Mary Hartnett and Wendy Williams with Ruth Bader Ginsburg (Aug. 4, 2004) (on file with authors).

7. The Role of Dissenting Opinions

1. Linda Greenhouse, *Oral Dissents Give Ginsburg a New Voice*, N.Y. Times, May 31, 2007 at A1.

8. Highlights of the U.S. Supreme Court's 2015–16 Term

1. Interview by Mark Sherman with Ruth Bader Ginsburg, Associated Press, July 8, 2016, http://bigstory.ap.org/article/0da3a641190742669cc0d01b90cd57fa/ap-interview-ginsburg-reflects-big-cases-scalias-death.

Conclusion

1. Joan Biskupic, *Ginsburg 'Lonely' Without O'Connor*, USA Today, Jan. 26, 2007, at A1.
2. Jessica Weisberg, *Supreme Court Justice Ruth Bader Ginsburg: I'm Not Going Anywhere*, Elle Magazine, Sept. 23, 2014, at 358, 360.
3. Ruth Bader Ginsburg, 2nd Annual Dean's Lecture to the Graduating Class, Georgetown University Law Center, Feb. 4, 2015, *available at* http://apps.law.georgetown.edu/webcasts/eventDetail.cfm?eventID=2559.
4. Weisberg, *supra* note 2, at 362.

Index

Page numbers in *italics* refer to illustrations.

Illustration Credits

Throughout text

iv Steve Petteway, Collection of the Supreme Court of the United States
18 Courtesy of Joan and Stuart Danoff
30 Courtesy of Justice Ginsburg's Personal Collection
31 Courtesy of Justice Ginsburg's Personal Collection
33 The Boston Globe / Getty Images
42a Courtesy of Collection of the Supreme Court of the United States
42b AP Photo / Stephen R. Brown / File
93 Courtesy of Collection of the Supreme Court of the United States
177 White House Photo, Courtesy of Justice Ginsburg's Personal Collection
333 Courtesy of Wendy Williams
334 Courtesy of Mary Hartnett

Insert

1 Courtesy of Collection of the Supreme Court of the United States
2 Courtesy of Si and Roz Bessen
3 Courtesy of Justice Ginsburg's Personal Collection
4 Courtesy of Justice Ginsburg's Personal Collection
5 Courtesy of Collection of the Supreme Court of the United States
6 Courtesy of Collection of the Supreme Court of the United States
7 Courtesy of Justice Ginsburg's Personal Collection
8 Courtesy of Wendy W. Williams
9 Courtesy of Justice Ginsburg's Personal Collection
10 Courtesy of Collection of the Supreme Court of the United States
11 Stephen Crowley / The New York Times / Redux
12 White House Photo, Courtesy of Justice Ginsburg's Personal Collection
13 White House Photo, Courtesy of Justice Ginsburg's Personal Collection
14 Courtesy of Justice Ginsburg's Personal Collection
15 Courtesy of Collection of the Supreme Court of the United States
16 Courtesy of James Ginsburg and Patrice Michaels
17 Courtesy of Collection of the Supreme Court of the United States

About the Authors

Steve Petteway, Collection of the Supreme Court of the United States

Ruth Bader Ginsburg was nominated by President Bill Clinton as Associate Justice of the United States Supreme Court in June 1993 and took the oath of office on August 10, 1993. Prior to her appointment to the Supreme Court, she served on the bench of the United States Court of Appeals for the District of Columbia Circuit for thirteen years. She was a law professor before that, teaching at Columbia University School of Law (1972–80) and at Rutgers, the State University of New Jersey (1963–72). In 1972, then-Professor Ginsburg was instrumental in launching the Women's Rights Project of the American Civil Liberties Union. Throughout the 1970s she litigated a series of cases solidifying a constitutional principle against gender-based discrimination. She has a Bachelor of Arts degree from Cornell University, attended Harvard Law School, and received her LL.B. (J.D.) from Columbia Law School. After law school she served as a law clerk to the Honorable Edmund L. Palmieri, in the U.S. District Court, Southern District of New York. She then served as a research associate and associate director of the Columbia Law School Project on International Procedure. She holds honorary degrees from more than thirty universities, including Columbia, Harvard, Princeton, Yale, and Lund University (Sweden). Justice Ginsburg's late husband, Martin D. Ginsburg, was a professor of tax law at Georgetown University Law Center; her daughter, Jane C. Ginsburg, is a professor of literary and artistic property law at Columbia Law School; and her son, James S. Ginsburg, is a producer of classical recordings.

Courtesy of photographer Holly Eaton

Mary Hartnett has been at Georgetown Law since 1998, first as Executive Director of the Women's Law and Public Policy Fellowship Program (WLPPFP), and now as an Adjunct Professor of Law and Advisory Board Member of WLPPFP. She has also served as a Public Policy Scholar at the Woodrow Wilson International Center, as a Visiting Professor at the Riga Graduate School of Law (Latvia), and as Vice-Chair of the ABA Committee on the Rights of Women. Prior to 1998, she was of counsel to the international law firm Coudert Brothers, represented low-income clients in federal court through her service on the Civil Pro Bono Panel for the U.S. District Court, D.C., and counseled victims of domestic violence. She is a recipient of the ABA's Rasmussen Award for the Advancement of Women in International Law, and the Grinnell College Alumni Award. She attended New York University School of Law for her first year as a Root-Tilden scholar, and graduated from Georgetown University Law Center *magna cum laude.*

Courtesy of Georgetown University Law Center

Wendy W. Williams, Professor Emerita, Georgetown University Law Center, is best known for her work in the area of gender and law, especially concerning issues of work and family. She is coauthor of a 1996 casebook on gender and law and a 2016 book on gender in American legal history. She helped draft and testified before Congressional committees on the Pregnancy Discrimination Act of 1978 and the Family and Medical Leave Act of 1993. Before joining the Law Center faculty in 1976, she was a law clerk for California Supreme Court Justice Raymond Peters, a Reginald Heber Smith Poverty Law Fellow, and a founder of Equal Rights Advocates, a public interest law firm in San Francisco. She received her A.B. and J.D. from the University of California at Berkeley. She is a past president of the Society of American Law Teachers and served as Associate Dean of Georgetown's Law Center from 1989 to 1993. A cofounder of the Women's Law and Public Policy Fellowship program, she has been a member of its board since 1993.